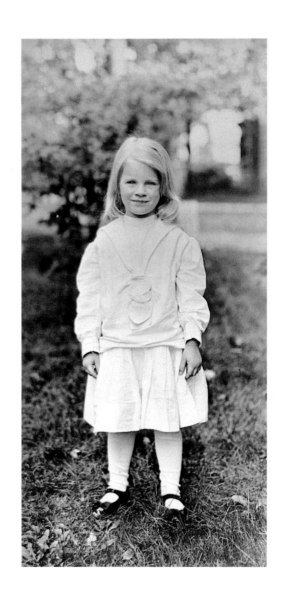

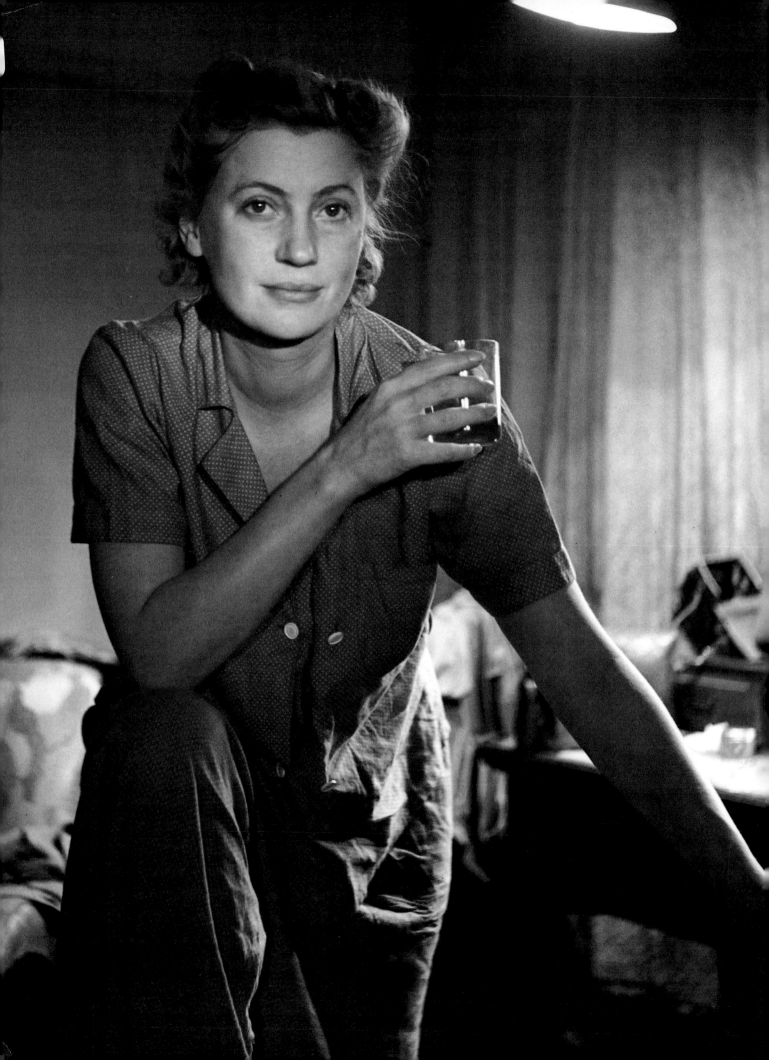

The Lives
of Lee Miller

Antony Penrose

with 171 illustrations in duotone

Thames and Hudson

For David E. Scherman, who gave me the title and the courage to write the book around it, and for Suzanna – without her it could never have happened.

© 1985 Thames and Hudson Ltd, London

First published in paperback in the United States of America
in 1989 by Thames and Hudson Inc., 500 Fifth Avenue,
New York, New York 10110
Reprinted 1999

Library of Congress Catalog Card Number 88-51525
ISBN 0-500-27509-2

Printed and bound in Japan

Contents

Acknowledgments

After Lee's death we uncovered many boxes and trunks full of negatives, original prints and manuscripts that were often in shreds from the censor's razor. Thanks to Alex Kroll at *Vogue*, the collection was augmented by the addition of negatives from the *Vogue* Archives which the magazine no longer had space for, and thus the Lee Miller Archive was created. Everything was so hopelessly jumbled that it took two years of patient sorting by Kenneth Clarke before any of the 40,000 negatives and 500 prints could be catalogued. My wife, Suzanna, tackled this with the help of Valerie Lloyd (ex Royal Photographic Society), Tim Hawkins, Delia Hardy and Sylvia Masham. Our greatest piece of luck was meeting Carole Callow, a photographic printer of the highest ability. Aided initially by the expert guidance of Helen McQuillan, Carole Callow has made all the fine prints for our exhibitions and for this book. These prints have been retouched by Helen McQuillan and Terry Boxall.

So many people have contributed to the research and production of this book that it is impossible to convey my indebtedness to everyone in detail. I must, however, particularly acknowledge the help of Roland Penrose, whose *Scrapbook* (London 1981) I have freely drawn on for information about Lee. I also gratefully acknowledge the help of the following:

USA: Erik and Mafy Miller, John and Edith Miller, Simon Bourgin, Alfred de Liagre, Bill Ewing, Deborah Frumkin, Robert Halmi ('Chespy'), Horst P. Horst, John Houseman, Tanja McKee (formerly Ramm), Cipe Penellis, John Phillips, Oreste Puciani, Kate Quesada, David and Rosemarie Scherman, Allene Talmey, David Travis.

PARIS: Lucien Clergue, Philippe and Yen Hiquily, Peter and Ninette Lyon, Juliette Man Ray, Marc Riboud, Lucien Treillard.

GREAT BRITAIN: Fred and Joan Baker, Sir Bernard and Lady Burrows, Carole Callow, Kenneth Clarke, Elsa Fletcher, David Hurn, Constance Kaine, Alex Kroll, Catherine Lamb, Alastair and Julie ('Tommy') Lawson, Valerie Lloyd, Henry and Bettina McNulty, Claudia McNulty, Helen McQuillan, Patsy Murray, Terry and Timmie O'Brien, Suzanna Penrose, David Sylvester, Allan Tyrer, Gertie Wissa, Audrey Withers.

Page 1:
Lee, aged 3 years 5 months, posing for her father at 40 South Clinton Street, Poughkeepsie, New York. 1910. (Theodore Miller)

Frontispiece:
Lee on the 'Wrens in Camera' assignment. Scotland, 1943. (Dave Scherman)

Opposite:
Lee, aged 11. 1918. (Photographer unknown)

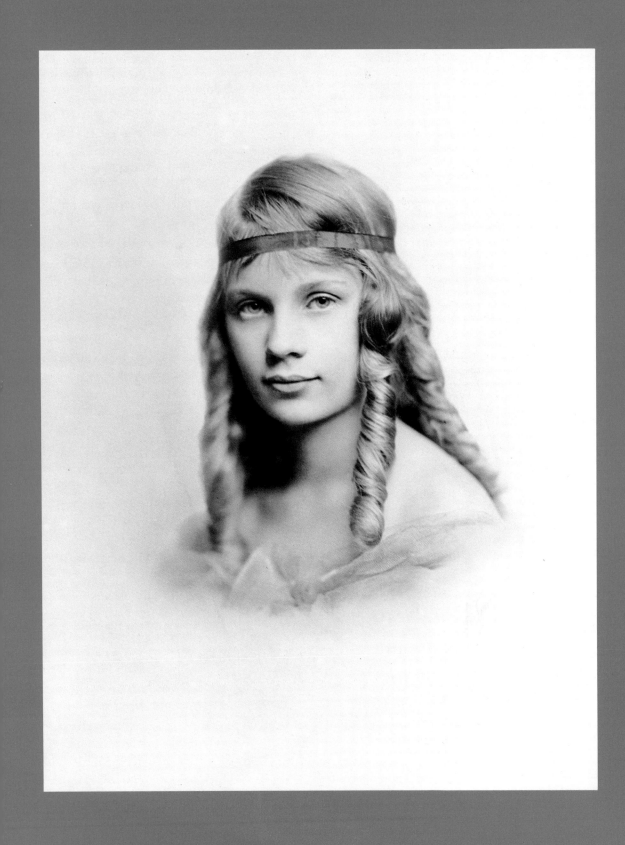

Lee Miller, fashion model. Lee Miller, photographer. Lee Miller, war correspondent. Lee Miller, writer. Lee Miller, aficionado of classical music. Lee Miller, *haute cuisine* cook. Lee Miller, traveller. In all her different worlds she moved with freedom. In all her roles she was her own bold self.

A paradox of irascibility and effusive warmth, of powerful talent and hopeless incapability, Lee rode her own temperament through life as if she were clinging to the back of a runaway dragon. Sometimes the dragon triumphed and Lee was plunged into bleak weeping despair, but mostly she took control and won a close run victory against herself first and adversity second. Her successes always left an enduring impression. She loved to learn, create or take part, and then move on to something else. Some of her 'jags', as she called her current obsessions, would last only days; others stretched for years. Photography was her supreme jag, and she deserted it only when, after thirty years, she had exhausted all its abilities to provide excitement.

Lee's spread of interests amounted to much more than the desultory pecking of a dilettante. Whatever she became involved in, her commitment was total and the consequence to herself and others was of only minor consideration. Though Lee had an immense capacity to learn from other people, few can be seen to have had much influence on her. She herself changed little as she moved among the giant-sized characters that peopled her different worlds. The core of her character had been assembled, stamped and sealed for life at an early age under the supervision of a remarkable mechanical engineer: her father, Theodore Miller.

Theodore Miller was descended from a Hessian soldier who settled in Lancaster, Pennsylvania, after the Revolution. His father was a bricklayer from Richmond, Indiana, but Theodore started his working life as a machine operator making wooden wheels for roller skates. With tenacious application he worked his way into progressively better jobs with the help of qualifications obtained through the International Correspondence School. In later years, when accused of being stubborn, he would dismissively say that stubbornness was just applied determination. This wilfulness, an insatiable curiosity about all things mechanical and scientific, and a completely unabashed manner of asking questions were traits that his daughter inherited.

In about 1895, when Theodore was in his middle twenties, he made up his mind to travel around the world. His limited means took him no further than Monterey in Mexico, where he got a job working in a steel mill. Unfortunately, this great adventure was short-lived. He contracted typhoid and ended up in the local hospital. It was the custom for patients to rely on their families for food, and with no family at hand it was lucky for Theodore that his friends from the steel mill brought him things to eat from time to time, and that the nuns from a nearby convent were kind enough to overlook his atheism and supplement his meagre rations.

As soon as he was well enough to stand the journey he returned to the United States. Career opportunities caused him to shelve his travel plans and he first took a job as foreman with the Mergenthaler Linotype Company in Brooklyn, New York, and then moved on to the Utica Drop Forge and Tool Company where he was rapidly appointed General Manager. Adding to the attractions of Utica was a Canadian nurse at Saint Luke's Hospital – Florence MacDonald. A kindly and industrious person, she was the daughter of Scottish–Irish settlers from Ontario. Their courtship was a long one, because Theodore refused to consider marriage until he was in a sufficiently advanced position to offer his wife-to-be a secure home. To help while away the years of waiting, he persuaded her to indulge his most cherished hobby – photography. Posing nude for him in a discreet but self-assured manner, she became the subject for an elegant sepia-toned portrait in the exact mode of the period.

At this time the De Laval Separator Company in Poughkeepsie was beset with labour difficulties and strikes, and, hearing about the bright young man in Utica who had rare managerial talents, sent for him. As soon as he was appointed Works Superintendent, Theodore radically improved the workers' pay and conditions, firing those who remained unsatisfied.

In 1904, after a year's separation while Theodore got established in Poughkeepsie, he and Florence were married. She did not immediately take to life in her new home; while waiting in Utica she had met someone else and could not be sure that she had made the right choice. With true pragmatism, Theodore sent her back to Utica to make up her mind. She returned a few weeks later completely reassured that she preferred the husband she already had.

The De Laval Separator Company was the largest and most prestigious business in the town with about eleven thousand employees and a massive

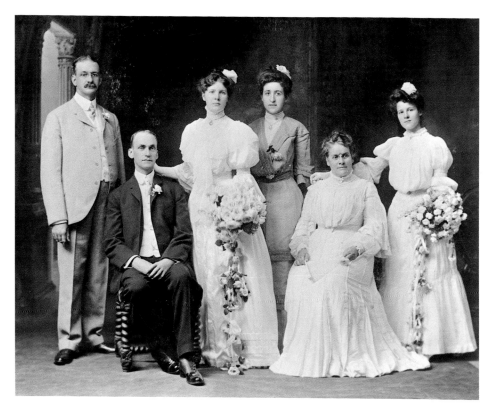

The wedding of Theodore Miller and Florence MacDonald. Poughkeepsie, New York, 10 August 1904. (Photographer unknown)

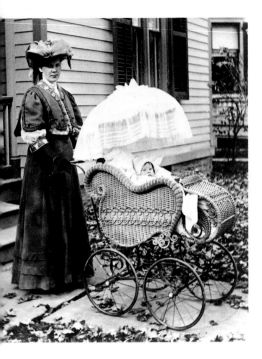

Lee, aged 6 months, with her mother.
Poughkeepsie, New York, 1907.
(Theodore Miller)

Kalamazoo Royal Range in the
kitchen of the Miller house,
Poughkeepsie, New York. (Theodore
Miller)

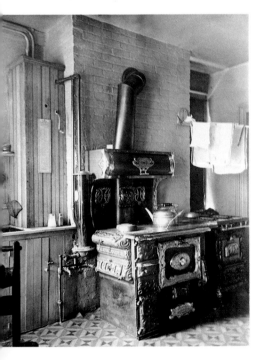

sales network. It may have been the newfound status of their company connections that brought the young couple to the flattering attention of the Daughters of the American Revolution. Florence was invited to join this elite social group founded on the filiation of loyal Americans. She gratefully accepted and all was well until they came to investigate her ancestry. Alas, her parents were Canadian and had therefore fought against the revolutionaries, and, worse still, Theodore's parents were descended from the Hessian mercenaries sent to quell the rebels. Florence's application was summarily dismissed, but the incident remained forever the key family joke.

John MacDonald was their firstborn, in 1905, and on 23 April 1907 Elizabeth was born. To begin with she was called Li Li; then she became Te Te to her parents; but everyone else always knew her as Lee. She was followed by Erik in 1910. Theodore's talent and industry earned his promotion to Works Manager, and the family moved to a small farm of 165 acres outside of Poughkeepsie on the Albany road.

The management of the farm was left to a Canadian, 'Uncle' Ephraim Miller, who despite his surname was no blood relation. Uncle Ephraim did not share Theodore's love of innovation, preferring the time-honoured methods. This was unfortunate, for though Theodore was known to be wonderfully tolerant of other people's views, failure by another to grasp progressive methods was absolute anathema to him. Uncle Ephraim had to go, and was eventually replaced by a more forward-looking manager, Jimmy Burns. The farm quickly became the test bed for all the new milking and cream separating equipment produced by De Laval.

Theodore's position in De Laval earned him several visits to the parent company in Stockholm and he took these opportunities to see as much of Scandinavia as he could, quietly storing up all the new ideas that he could find. One winter, soon after a Stockholm trip, word went round that Mr Miller had gone nuts: he was seen sliding down a hill on a couple of planks with pointed ends. This was Poughkeepsie's introduction to skiing, and it was not long before the three children and several neighbours were fitted out with skis made for them by Theodore.

The farm was one huge playground for Lee and her brothers. Their father encouraged their adventures, fostering every possible interest in science. With John as superintendent, they built a water-wheel beside a small stream and constructed a wooden railway track down one side of a valley and up the other. The wheels of the loco and tender were cast at the De Laval factory, but there was no motor. The children provided the power by dragging the loco up to the top of the track, piling on board and jerking a chock out from under the wheels. On the flat ground between the two gradients, John made a passing place by laying a short parallel track with two sets of points. This allowed the loco and the tender to be launched simultaneously from opposite ends of the track, relying on the split second timing of two friends switching the points to avoid a head-on collision.

Games were dangerous, thrilling and usually involved some kind of applied technology. Lee's favourite toy was a chemistry set, a wonderful and elaborate collection of apparatus and chemicals. She used to spend

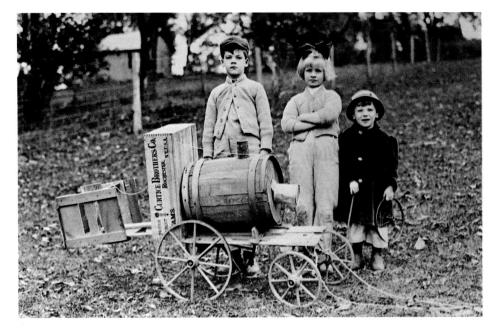

John, Lee and Erik Miller, 19 October 1913, at Sycamore Lodge, South Road, Poughkeepsie, New York. This loco was the forerunner of the one with flanged wheels and was mainly built by John. (Theodore Miller)

days at a time during the long winter months mixing potions and producing pungent smells, good-naturedly tolerating the interferences of Erik. Unwittingly they were laying the foundations not only for their later photographic work, but also for the technique of working together.

Photography came to Lee like everything else – as part of her surroundings. Theodore had installed a darkroom in a cramped cupboard under the stairs. His carefully annotated albums are crammed with photographs of locomotives, battleships, bridges, dams, roadways or marvels like an early biplane captioned 'First flight in a heavier-than-air machine' taken in 1910 at a fair. But these feats of modern engineering came a poor second to the studies of Lee which fill the books. Every possible event like 'Te Te's 3-month birthday' was lovingly recorded by a small snapshot and carefully typed caption. With the mass of tiny photographs he indulged his parental adoration.

Theodore and Florence shared an undemanding enjoyment of the theatre, and frequently took the children to shows. Nearly fifty years later Lee wrote:

The first theatrical performance I ever attended was in the Poughkeepsie Opera House. It seems highly unlikely, but is memorable and true that the 'bill' consisted of Sarah Bernhardt in person, playing 'the great passages from her greatest roles', from a chaise-longue; secondly, artistic, immobile nudes, imitating Greek sculpture (livid, quivering in the limelight); and as a curtain-raiser there was a guaranteed, authentic 'Motion Picture'. The Divine Sarah dying on a divan was of considerable morbid interest to me as a seven-year-old. Though I understood no French, her Portia, pleading, seemed urgent enough (she was propped up vertical for that); the nudes were just more ART. But the 'Motion Picture' was a thrill-packed reel of a spark-shedding locomotive dashing through tunnels and over trestles. The hero was the intrepid cameraman himself who wore his cap backwards, and was paid 'danger money'. On a curve across a chasm, the head of the train glared at its own tail . . . the speed was dizzy, nothing whatever stayed still and I pulled eight dollars worth of fringe from the rail of our loge, in my whooping, joyful frenzy.[1]

At the age of seven, during a brief illness of her mother's, Lee was sent to stay with some friends of the family, who lived in Brooklyn. They had a young son who was in the United States Navy, and during Lee's stay he was home on leave. The details and circumstances of his connection with Lee are not known, but what is certain is that she was the victim of a sexual molestation with savage consequences. On her return home, she was found to be infected with venereal disease. These were the days before penicillin was discovered, and the only cure was douching with dichloride of mercury. It fell to Florence, with her nurse's training, to administer the treatment. It was agony for them both.

To forestall the inevitable emotional trauma, Florence and Theodore sought the help of a psychiatrist. His advice was to convince Lee that sex and love were dissociated – sex was merely a physical act with no positive link to love. By trivializing sex it was hoped to ward off any backlash of guilt. The efficacy of this treatment is impossible to judge, because a few years later another tragedy struck at its core.

It was summer, and Lee in her early teens had fallen in love for the first time with a young local boy. To her he was all she could wish for – good-looking, fun and, like herself, adventurous. One hot afternoon they were out on a lake in a rowing boat. No one knows if he fell over the side or jumped in for a joke. His heart failed and he died instantly. Lee carried the combined scar from both events to her grave.

In their attempt to help her through these horrors, her parents indulged her shamelessly and, not surprisingly, Lee was quick to take advantage of their leniency. With a logic entirely normal in a child, she saw that her special position allowed household chores to be ducked and most other family matters manipulated to her advantage.

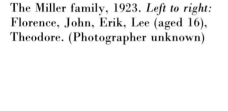

The Miller family, 1923. *Left to right:* Florence, John, Erik, Lee (aged 16), Theodore. (Photographer unknown)

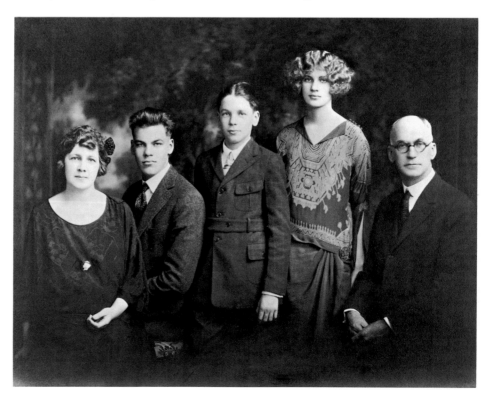

No matter how successful she was at getting things her own way at home, school was a different problem. If a subject failed to interest her, no amount of coercion could make her absorb it. At home Lee would immerse herself in her own projects with total dedication, but at school nothing would make her submit to authority. Her indignation channelled itself into a series of often ingenious and high-spirited practical jokes, and inevitably she was expelled from one school after another.

Theodore was torn between pride in the young rebellious spirit he had fostered, and exasperation. He kept finding new schools of increasing severity, mainly run by religious orders, despite his commitment to atheism. The final blow fell when Lee obtained some diagnostic blue dye and surreptitiously fed it to a rather prim classmate. The poor girl was stricken with hysterics at the sight of her bright blue urine. Enough was enough. Lee was expelled again, and this time there were no more schools left to go to.

Rescue came from an unexpected quarter in the shape of Madame Kockashinski, a Polish spinster who had taught French at Putnam Hall Private School which Lee had briefly attended. She proposed that she and a companion be allowed to take Lee to Paris and there expose her to the steadying effects of European classical art and culture. The trip was to conclude with a spell in a finishing school in Nice. Lee was wildly enthusiastic and Theodore and Florence were soon persuaded to disregard their misgivings. After all, this could be a solution to the sticky problem of furthering Lee's education, and with two such upright chaperons Lee could not possibly come to any harm.

On 30 May 1925 the entire Miller family went to New York to see Lee off on the S.S. *Minehaha*. Lee had known all along that she would not find it difficult to run rings round her chaperons, and she was soon proved right. When the ship docked at Boulogne, Madame Kockashinski's French was so bad that she could not even get a taxi. One farce led to another, and Lee recalled: 'Somehow their first hotel in Paris turned out to be a *maison de passe*. It took my chaperons five days to catch on, but I thought it was divine! I was either hanging out of the window looking at the clients come and go or watching the shoes being changed in the corridor with amazing frequency.'[2]

This first visit to Paris was intoxicating. It was the catalyst Lee had been waiting for. Far from being the cultivating influence for which her parents had hoped, it offered the first contact with a world Lee had unconsciously craved. She stayed with her chaperons just long enough to become familiar with the city. Then she escaped.

She quickly learned to fend for herself and announced to her parents that she wanted to become an artist. Once over their initial shock, they grudgingly assented and paid her fees at the newly opened L'Ecole Medgyes pour la Technique du Théâtre in the Rue de Sèvres, run by Ladislas Medgyes, a talented stage designer, with Erno Goldfinger, who later became a famous architect and town planner, listed as 'architecte'.

Lee was not one of the school's star pupils. She was eighteen, gregarious, fabulously beautiful in exactly the style of the period and far more

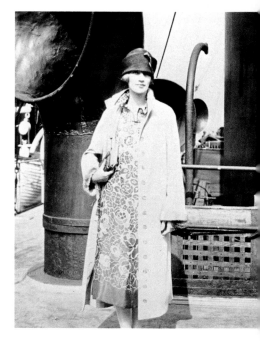

Lee setting off for Paris on the S.S. *Minehaha*. New York, 1925. (Theodore Miller)

13

interested in celebrating her newfound freedom than in formal studies. Informally, what she was learning was what it meant to be a fully emancipated woman in charge of her own destiny. She had arrived in Paris in the heyday of the survivors of 'the lost generation' – the people whom F. Scott Fitzgerald described as 'a generation grown up to find all Gods dead, all wars fought, all faiths in man shaken'. Easy living was a virtue, pleasure-seeking an obsession.

Paris was the hotbed of artistic revolution. The nihilistic Dada movement, born of revulsion against the slaughter of the First World War, had given way to Surrealism. André Breton, using the words of Apollinaire, described the movement as 'Pure psychic Automatism, by which it is intended to express verbally, in writing or in any other way, the true process of thought. It is the dictation of thought, free from the exercise of reason, and every aesthetic or moral preoccupation.' Dreams, hallucinations and fantasies were the fabric of the movement, libertarianism was its style. Lee could not have sought her personal freedom at a more propitious moment.

Artists whose works were later to be regarded as pivotal were on the springboard of their fame. Giorgio de Chirico's dreamlike landscapes signalled the start of an era. The poets Paul Eluard and André Breton and the painters Max Ernst, Marcel Duchamp, André Masson, Yves Tanguy and René Magritte, to name but a few, were youthful champions of exciting iconoclastic ideas. Picasso, Braque and Miró set their own pace, the stream of their work touching like tangents with the work of the Surrealists.

The photographic scene was dominated by Man Ray, a young American photographer who preferred to be thought of as a painter. In addition to strong portraiture, he was making camera-less photographs which he called 'rayographs'. His method was to place assemblies of objects on photographic printing paper which he first exposed to light and then developed in the normal way. The result, often a conglomerate of more than one exposure, was that the objects' white or grey shadows formed strange dreamlike patterns. The use of random juxtapositions in this way appealed greatly to the Surrealists, but the established photographers sneered at Man Ray, referring to him as 'no more than a clever darkroom trickster'.[3]

The tempo of *haute couture* was set by Chanel, Patou and Lelong, who created a style of boyish simplicity with sportswear-type day clothes. Both this clean-cut active look and the bead-embroidered sheath evening dresses suited Lee so well that it seemed as if the whole *mode* had been designed specially for her. On the stage, the ballets of Diaghilev and Massine were all the rage. Jean Cocteau and Christian Bérard were the rising stars of design, although at this point Cocteau was best known for his poetry. Gertrude Stein, Ezra Pound, Ford Madox Ford and Ernest Hemingway glittered in the literary constellation.

It is hard to know how many, if any, of these creative people, whom history was later to make so eminent, Lee actually came into contact with. Whether she met them or not, she was certainly fascinated by them and

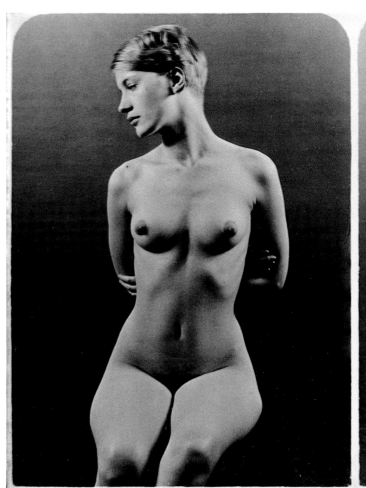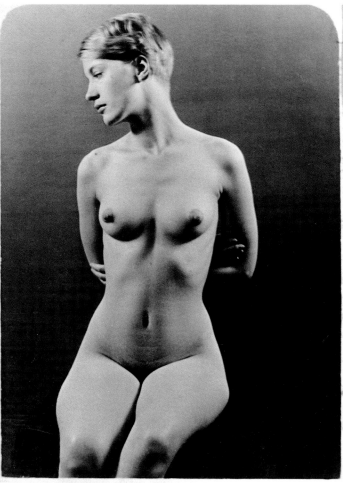

touched by their influence. It is not surprising that she refused to come home until, in the winter of 1926, Theodore arrived in Paris and dragged her back to Poughkeepsie.

Life on the farm was no substitute for Paris, so Lee set about weaning her parents from her by making trips of ever increasing duration to New York, finally enrolling in the Art Students League. The course concentrated on theatrical design and lighting, but for her it was an excuse to resume life in a big city. She swung into it with gusto, rushing through student social life in a whirl of hedonism. Theodore gave her modest but adequate support which allowed her to rent a small flat in a brownstone building on East 49th Street. To add to the excitement she started training as a dancer for the Hippodrome Spectaculars, appeared briefly in the George White Scandals variety show, and also took part in a night-club production called 'The Great Temptation'.

During weekends at Kingwood Park, Lee would help Theodore indulge his passion for photography. He had bought a stereoscopic camera which photographed two images simultaneously on to an 85mm × 170mm nitrate negative. When the contact print was viewed through a device with prismatic lenses, the images combined to give a three-dimensional effect. Bridges and other civil engineering marvels were obvious subjects, but his secret passion was nudes. Lee posed for him countless times,

Nude study of Lee by her father, 1 July 1928, Kingwood Park, Poughkeepsie, New York. A stereoscopic photograph which when looked at through a viewer gives a three-dimensional effect. (Theodore Miller)

15

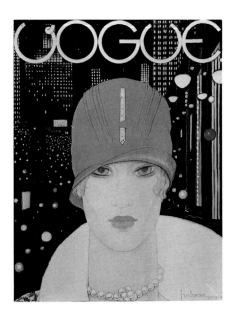

American *Vogue*, March 1927.
Designed by Georges Lepape.

indoors and out; cool, poised and at times a little solemn. Her self-consciousness only creeps into the shots where she is posing together with nude girlfriends.

Years of Lee's life might have slipped away in this rather purposeless way had it not been for a near accident that changed everything. One day, crossing the street in New York, she carelessly stepped into the path of an oncoming car. A bystander yanked her back with only inches to spare, and Lee collapsed into his arms. Her rescuer was the new self-made king of magazine publishing, Condé Nast.[4] The fright induced Lee to babble away in French, and this, plus the fact that she was dressed in European-style clothes, must have intrigued Condé Nast. He befriended her and offered her modelling work on *Vogue*. She was an instant success and her face appeared immediately on the front cover of the March 1927 issue, designed by Georges Lepape. The background is the glittering lights of Manhattan, and the penetrating determination of her gaze from under the brim of a blue cloche hat counterpoints the sophisticated fripperies of her costume.

Edward Steichen vied with Baron de Meyer for the title of the world's highest-paid photographer. Steichen was also a close friend of Condé Nast and the main photographer for *Vogue*, so it was a double honour for Lee when she was sent to him as a model. She was soon posing regularly for him and appearing in the pages of *Vogue* and other Condé Nast magazines. For Steichen, Lee was the ideal model for the mid-twenties *mode*. She was tall, carried herself well, and her strong profile and fine blond hair exactly suited his clear, elegant style. There was an air of detachment about her, and she was wonderfully photogenic. Steichen gave her a look of worldly sophistication way beyond her years, which fitted in perfectly with the uninhibited and relaxed look that was ousting the remnants of the *belle époque*. Thinking back on this period many years later, Lee said, 'I was terribly, terribly pretty. I looked like an angel, but I was a fiend inside.'

Arnold Genthe, on the other hand, was one of the few photographers who allowed Lee to look like a romantic young girl. The low key and soft focus of his portraits, and also, perhaps, the fact that he photographed her for love, not money, give her image a delicacy and sense of vulnerability that no one else ever achieved. Genthe was well into his seventies, but could often be discovered at the head of the stairs leading up to Lee's flat with three red roses clutched in his hand. Lee adored this wise, gentle old man and used to listen for hours to his comments on art and culture.

She also met and formed an enduring friendship with Frank Crowninshield, the editor of *Vanity Fair* and another man well worth listening to, who was sometimes described as 'Condé Nast's Svengali'. Nast, whose manners were less polished than he felt desirable, allowed himself to be guided by Crowninshield's immensely sophisticated ideas of good taste.

In addition to these erudite people, Lee had many other friends of her own age. From Poughkeepsie Belle Van Der Water and Artida Warner were good friends, but it was with Tanja Ramm whom Lee met at the Art Students League that she formed the closest bond. Tanja, whose parents

Opposite: Lee. New York, *c.* 1928.
(Edward Steichen)

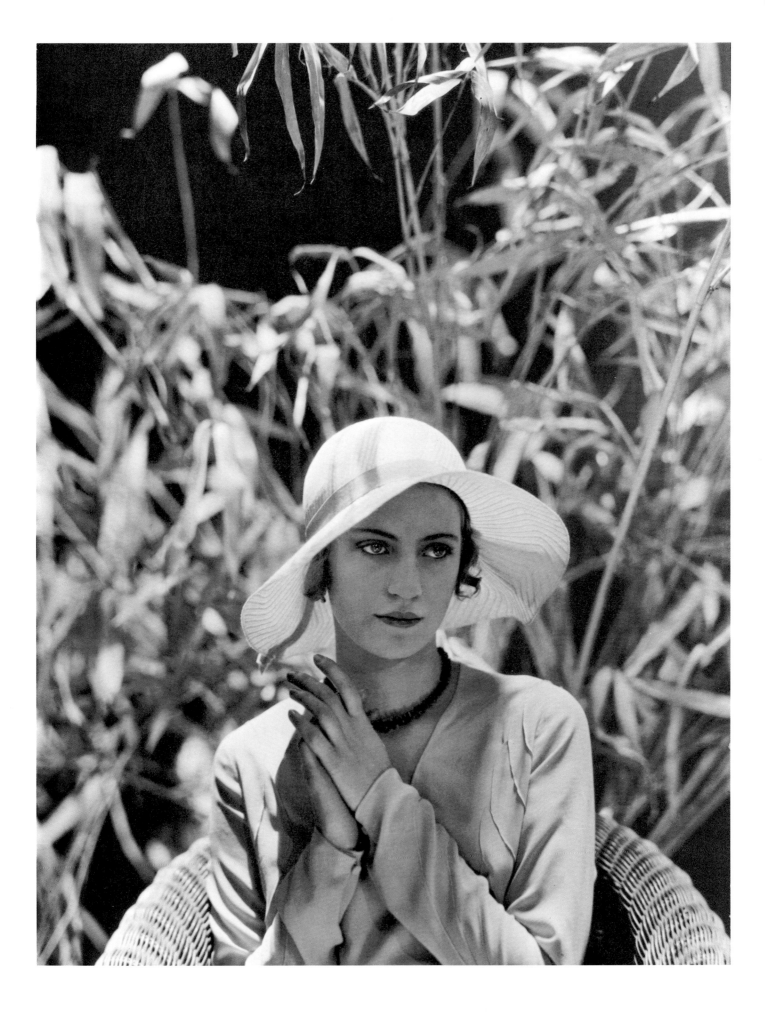

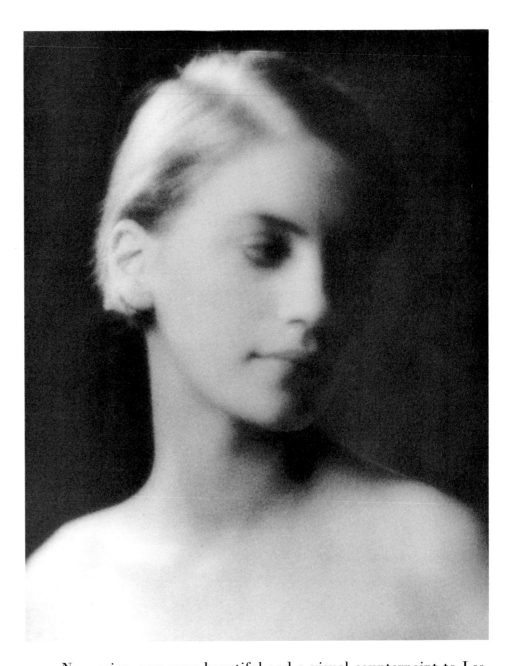

Lee. New York, *c.* 1927. (Arnold Genthe)

Opposite: Lee. New York, *c.* 1927. (Nickolas Muray)

were Norwegian, was very beautiful and a visual counterpoint to Lee, having dark hair and eyebrows. Together they went to the fashionable parties at Condé Nast's apartment at 1040 Park Avenue. Nast mixed his guest list in the way a master painter blends colours on a palette. The pages of his magazines seemed to come to life, with a blend of brilliant people from society, business and the theatre, and a dash of beautiful young girls like Lee and Tanja thrown in for added dazzle.

Weekends were usually spent at Kingwood Park, where Theodore and Florence unfailingly welcomed all Lee's friends, particularly the girls, whom Theodore would beg to pose nude for his stereoscopic photos. John had become an aviation pioneer and in one of the barns had rebuilt a wrecked two-seater Standard J1 biplane. He became a highly proficient flyer and eventually owned several different types of aircraft, including a gyrocopter. Occasionally Lee and her pals would be treated to a flip

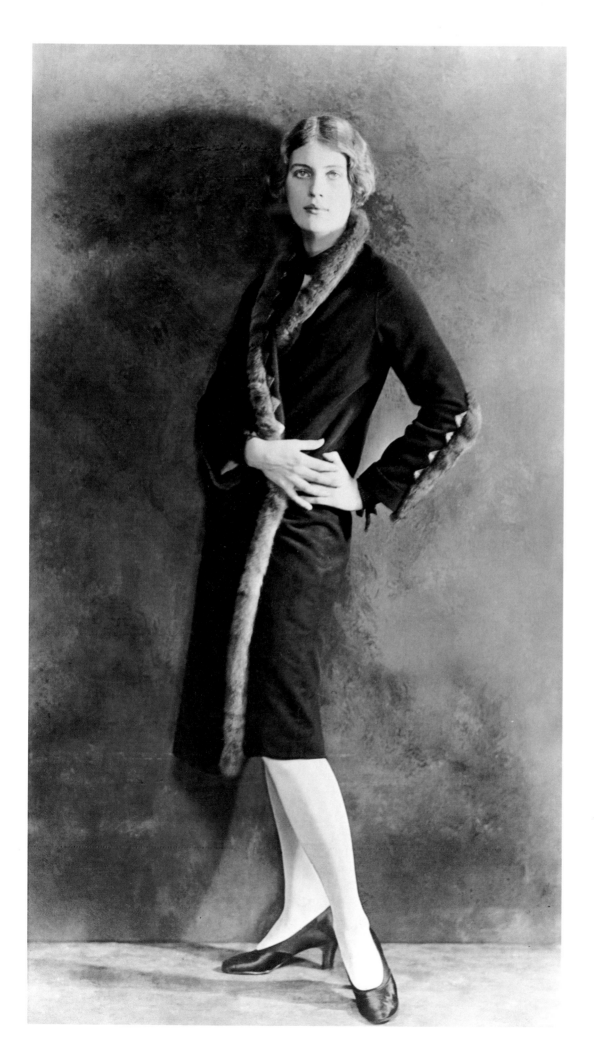

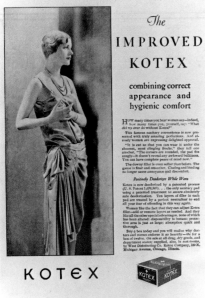

The Kotex advertisement with
Steichen's photograph of Lee which
created a scandal when it was
released nationwide in 1928.

Lee, modelling for Jean Patou. Paris,
c. 1930. (Man Ray)

around the neighbourhood which usually culminated in looping the loop
over the family home.

Despite her uninhibited lifestyle, Lee was horrified in July 1928 to
discover that a Steichen photograph of herself had been used as an
advertisement for Kotex sanitary towels. It was the first time a
photograph of a model had been used for this purpose. At that time these
feminine matters were considered far too delicate to discuss and any
woman who allowed her image to be used to endorse such a product was
likely to be regarded as utterly debased. The advertisement appeared
nationwide in all the fashionable magazines – today such coverage would
be equalled only by the saturation achieved in a massive television
advertising campaign. Letters of protest poured in to the magazine and
the advertising agency, one of the strongest representations coming from
Lee's beau, Alfred de Liagre, who actually bearded Condé Nast on the
matter. No protest prevailed; Lee had signed the model's release form and
the agency was well within its rights. The advertisement ran until
December, but by that time Lee had become quite proud of the fact that
she had ruffled so many prudish feathers.

For Lee her success in New York was little more than marking time. She
loved the excitement of life in the big modelling studios and her contact
with the social and intellectual elite, but it still did not compare to those
heady student days in Paris. She was now twenty-two, and obsessed with
the idea of returning. Steichen had given her an introduction to Man Ray,
Condé Nast had directed her to George Hoyningen-Huene who ran the
French *Vogue* studio, and a fashion designer had offered her a small
research assignment which promised a little money. With all this firmly in
her grasp, and the assurance of Tanja as a travelling companion, she
booked a passage on the *Comte de Grasse*.

Lee's love affair with de Liagre, who was later to become a successful
and tasteful producer of the Broadway theatre, had always been
tempestuous, full of recriminations and passions. With his complicity, she
divided her affections between him and a young Canadian flyer called
Argylle, an arrangement made easier by the fact that the two men were
great friends. When the day of Lee's departure came, they tossed a coin to
decide which of them should see her off at the pier. De Liagre won, but
Argylle consoled himself by swooping his Jenny biplane low over the liner
as it headed down the Hudson River and showering red roses on the
sundeck. His mission accomplished, he returned to the Roosevelt airfield
to pick up a pupil. On solo flights, the Jenny was normally flown from the
front cockpit, but when a pupil is learning he takes the front so that the
instructor can knock him out with a spanner if fear causes him to freeze on
the controls. On this occasion, perhaps overcome by the excitement of the
farewell, Argylle stopped the plane only long enough to allow his pupil to
climb into the rear cockpit. A few minutes after take-off, the Jenny spun
into the ground. Argylle and his pupil were killed instantly. Lee,
meanwhile, threw herself into shipboard social life, completely unaware of
the tragic death of her lover.

Chapter Two

Photography in Surrealist Paris
1929–1932

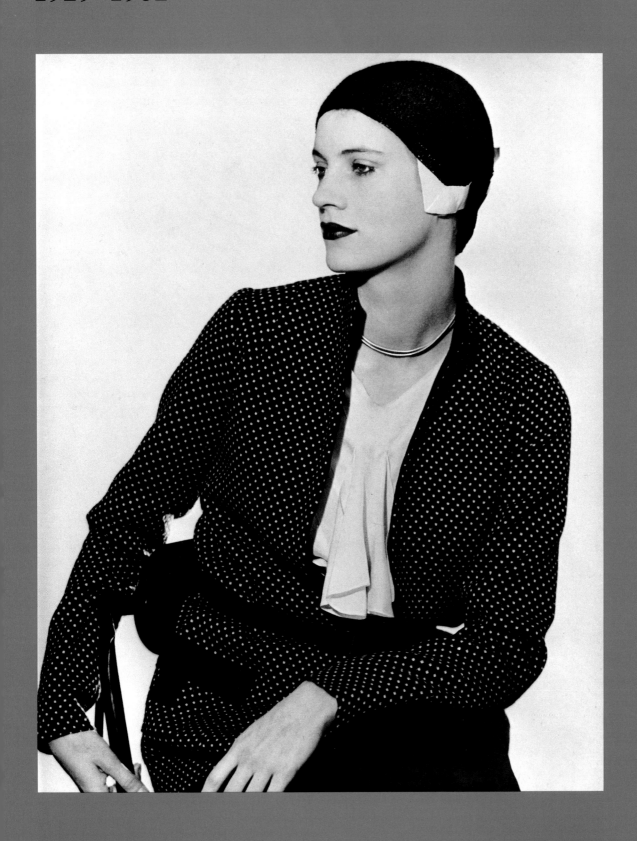

Lee and Tanja halted briefly in Paris, then boarded the train for Florence. Under the tutelage of an elderly art dealer they toured the city and the nearby hill towns. Lee's research assignment, which could hardly be called significant in itself, was by chance a vital catalyst.

Her task was to make meticulously detailed drawings of buckles, bows, lace and other costume adornments in Renaissance paintings and send the drawings back to the United States for use in contemporary fashions. It was tedious and exacting work, and before long Lee began to experiment with using a camera. Today this seems a glaringly obvious step, but the only equipment available to her at the time was a folding Kodak and the spindliest of portable tripods. Taking close-ups in poor light with low-speed film must be about the most difficult starting point from which to explore a technique, but it was entirely characteristic of Lee to want to begin in the middle of a new skill. By all accounts the results seem to have satisfied her sponsor.

From Florence they went to Rome, where Tanja departed to visit friends in Germany, and Lee returned to Paris. Her original intention had been to carry on working as a fashion model, but now another idea had taken hold: she had decided to become a photographer. Man Ray was regarded as the most exciting photographer in Paris; instead of modelling for him, she would become his pupil.

She found her way to his studio on the ground floor of 31bis Rue Campagne Première, which must be the ugliest Art Nouveau building in Paris. To her disappointment the concierge announced that Man Ray had left for Biarritz. Lee's impatient expectations were dashed: things always had to happen NOW to engage her; in a month's time when Man Ray returned the bold intention would have evaporated. Disconsolately she retired to the Bateau Ivre, a small café nearby, and ordered a Pernod with plenty of ice. Suddenly Man Ray appeared.

He kind of rose up through the floor at the top of a circular staircase. He looked like a bull, with an extraordinary torso and very dark eyebrows and dark hair. I told him boldly that I was his new student. He said he didn't take students, and anyway he was leaving Paris for his holiday. I said, I know, I'm going with you – and I did. We lived together for three years. I was known as Madame Man Ray, because that's how they do things in France.[1]

In reality it was not quite that easy, because at this time Man Ray was living with Kiki de Montparnasse, the cabaret artist, who was well known for giving her lovers both her affection and her jealousy with equal passion. There were several scenes in cafés, where Kiki ferociously hurled abuse and dinner plates at Man Ray, but after a while she simmered down and eventually became quite amiable towards Lee.

In many ways there were striking similarities between Man Ray and Lee's father, quite apart from their both being devotees of engineering and science. As Henry Miller says in 'Recollections of Man Ray in Hollywood', 'He had a way of making everything new and, if not important, certainly worth considering, worth pondering. . . . He had no difficulty in

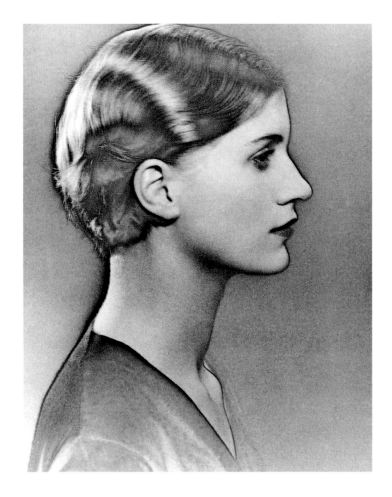

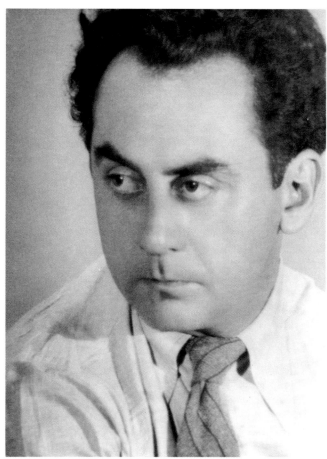

understanding what was alien because nothing was or is alien to him. . . . His curiosity was unquenchable, and often led him far afield. He was never just a painter or a photographer, he was an adventurer and explorer.'[2] These words exactly describe Theodore and, of course, Lee.

Lee and Man Ray made a fruitful partnership: she posed for him, and he tutored her. They lived and loved together, but it cannot have been easy. Even for the totally dedicated Surrealist, the basic tenet of free love must have conflicted with the basic instincts of possession and jealousy. Lee was more successful than most in upholding this principle. She rarely allowed loyalty to a current lover to conflict with her sexual desires, stating that she went to bed with whomever she chose, and why should that affect the person she loved? The doctrine of free love had largely been constructed from a male standpoint. Lee exposed the hypocrisy of its double standards, to the chagrin and bewilderment of the men around her. Man Ray's honesty is tinged with a touch of pique as he describes the occasion of the elaborate costume ball given by the Count and Countess Pecci-Blunt:

The theme was white; any costume was admitted but it had to be all in white. A large white dance floor was installed in the garden with the orchestra hidden in the bushes. I was asked to think up some added attraction. I hired a movie projector which was set up in a room on an upper floor, with the window giving out on to the garden. I found an old hand-coloured film by the pioneer French

Left: Photograph of Lee, using the solarization technique which she and Man Ray invented. Paris, *c.* 1929. (Man Ray)

Right: Man Ray. Paris, *c.* 1930. (Lee Miller)

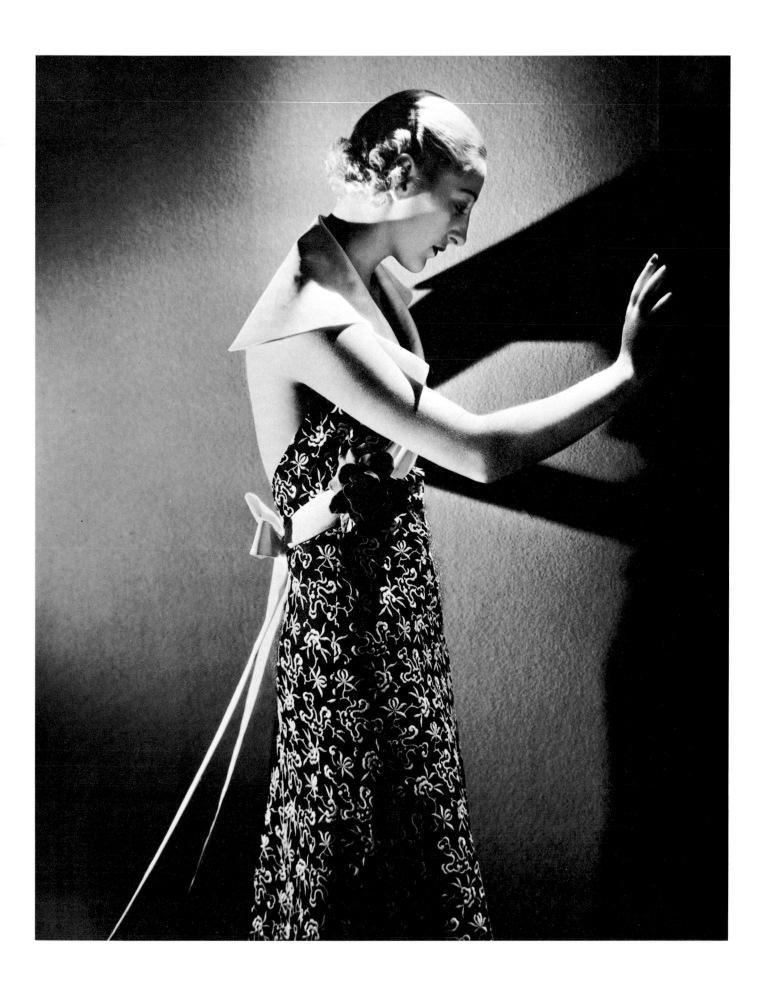

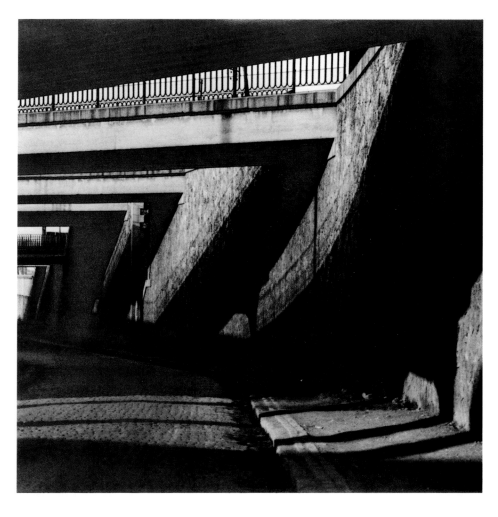

Walkway. Paris, n.d. (Lee Miller)

film maker, Méliès. While the white couples were revolving on the white floor, the film was projected onto this moving screen – those who were not dancing looked down from the windows of the house. The effect was eerie – figures and faces in the film were distorted but recognizable. I had also set up a camera in a room to photograph the guests.

In keeping with the theme of the ball, I was dressed in white as a tennis player, bringing as assistant a pupil who studied photography with me at the time – Lee Miller. She too was dressed as a tennis player in very smart shorts and blouse especially designed by one of the well-known couturiers [Mme Vionnet]. A slim figure with blond hair and lovely legs, she was continually being taken away to dance, leaving me to concentrate alone on my photography. I was pleased with her success, but annoyed at the same time, not because of the added work, but out of jealousy; I was in love with her. As the night progressed I saw less and less of her, fumbled with my material and could not keep track of my supply of film holders. I finally ceased taking pictures, went downstairs to the buffet for a drink, and withdrew from the party. Lee turned up now and then between dances to tell me what a wonderful time she was having; all the men were so sweet to her. It was her introduction to French society.[3]

Lee learned fast. The technical side of photography came easily to her and she regarded the exacting standards of the darkroom work as a challenge rather than a chore. But more importantly, Man Ray gave her confidence in her own eye and contact with his Surrealist friends stimulated her imagination.

Opposite: Fashion study. Paris, 1932. (Lee Miller)

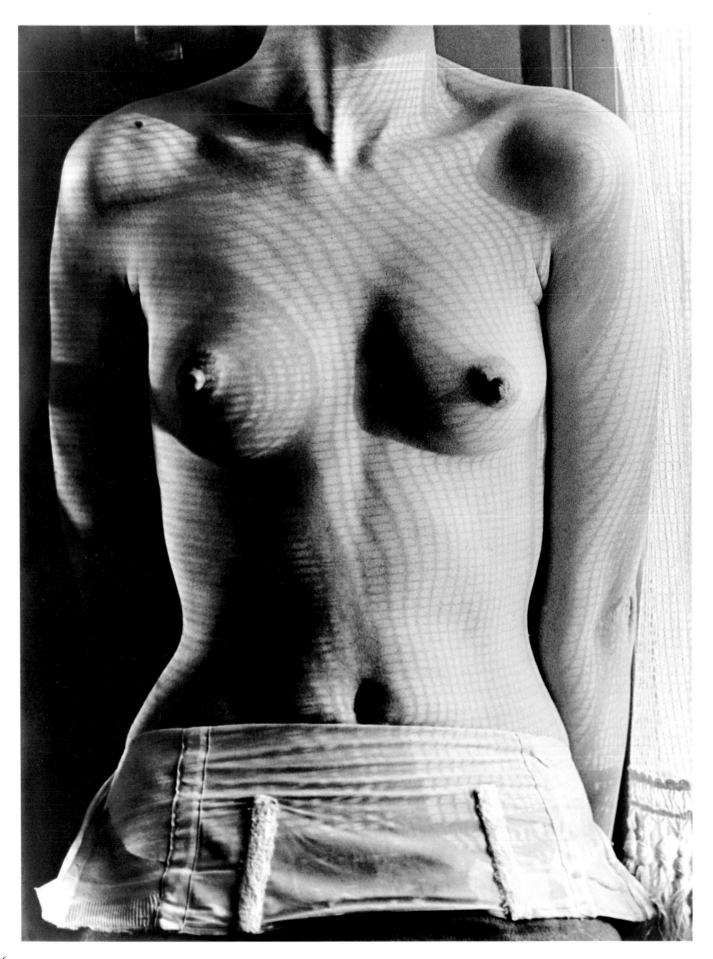

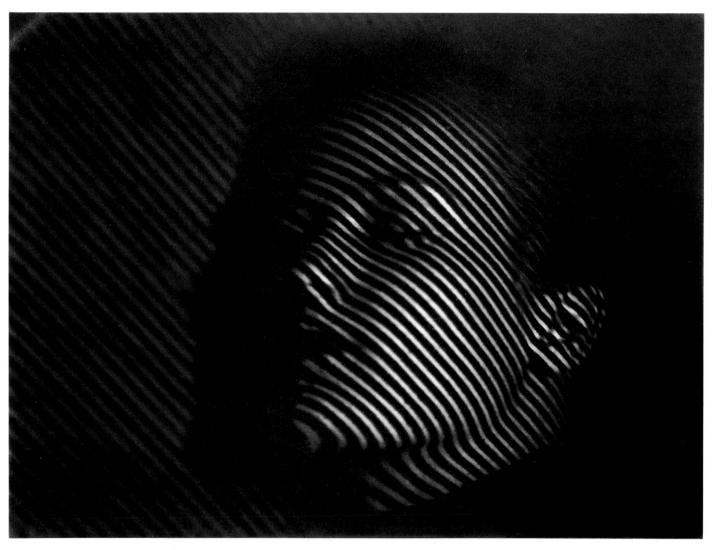

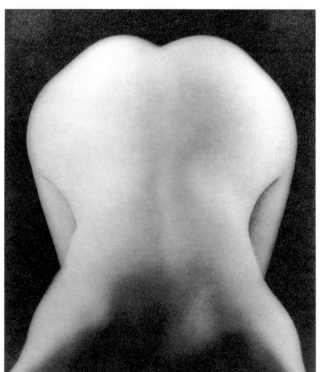

Opposite: Shadow patterns on Lee's torso. Paris, *c.* 1930. (Man Ray)

Above: 'Leebra'. Paris, *c.* 1930. (Man Ray)

Left: Nude bent forward. Paris, *c.* 1931. (Lee Miller)

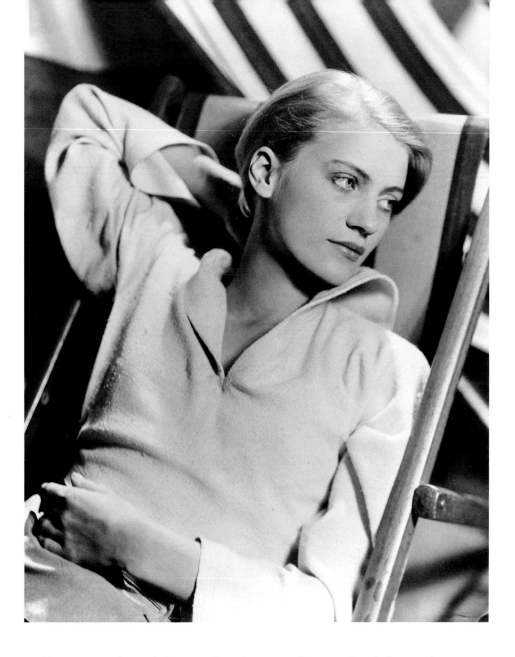

Lee. Paris, *c.* 1930. (George Hoyningen-Huene)

Few examples of her early photographs survived her subsequent travelling and the strange contempt in which she held her own work. Those that remain show that she saw her world with a delicate, cool elegance. The images are direct and perceptive, and the Surrealist influence is often present in the form of some witty juxtaposition. The style is pure and innocent, the photographs made simply for their own sake.

Most of the work was done on the smaller sizes of glass plates and then enlarged. According to Lee's description of Man Ray's set-up, 'The darkroom wasn't as big as a bathroom rug. There was a wooden sink lined with acid-proof paint, a big print developing basin and a tank above that where the water could run through and rinse. Man was absolutely meticulous about how photos were fixed and washed.'[4]

At regular intervals she would interrupt her apprenticeship with Man Ray and go to the Paris *Vogue* studios to model for George Hoyningen-Huene, a White Russian baron who had become a renowned fashion photographer. Part of the aura that surrounded him was a fearsome reputation for intimidating his models. Lee was unimpressed by his outward show of antipathy and the warmth of her personality won an enduring friendship. She continued to model for him all the time she was in Paris, and though Hoyningen-Huene did not like his models to pose for other photographers, he thought highly enough of Lee to ignore the fact that she did so.

One of the keys to Hoyningen-Huene's success was his mastery of studio lighting, and from their work together Lee quickly absorbed much of his technique. Her charm and curiosity were coupled with a knack for getting people to talk and explain what they were doing. These modelling sessions with Hoyningen-Huene were rather like a privileged tutorial, allowing Lee to experience the work on both sides of the camera at the same time. For the next three years her image was highly celebrated in the pages of glossy magazines and photographic art publications. Cecil Beaton, writing many years later about that period, stated: 'At this time another American, Lee Miller . . . cut short her pale hair and looked like a sunkissed goat boy from the Appian Way. Only sculpture could approximate the beauty of her curling lips, long languid pale eyes and column neck.'[5]

Hoyningen-Huene's assistant at this time was a handsome young German, Horst P. Horst, who was just taking on his first assignments. To augment his portfolio, he asked Lee to pose for him. He put every possible effort into the portrait, a wistful study of Lee clutching some lilies of the valley, and when he proudly showed her the finished print, she exclaimed approvingly, 'Wow! that's a howl!' Mistaking this for disapprobation, Horst resolved never to photograph her again. He was even more put off a

Lee. Paris, *c.* 1930. (Horst P. Horst)

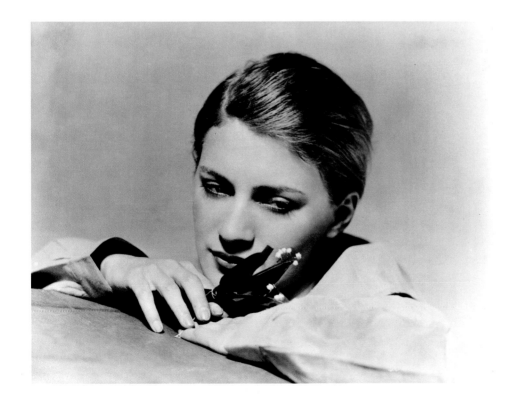

few weeks later when she came into the studio bearing a breast on a dinner plate. She had been watching a radical mastectomy at a hospital and had asked the surgeon for his leavings, carrying the breast through the streets under a cloth. The idea was to photograph it surrounded by a place-setting as a Surrealist object. Michel de Brunhoff, editor-in-chief of French *Vogue*, was horrified and threw Lee and the breast out, but not before she had managed a quick shot of it.[6]

After about nine months of apprenticeship to Man Ray, Lee began to take on assignments of her own for *Vogue* and other magazines. A measure of Lee's and Man Ray's mutual respect was that neither of them was seriously concerned when their credits were wrongly ascribed. Man Ray passed quite a lot of his own work over to Lee to free himself for painting, though Lee claimed she was given only the jobs he did not want or which did not pay enough. They worked together on a brochure for the Compagnie Parisienne de Distribution d'Electricité. It took the form of an edition of five hundred albums with a preface by Pierre Bost, to be given to the company's top customers. Lee recounted later that 'the use of a nude – that was me – was a little tough for the officials because they were a public utility company. And we were pretty shaken because we went and took a beautiful picture one night of the Place de la Concorde (I borrowed somebody's roof to do it from) and later discovered it was lit by gas!'[7]

One of their best-known joint achievements was the development of the 'solarization' technique. Several years earlier, Man Ray had seen a solarized photograph by Stieglitz that had been discarded as ruined, but it did not occur to him to try to make use of the technique until Lee had a lucky accident:

Something crawled across my foot in the darkroom and I let out a yell and turned on the light. I never did find out what it was, a mouse or what. Then I realized that the film was totally exposed: there in the development tanks, ready to be taken out, were a dozen practically fully developed negatives of a nude against a black background. Man Ray grabbed them, put them in the hypo and looked at them: the unexposed parts of the negative, which had been the black background, had been exposed by this sharp light that had been turned on and they had developed and came right up to the edge of the white nude body . . . It was all very well my making that one accidental discovery, but then Man had to set about how to control it and make it come out exactly the way he wanted to each time.[8]

The results are the hallmark of their artistic association.

On one occasion Man Ray took a low-angle, soft-focus photograph of Lee's head, featuring her neck prominently. The result was not to his liking so he threw away the negative. Lee retrieved the plate and carefully made a print, working hard to enhance and perfect it until she was satisfied with the image. Man Ray was impressed, but then infuriated because Lee claimed it had become *her* work of art, not his. The row was short and furious, and ended with the usual procedure of Man Ray throwing Lee out of the studio. A few hours later, when she returned, she found the image pinned to the wall with its throat slashed by a razor and streams of scarlet ink cascading from the wound.[9] As with so many other

Lee. Paris, 1929. (Man Ray)

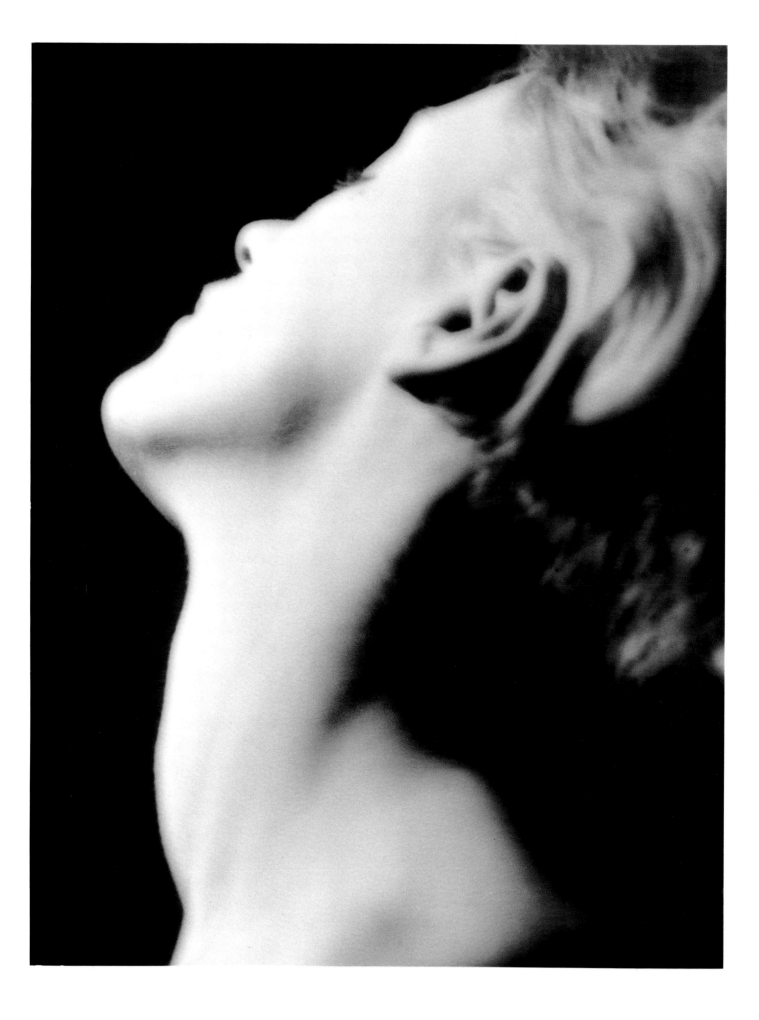

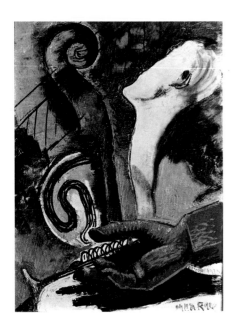

Le Logis de l'artiste, by Man Ray, *c.* 1931. Lee, her neck slashed, is shown in the artist's studio among his possessions.

traumas in his life, Man Ray sought to sublimate this experience in his work. His painting *Le Logis de l'artiste* (The Artist's Abode) shows the delicate soft neck stretching up out of a jumble of objects recognizable as the familiar clutter of the studio. The reduction of Lee's head to an object and its inclusion in this visual context reveal even more perhaps than Man Ray intended.

In spite of all Lee's work as a photographer, it was as a model that she created the most vivid impressions, then as now. She posed for many of Man Ray's most striking portraits and nudes; the fame of her image became widespread. One of the first Man Ray objects to be made as a multiple was his *Boule de Neige*, which 'consisted of a glass ball filled with water in which floated a photograph of a girl's eye (Lee Miller's), larger than life, enveloped in a snow-storm of white flakes when the globe was agitated.'[10]

A glass manufacturer designed a champagne glass inspired by the shape of her breast, and *Time* magazine ran an article about Man Ray, with a photograph of him by Lee. The concluding comment was that Lee Miller was 'widely celebrated for having the most beautiful navel in Paris'.[11] Theodore was not amused. He obliged *Time* to publish a letter from him stating that 'the article contained a very offensive and quite untruthful reference to Miss Lee Miller',[12] followed by an apology from the editor claiming that the piece was based on erroneous information.

By now Lee had her own apartment and studio, ten minutes' walk from Man Ray's studio, at 12 Rue Victor Considérante. The tall 1920s cement-faced building stands at the end of a street of old stone houses, overlooking the adjacent Cimetière du Montparnasse: at the other end the Lion de Belfort guards the Place Denfert-Rochereau. In common with many buildings in Montparnasse, it was designed for artists and had six individual duplex studios. Lee adapted hers easily for photographic purposes. Her installation was basic – a few lights, a roll of backdrop paper and a small darkroom. For the more demanding assignments she used to borrow Man Ray's equipment. She decorated the walls with rainbow-coloured chiffon, studded with coloured German gramophone discs like giant jelly lozenges. Above the bed was a tapestry wall hanging made to a design by Cocteau.

Lee discovered immediately that her portrait clients came in cycles. First there was a run of royalty, the Maharanee of Cooch-Bihar, the Manee of Mindi, Duke Vallombrosa, the Duchess of Alba. Then literary people began arriving, after them children by the dozen, and then by chance, despite Lee's dislike of all animals except cats, pets became a subject. This trend started when she photographed a socially prominent Frenchwoman who returned a few days later to have a portrait made of her pet lizard. Lee photographed the creature perched on a Stylosa flower and was bold enough to charge $100, the full fee for a child.

The studio gave Lee the independence she craved, and though Man Ray stayed there most nights, they both lived their own lives and had their own groups of friends. Tanja Ramm returned to Paris the following spring and moved in with Lee for a few weeks while she got established working

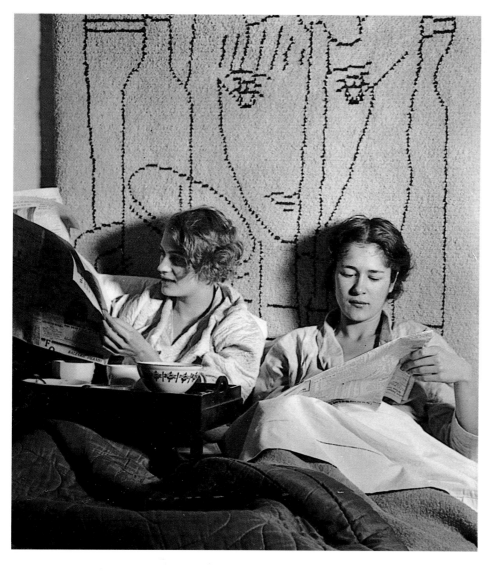

Lee and Tanja Ramm having Sunday breakfast in bed at Lee's studio. Paris, 6 January 1931. The wall hanging is from a design by Jean Cocteau. (Theodore Miller)

as a model and apprentice designer for the *Vogue* editor turned couturier, Mainbocher.

Lee's brother Erik visited Paris in 1930, and Lee and Man Ray met him off the ship. He had just turned twenty and was at the perfect stage of life to become utterly enamoured of the romance and beauty of France. Added to the impact of his first impressions was the fact that on the liner from New York he had fallen in love with his bride-to-be, Mary Frances Rowley (known as Mafy), from Ohio.

One of the first people Lee took Erik and Mafy to meet was Hoyningen-Huene at the *Vogue* studios. They all went to have lunch outdoors at a nearby restaurant, where, Erik recalled, 'Hoyningen-Huene had a glass of warm champagne, and it had a head on it. He asked for a block of cheese from which he cut little tiny squares, they could not have been more than 2mm cubes. He delicately dropped them on the champagne and the head disappeared just like that. Then he calmly drank it. I thought it was the epitome of sophistication.'[13] After lunch they returned to the studio and Hoyningen-Huene generously took portraits of Lee and Erik, Erik and Mafy, and Mafy alone.

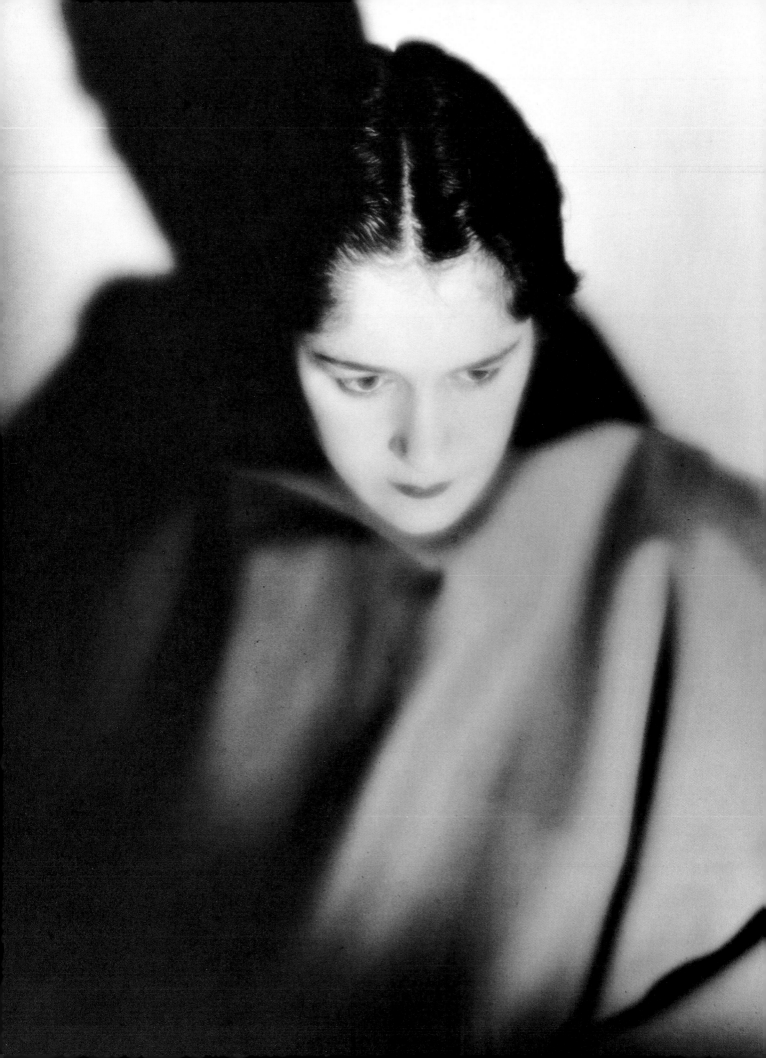

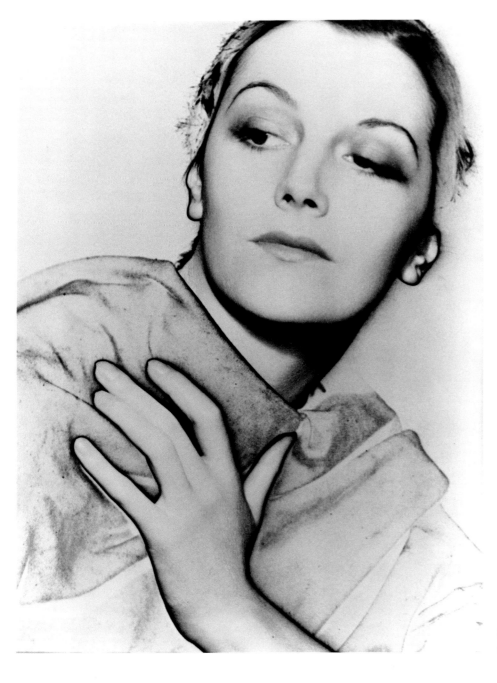

Solarized photograph. Paris, 1930.
(Lee Miller)

Lee had made many friends among the Surrealists, but she refused to be drawn into their feuds. When Jean Cocteau cast her in the female lead role in *Blood of a Poet*, there were howls of protest from her friends and a bitter row with Man Ray, who held Cocteau in jealous contempt. The opportunity for Lee to act in the film arose by chance one evening in the Boeuf sur le Toit night club when Cocteau was ostentatiously asking his friends whom he should audition for the part of the statue. Lee jumped to her feet and quickly convinced Cocteau that she was made for the role. It must have been doubly galling for Man Ray, a film-maker himself, to find that the production was backed by his own ex-patron, the Vicomte Charles de Noailles. The feuding with Man Ray lasted for months but Lee went ahead with making the film.

Opposite: Tanja Ramm. Paris, 1931.
(Lee Miller)

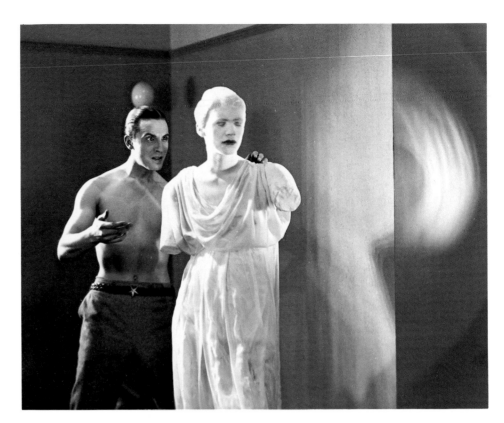

Enrique Rivero and Lee. A still from Cocteau's film *Blood of a Poet*. 1930.

The costume and make-up hardly enhanced Lee's looks and the role gave her little scope, but she emerged as a powerful, dominant image. She willingly suffered being trussed up and draped to create the effect of an armless statue in the first scene. The butter and flour mixture that joined her sculptured *papier-mâché* hair to her forehead melted rancidly and stained the plasterwork of her broken arms. The scenes that followed allowed her the use of both arms for a game of cards, and were fairly straightforward to perform. The difficulties arose with the finale in which the statue makes her exit accompanied by a bull. A huge ox was given a temporary reprieve from the local abattoir and brought to the studio. It had a horn missing, so the props department had to make one and fix it to the animal's head. Then they found that the ox could not be persuaded to move at the right moment. A wire was attached to its head so that it could be pulled on cue to encourage it to walk forward. The ox had other ideas. As soon as the wire was tightened, it bucked and stomped across the set, crashing into Lee and knocking her flying. In desperation an assistant was sent motoring off into the country. He returned with an ox driver who stood in the wings and immediately exerted complete control over the animal with a series of grunt-like commands.

Many years later, Lee recalled:

The script was constantly altered. Feral Benga, the black jazz dancer, had sprained his ankle and had to be a limping angel . . . Cocteau liked it better that way, but people have read all kinds of things into it. The star on Enrique Rivero's back was put there by Cocteau to cover a scar . . . he had been shot by his mistress's husband. After nineteen re-takes of the card playing scene, Rivero tore up the cards so there wouldn't be a twentieth . . . there was a party he wanted to go to.[14]

She also wrote in *Vogue*:

If poems and masterpieces are traditionally made in sordid surroundings such as garrets and jails; if chaos and misunderstanding is the poet's lot, this film was blessed . . . all augured well. The studio had been emergency soundproofed: lined with all of the available second-hand mattresses in Paris. They in turn were stuffed with the kind of insect life typical of mattresses; we were devoured, itchy and stoical. The magnificent crystal chandelier for the card game arrived in the nick of time, but in three thousand numbered pieces, each wrapped separately in acid free tissue paper.

Then, when the film was finished,

The church threw fits, the 'patrons' were persecuted and the finished picture languished in the vault for a couple of years. . . . None of the mishaps or accidents of production found Cocteau without an improvisation which was to his advantage. He himself, elegant, shrill, and dedicated, knew exactly what he wanted and got it. He screamed and cajoled. He electrified everyone who had anything to do with the film, from sweepers to tax-collectors. In a state of grace we participated in the making of a poem.[15]

The ox resumed its trip to the abattoir, and *Blood of a Poet* received both violent condemnation and great critical acclaim. But Lee never became involved in another film. 'I just can't act,' she would say when asked. Perhaps the truth was nearer to the fact that acting was too much a part of her natural behaviour for her to be able to do it on demand. Nevertheless, her star was rising – she had become well-known and well-liked.

Lee pursued her own flourishing career as a photographer. Her reputation was now well established and, helped by her first-hand working knowledge of fashion, she regularly got assignments from top clients like Patou, Schiaparelli and Chanel. At times she successfully combined both arts, and appeared as the model in her own pictures. Photographs in the Surrealist genre became fewer as pressure from commercial competition mounted, but she was making the right contacts.

The art dealer Julien Levy, who was later to mount her first exhibition of photographs in his Madison Avenue gallery in New York, described a meeting with Lee:

The morning after my arrival the photographer Lee Miller appeared. Suddenly there she was, walking just ahead of me down the Boulevard Raspail in a bold bright aura. In every way Lee seemed bright. Her spirit was bright, her mind, her photographic art, and her shining blond hair. She had the right kind of hair, springy and not wiry, fine but not straight or lifeless. She was the kind of blonde about whom one didn't sing 'pourquoi les femmes blondes . . .?' But instead one would hope to sing 'Auprès de ma blonde . . .' . . . I caught up with her and made a date for that evening at the Jockey [Night Club].[16]

In December 1930 Theodore arranged one of his trips to Sweden so that he passed through Paris and collected Lee. They spent Christmas in Stockholm at the Grand Hotel, where Theodore took the opportunity of making several stereoscopic nude studies of his daughter. Back in Paris for a few days around New Year's Eve, Theodore and Man Ray were inseparable. It seemed an unlikely combination, but with Man Ray's passion for engineering and Theodore's love of photography, they found

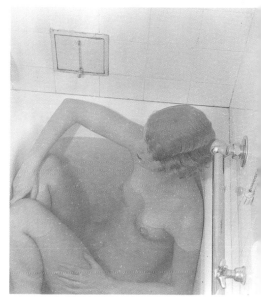

Lee in the bath at the Grand Hotel, Stockholm. 30 December 1930. (Theodore Miller)

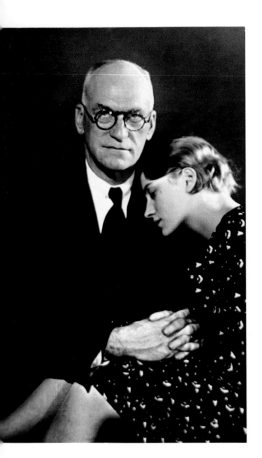

Lee with her father. Paris, January 1931. (Man Ray)

plenty to talk about. Theodore was impressed by Man Ray's inventiveness. Among the gadgets he had designed was a tripod with its centre column elevated by a rack and pinion which was years ahead of its time. Man Ray was also the first to hit on the idea of connecting a low-voltage light bulb to the mains in order to produce the brilliant illumination of the photoflood.

Of this interlude it is not Theodore's rapport with Man Ray that leaves the greatest impression, but the unassailable position Theodore clearly held in his daughter's affections. The images of Lee, resting her head on his shoulder, affirm for us that, of all the men in her life, he was undoubtedly the one she loved the most. The totally abandoned way she nestles her head into his shoulder like a drowsy puppy tells us that here is where she felt safest, tenderest and happiest. Throughout her life there remained a fundamental inability to form stable relationships with her lovers. There were many times when she wanted these relationships to endure, but there was always some unexplainable inhibition that prevented them from becoming completely satisfactory.

Man Ray suffered grievously from Lee's capriciousness. He tried hard not to be hurt by her affairs, but they were more than he could bear. During those brief absences of hers which usually followed a row, he poured out his soul in letters:

I have loved you terrifically, jealously; it has reduced every other passion in me, and to compensate, I have tried to justify this love by giving you every chance in my power to bring out everything interesting in you. The more you seemed capable the more my love was justified, and the less I regretted any lost effort on my part. In fact it was a much more satisfactory form of realisation, for me. You met me half-way on every occasion – until this new element appeared [Man Ray is referring to a Russian refugee interior decorator named Zizzi Svirsky with whom Lee had a brief affair], which has given you the illusion that you are freeing yourself from being an accessory to me. I have tried to make of you a complement to myself, but these distractions have made you waver, lose confidence in yourself, and so you want to go by yourself to reassure yourself. But you are merely getting yourself under someone else's control, much more subtle and indispensable. I can see you becoming one of these women, helpless and decorative, that surround Zizzi, devitalising you until you will care for nothing, but just drift along accepting the distractions of each new moment, tolerant of everything, helpful to all intrigues, because lacking any fixed attachment yourself, always tired and with a bad taste left over. You know well, since the beginning I promoted every possible occasion that might be to your advantage or pleasure, even where there was a danger of losing you; at least any interference on my part always came afterward, and stopped before it could produce a break, so we could easily come together again, because every quarrel and making-up is a step towards a final break, and I did not want to lose you.

Lee's reputation was earning her some worthwhile assignments and she made several trips to London for various clients. She went to Elstree studios to photograph the stars of Paramount's movie *Stamboul* for a spread in the 1 July 1931 issue of *The Bioscope*, and photographed the English summer sports clothes collection for the June 10 issue of British *Vogue*, in which she also appeared as the model for Rodier's tennis ensemble. Man Ray wrote to her frequently, chiding her for infidelities, real or imagined, begging her to live with him for ever, married or unmarried, or giving her useful technical advice. In one letter he joyfully proclaims that Mehmed Fehmy Agha, Condé Nast's new chief of art direction, was taking a big interest in his work:

He thinks my school of flat lighting in three or four tones only and printing on rough paper the coming thing – very tired of the Steichen school. He referred several times to your first things in *Vogue* and hopes you will get back to my influence. He took a copy of the Electrical book which may be reproduced in *Vanity Fair*, and with one of the inversions [solarized photographs], the large head on rough paper with the arm coming up the side that you thought was mysterious. In any case, the policy is changing in America and you and I must be ready by the fall to swamp the market. Agha seemed to think that my return to America was ripe, that I was liked and understood now, but I don't think one ought to move without a definite proposition.

The letters were reinforced by frequent telephone calls. Lee was lying in bed in a Park Lane hotel early one morning talking to Man Ray in Paris when the room was shaken by a violent shudder. 'We're having an earthquake,' she squawked. 'Don't be stupid,' replied Man Ray, 'they don't have earthquakes in England.' The date was 7 June 1931, and it was in fact a real tremor, but nothing compared to the one that was about to shake the life of Man Ray.

Tanja Ramm introduced Lee to an Egyptian, Aziz Eloui Bey. Aziz lived on the first floor of Anatole France's house, the Villa Said, and his beautiful wife Nimet, who was of Circassian descent, lived on the second floor. Nimet was already known to Man Ray, Hoyningen-Huene and Horst, because her haughty, aristocratic features had attracted them to use her as a model. She was tagged as 'one of the five most beautiful women in the world'. 'She should be,' remarked Aziz, 'she spends all her

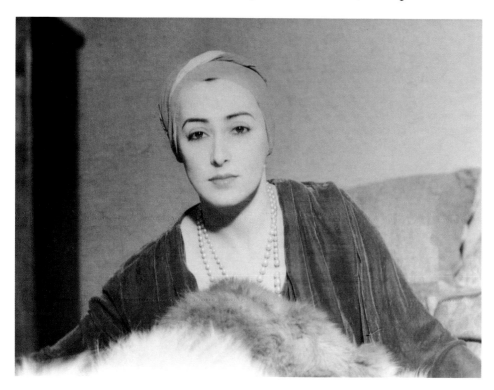

Nimet Eloui Bey, Aziz's first wife. Paris, 1931. (Lee Miller)

time painting her face.' The doting admirers who surrounded her as she reclined, holding court on her *chaise-longue*, were less cynical.

No one, least of all Man Ray, suspected that this gentle, quiet, unremarkable Egyptian, who was nearly twenty years older than Lee, would ever have any lasting effect on her. By accident or design, Lee turned up in Saint Moritz where Aziz was on holiday with Nimet in their chalet Villa Nimet. Aziz numbered Charlie Chaplin among his friends. Chaplin, who had just finished making *City Lights*, took a liking to Lee, who took several portraits of him in both serious and jokey moods.

Before anyone knew what was happening, Aziz was infatuated with Lee and she with him. Back in Paris, the row that followed was explosive. Man Ray let it be known that he had a pistol, but no one was quite sure if in his madness he intended to use it on himself, Lee or her new lover. He was known to have a fascination with suicide so there was concern that his threats might turn to reality. One of his self-portraits from that period shows him with an expression of utter defeat on his face, a pistol in his hand and a rope around his neck. For weeks he alternated between wild ravings and long sulks. He sent Lee a page torn from his notebook. Her eyes and mouth, drawn in pencil and arranged like a mask are nearly obliterated by the words in ink, 'Elizabeth Elizabeth Elizabeth Elizabeth Lee Elizabeth', repeated again and again in wild handwriting, tumbling back and forth across the whole page until it is filled. On the back it reads, 'Accounts never balance one never pays enough etc etc, love Man.' Tucked into the folded page was a photograph of Lee's eye, slightly larger than lifesize, on the back of which was written in red ink:

Postscript: Oct.11.1932:

With an eye always in reserve
Material indestructible. . . .
Forever being put away
Taken for a ride. . . .
Put on the spot. . . .
The racket must go on –
I am always in reserve.

MR

Aziz, using the Moslem husband's prerogative, and with all the lack of ceremony inherent in a Moslem divorce, severed his ties with Nimet. Distraught, she took a room in the Hôtel Bourgogne et Montana where, with liquor supplied by a Russian friend, she drank herself to death in the space of a few weeks.

Lee was tossed about in the centre of a storm of passion. Her own feelings for Aziz were far from clear and she had certainly not expected his hasty reaction and the death of Nimet. Fond of Man Ray as she unquestionably was, she was not in love with him. Other peripheral love affairs added to the confusion. Whichever way she turned she seemed confronted by men who were besotted with her and prepared to go to any lengths to pin her down. Only one solution was open to her – to move on.

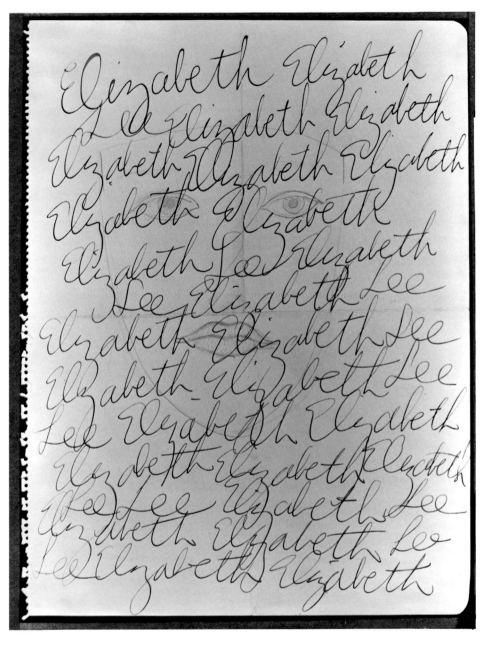

Page from Man Ray's notebook.
Paris, 1932.

Object of Destruction, by Man Ray.
Paris, 1928. (Antony Penrose)

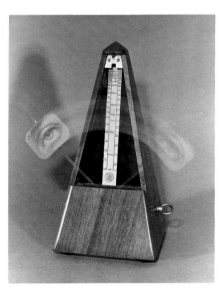

Mindful of Agha's interest in her work, Lee carefully considered returning to the United States. She had received some additional encouragement from Arnold Freeman, managing editor of *Vanity Fair*, and this looked like adding up to the opportunity she needed to make the break and set up her own studio in New York. In November 1932, she closed her Paris studio and, not without profound regrets, went back home.

Man Ray was at first inconsolable. Then his mad despair found an outlet. He took an object he had created – titled *Object of Destruction* – a metronome with a photograph of an eye pasted to the pendulum weight. He replaced the original eye with one cut from a portrait of Lee and, as if to insure against someone destroying the object, he made a drawing of it so that it could be reconstructed. On the back he wrote, 'Legend, Cut out the eye from a portrait of one who has been loved but is seen no more. Attach the eye to the pendulum of a metronome and regulate the weight to suit the tempo desired. Keep going to the limit of endurance. With a hammer well aimed, try to destroy the whole at a single blow.'[17] Lee claimed it was like making a wax effigy to stick pins into.

The creation of this object seemed to give Man Ray some relief although thoughts of Lee emerged elsewhere. Inspired initially by a red lipstick kiss left on his white collar by his former mistress Kiki, he started work on a huge canvas, about eight feet long, which he hung over his bed. It took two years of intermittent work to finish the painting, titled *Observatory Time – The Lovers 1932–34*. It showed a giant pair of lips floating in the sky above the twin breast-like domes of the observatory near the Luxembourg Gardens. The initial composition was of Kiki's rosebud lips, positioned horizontally, but as the months slipped by, the lips became Lee's – thinner, longer, more sensual, like the closely entwined form of two lovers, and tilted to enable them to fly freely in their serene mackerel sky.

Observatory Time – The Lovers, by Man Ray. Paris, 1934. (Man Ray)

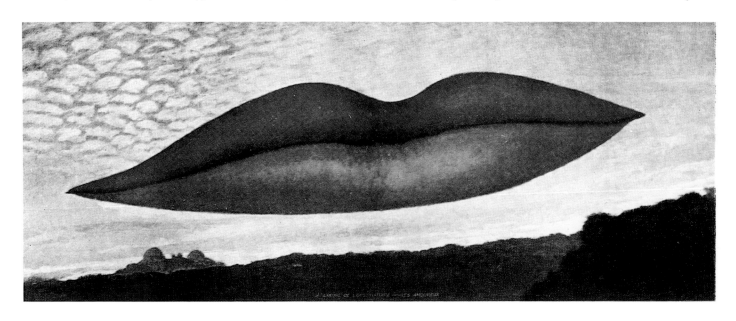

Opposite: Lee and her brother Erik. Paris, June 1930. (George Hoyningen-Huene)

Chapter Three
Photography in Fashionable New York
1932–1934

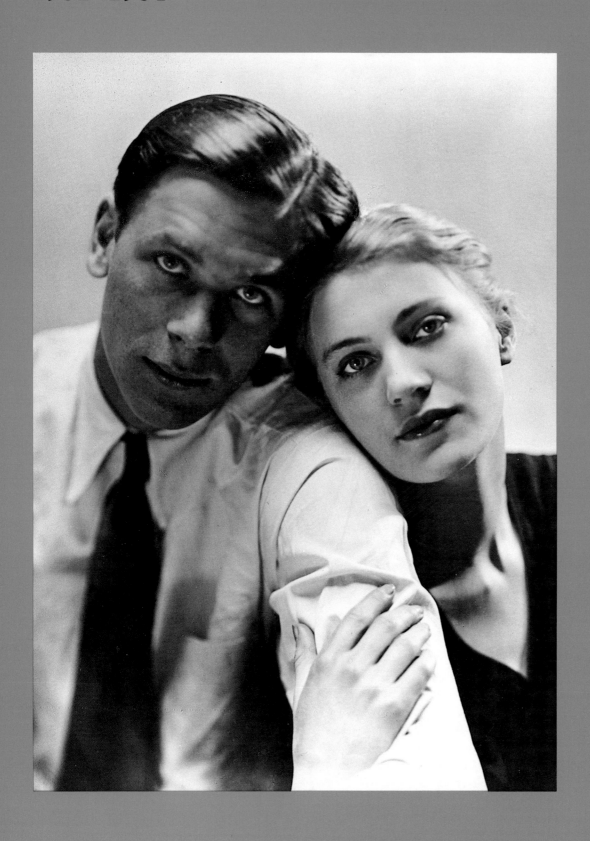

The after-effects of the Wall Street Crash of 1929 made the early thirties the worst possible time to be starting a business of any kind, least of all one as ephemeral as a photographic studio specializing in fashion. Fortunately, Lee was not without influential friends. Her contacts with the Condé Nast empire ensured that she would at least have an *entrée* into commercial circles, but she needed her starting capital, and it was here that her fellowship with the social elite rewarded her by providing two 'angels': Christian Holmes and Cliff Smith.

Holmes was an heir to the Fleischmann Yeast fortune, and his mother had set him up with a brokerage business in Wall Street. He used to commute in a yacht across Long Island Sound to Manhattan, where his chauffeur would meet him and drive him to the office. He was interested in photography and when Lee's studio was established he spent a lot of time there, just hanging around and watching. His fellow angel was playboy Cliff Smith, one of the heirs to the Western Union fortune. Between them they floated Lee Miller Studios on a share capital of $10,000 and helped Lee lease two apartments in a six-storey building at 8 East 48th Street, one block south of Radio City Music Hall. The apartments, which were both on the third floor, were connected by a small kitchen. Lee took over one side for her own living quarters and the other was converted into the studio.

The obvious choice for her assistant was her brother Erik, who had previously been working for Toni Von Horne, a German photographer who specialized in fashion and advertising. Lee took him on at a salary of $100 a month. At the start, the engineering skills Erik had learned from their father were his greatest contribution. He built the darkrooms and supervised the making of a row of cypress wood tanks, wide and deep enough for the 10″ × 8″ plates which were the standard format. Then he built all the props and backgrounds for the studio and installed the lighting. With the typical Miller love of innovation, the cables were concealed and the lights operated from a remote switchboard – no mean achievement when the dictates of large format cameras with slow film speeds called for enormous lights and fat cables. There was a practical reason for the concealment, as a lot of Lee's work was portraiture. She was always keen to have her sitters appear as natural and relaxed as possible, and despite her love of technology, she was aware that gadgets and equipment could be distracting and intimidating. Perhaps it was for the same reason that she 'decorated the windows with tubes of chiffon in the shades of the spectrum, like a row of Christmas stockings. The French doors [were] treated with the same tints in flat curtains'.[1]

Lee hired Jackie Braun, a secretary, to keep the books and, never being one to clear up for herself if she could help it, promptly engaged a cook/housekeeper. The girl was young, black and eternally cheerful, and the lunches she prepared soon became a central part of studio life for clients and visiting angels as well as for staff. When alone, Lee and Erik would eat at a card table in the studio. They would each try to destroy the other's appetite and gain the other's share of the food by telling lurid stories about such things as surgical operations or revolting biological parasites. It did

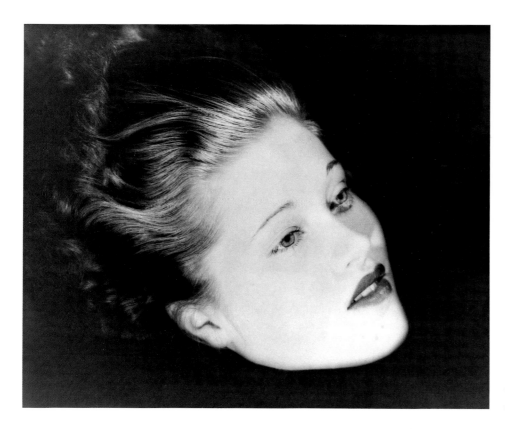

'Floating Head'. New York, 1933.
(Lee Miller)

not matter that neither won the contest; it was the outrageousness of the attempt that they found amusing.

Erik was soon presiding over the darkroom, and under Lee's guidance he became adept at fine printing. He recalled:

It was tough at first, because Lee was very insistent on getting the highest quality. She would come into the darkroom to examine the prints and she would grab hold of any that were even slightly defective and tear the corners off. I always used to marvel at the way she could pick out what was wrong with a print, maybe something that had completely escaped my notice, but when it was put right the whole print would be greatly improved. It was never a case of delicately dabbling away with print forceps. We always used to plunge right in, rubbing the surface of the print with our fingertips and sometimes blowing on it so the warmth would enhance the tone in a specific area. We had a vast array of chemicals which we used to dose up the normal proprietory solutions, and the resulting brew sometimes became quite deadly. We would cough and splutter in the fumes, and my finger nails would turn brown. Looking back on it, if there had been such a thing as safety inspectors in those days we would have been out of a job.[2]

Lee's first exhibition in New York was held at the Julien Levy Gallery from 20 February to 11 March 1932, while she was still in Paris. She was one of twenty photographers in a show entitled 'Modern European Photographers' which included Walter Hege, Helmar Lerski, Peter Hans, Maurice Tabard, Roger Parry, Umbo, Moholy-Nagy and of course Man Ray. Lee's second show at the turn of the year at the same gallery offered her greater prestige. It ran from 30 December to 25 January. Half the space was allocated to paintings and drawings by Charles Howard, with the remaining half solely for Lee's photographs. Frank Crowninshield wrote the announcement, elegantly printed in white ink on a long, narrow strip of dark pink paper.

Lee Miller left America for France four years ago . . . a girl in her earliest twenties. She has now returned . . . an accomplished artist and a versatile photographer. During those four years she lived in Paris, studying the camera's art in its every ramification. While there she came directly in contact with the artistic radicals of France, the Surréalistes, and their photographic leader, Man Ray; so that she passed quickly from apprenticeship into creative photography. In her French environment she learned not to restrict herself to formal photography, but to see artistic possibilities in all sorts of subjects. Her camera was constantly focussed upon landscapes, architecture, flowers, street scenes, still lifes; on subjects for advertising no less than for portraiture.

She has just opened a studio in New York where she will go on exercising her sensitive and rounded talent in an art in which she has shown herself naturally and peculiarly adept.

Woman with hand on head. Paris, 1931. (Lee Miller)

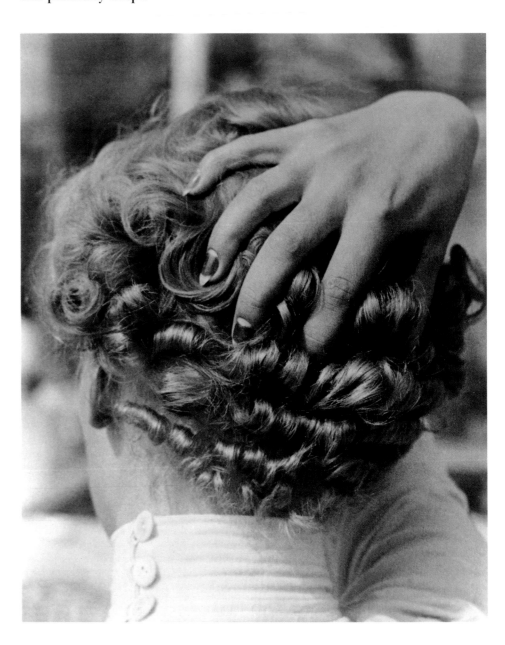

Opposite: Dorothy Hill, a friend of Lee's. A solarized photograph. New York, 1933. (Lee Miller)

46

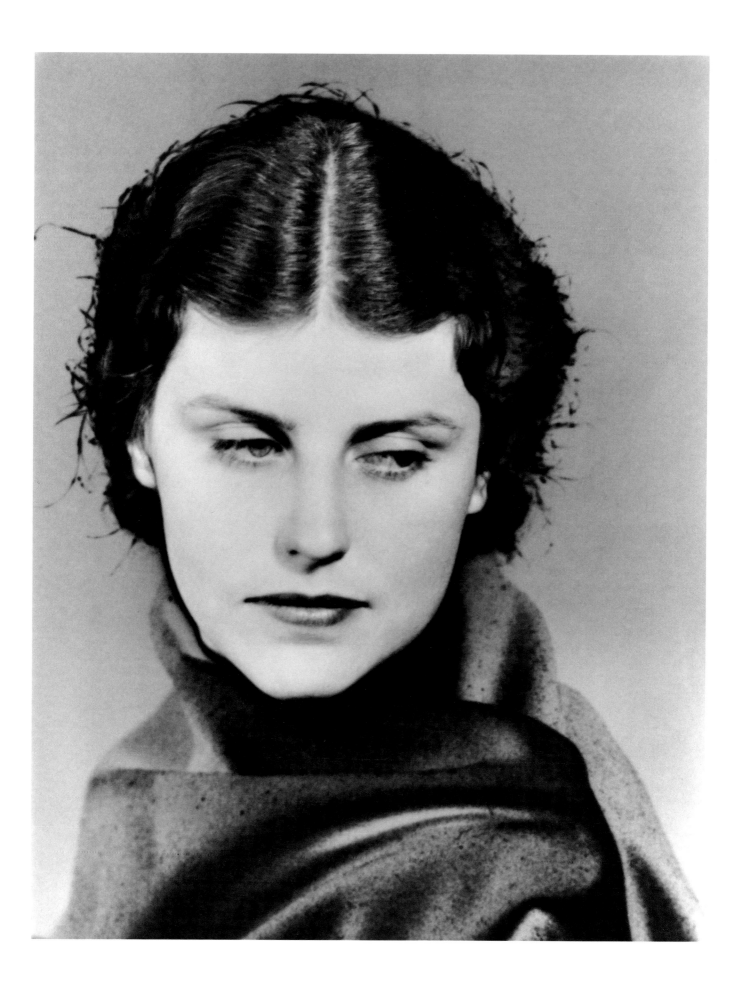

The photographs never sold at all well. At that time and for decades to come, despite Julien Levy's commitment to collecting and his bold, pioneering exhibitions, photography barely earned consideration as an art form. Surrealist painting and sculpture were becoming conspicuous and successful, but Surrealist photography never received its just recognition. Forty-five years later most of Levy's photographic collection was still unsold, a fact that did not worry him in the least because he had an intrinsic love of the photographs. It was typical of his vision that he donated many photographs from his collection to the Art Institute of Chicago, contributing to one of the world's finest archives of 1930s photographs.[3]

Lack of recognition for art photography forced most of the photographers who wished to pursue this genre to lead a double life. Lee, Man Ray and many others found that the only way to pay the large bills that beset all photographers was firmly and often secretively to do commercial work first and let it pay for the esoteric excursions into self-expression; certainly the commercial assignments always benefitted from the inventiveness of the artistic work.

Lee's commercial work in her new studio got off to a slow start. Many of her European fashion contacts withered as the effects of the Depression increased and most of the promised contracts of work were not honoured. Condé Nast's empire was going through its own spell of troubles and clothing and cosmetic companies were cutting back on their spending. It was Lee's old friends among the professional photographers, especially Nickolas Muray, a pioneer of colour photography, who saved her skin in the early days by sending her occasional assignments.[4] For photographers, personal recommendation is the only form of advertising that counts, so the first few months before word got round and work started to come in must have been agonizing for her. At first it was advertising pack shots for uninspiring products like perfumes, shoes, stockings, accessories and cosmetics. Then came fashion work for *Vogue, Harper's Bazaar* and *Vanity Fair* where Arnold Freeman continued his support. Sometimes Lee herself modelled, with Erik behind the camera under her direction. These photographs were always technically perfect and some have a refined beauty, but there is something stilted and self-conscious about them. At this time Lee's artistic and commercial styles were at their most divergent, neither nurturing the other. It was not until well into 1933, when she began to get a run of portrait clients, that the fetters on her imagination were broken.

Among her first sitters was 'Prince Mike Romanoff', known to the US Commissioner of Immigration as Harry F. Gurguson, who was wanted for questioning in connection with his illegal entry into the United States and his use of bogus titles. He had been a stowaway on the *S.S. Europa*, the German liner that had brought Lee back to New York. 'Gurguson was released from a Paris prison on December 9 after serving a term as a stowaway. The French authorities invited him to leave for the frontier. . . . Apparently he boarded the first liner whose appointments and passenger lists appealed to his taste . . . he is said to have confided that he

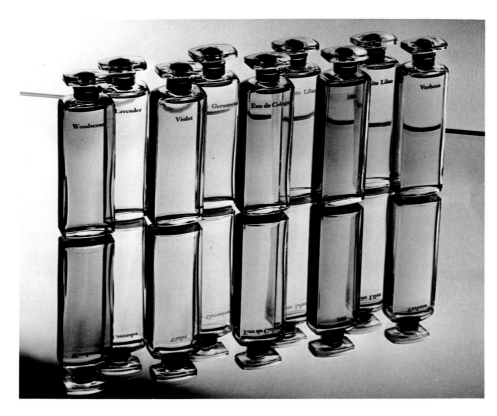

Scent bottles. New York, 1933.
(Lee Miller)

simply sauntered off the liner behind Marilyn Miller'.[5] Marilyn Miller was
a musical comedy star, no relation to Lee. Lee had met Gurguson on the
voyage and, as she was always attracted to outlandish characters, she
found him irresistible. Not all the friends she accumulated in this way
were as dubious as 'Prince Mike' though he was in fact more of an
adventurer than a crook. She arranged for him to hide out at Kingwood
Park for a few days before he slipped over the border into Canada, from
where he could make a legal entry into the United States. Once there, he
polished his phoney accent to a convincing perfection and got a job as a
salesman for Alfred Dunhill.

The sitters that followed were of quite a different calibre. The portraits
of the Broadway actresses Selena Royale and Claire Luce have that cool
romantic elegance typical of the period. Lilian Harvey, the British star of
German films, had the perfection of looks and figure that made her
resemble a beautiful porcelain doll. Her career was in full flood, so she
returned to the studio several times for portraits that her agent used
successfully to tempt Hollywood producers. One of the most striking
portraits from this sequence is possibly of the English actress, Gertrude
Lawrence. Lee posed her subject dressed in black, standing beside a vase of
metal flowers so that she appears to be the materialization of the spirit
lacking in the flowers.

One of Lee's most valued portrait clients was John Houseman, a young
businessman who had made a huge fortune in the wheat market, only to
lose every penny of it when the market crashed in 1929. In his
autobiography he describes attending

all-night poker games for negligible stakes in Lee Miller's apartment to which I was drawn less by passion for gambling than by an unrequited lust for my hostess. . . . She had a constant companion – the best of the poker players [John Rodell, a literary agent] – of whom I was bitterly jealous. In a reckless attempt to take her from him, I escorted her one night in a long white satin evening dress to the Casino in the Park, where we danced to the music of Eddie Duchin. The next morning, poorer by three-quarters of my week's budget, I was back in Lewis Galantiere's room, listening to Schnabel's Beethoven sonatas, waiting for a new wind to fill my sails.[6]

When that wind did blow for John Houseman, he made sure some of it filled Lee's sails too. Amid the prevailing gloom of the winter of 1933, he produced and directed a theatre production that stood out like a beacon. Sponsored by a group called 'The Friends and Enemies of Modern Music' and titled *Four Saints in Three Acts*, it was best described as a Surrealist opera. The libretto was a poem by Gertrude Stein set to music by Virgil Thomson. The cast, on Thomson's insistence, were all black, and rehearsals were held in Saint Philip's Episcopal Church on 137th Street in Harlem. Lee went there several times to photograph the cast for the programme. Houseman, Thomson and the choreographer, the young but already famous Frederick Ashton, went to the studio for their portraits. When the production opened, as the inaugural show of the Avery Memorial Theatre at the Wadsworth Athenaeum in Hartford, Connecticut, it proved to be one of those rare events that satisfied the intelligentsia and left the critics in raptures.

Lilian Harvey, film star. New York, 1933. Print from a solarized negative. (Lee Miller)

Opposite:
Top left: John Rodell, literary agent and one of Lee's boyfriends. New York, 1933. (Lee Miller)

Top right: John Houseman, impresario, for the programme of *Four Saints in Three Acts*. New York, 1933. (Lee Miller)

Bottom left: 'Prince Mike Romanoff'. New York, 1933. (Lee Miller)

Bottom right: Virgil Thomson, composer, for the programme of *Four Saints in Three Acts*. New York, 1933. (Lee Miller)

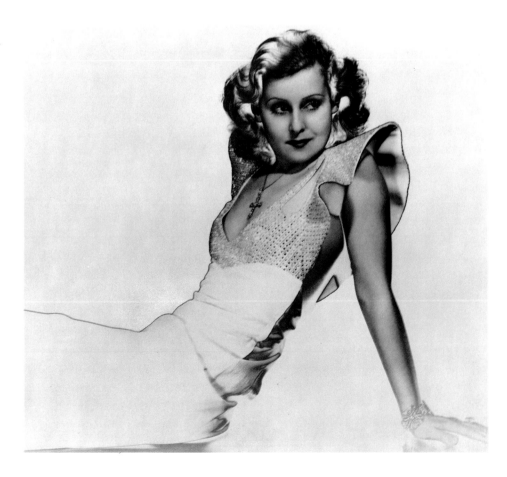

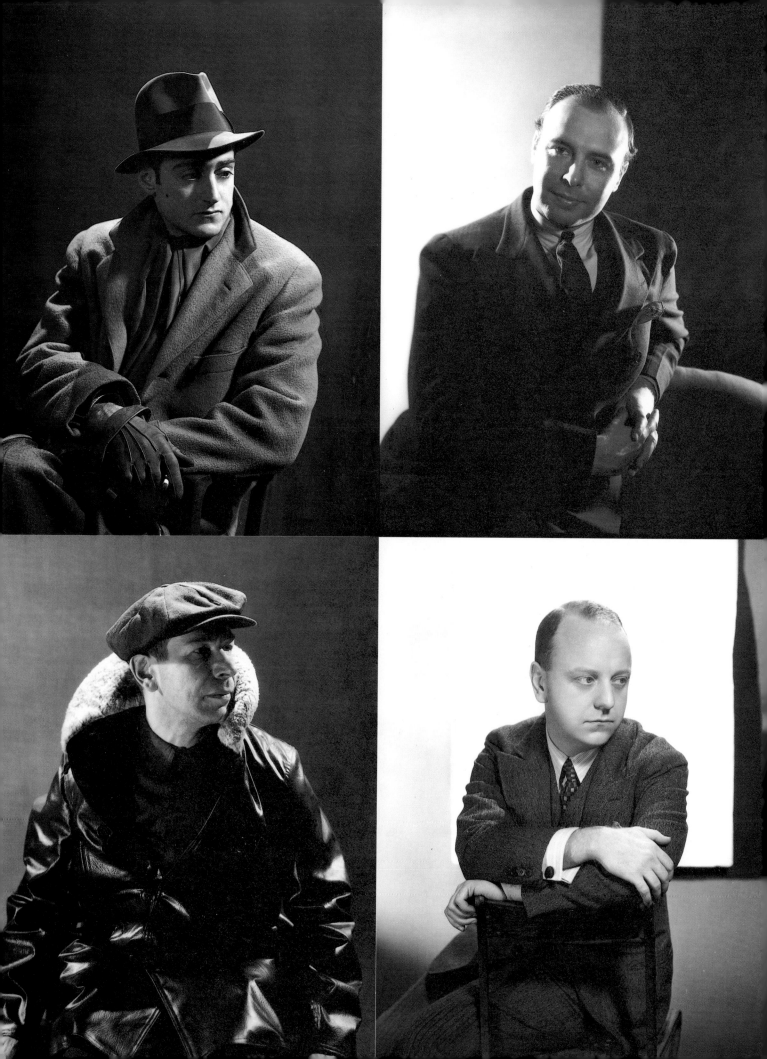

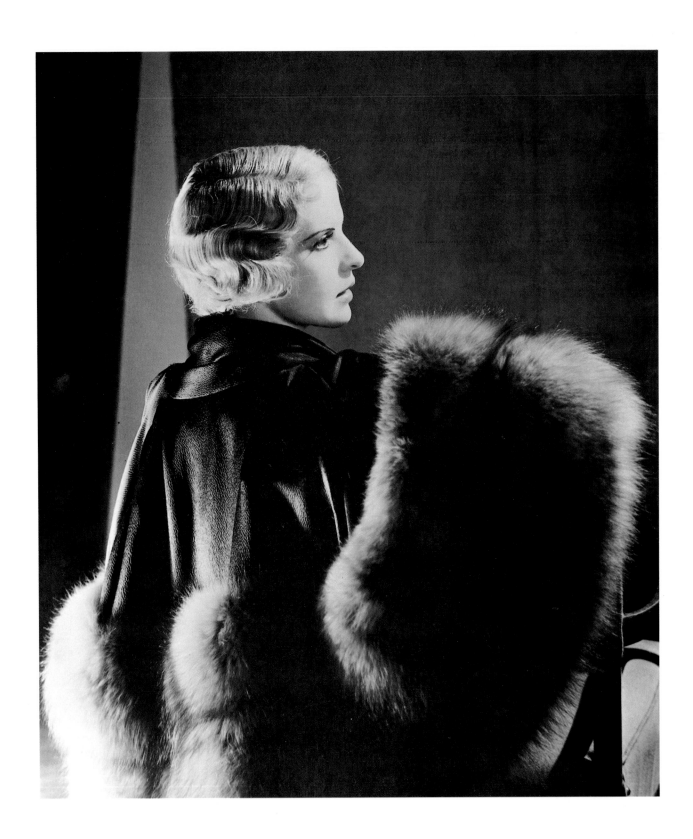

Portrait of unknown woman. New
York, 1933. (Lee Miller)

Opposite: Portrait inscribed by Lee,
'Gertrude Lawrence'. New York,
1933. (Lee Miller)

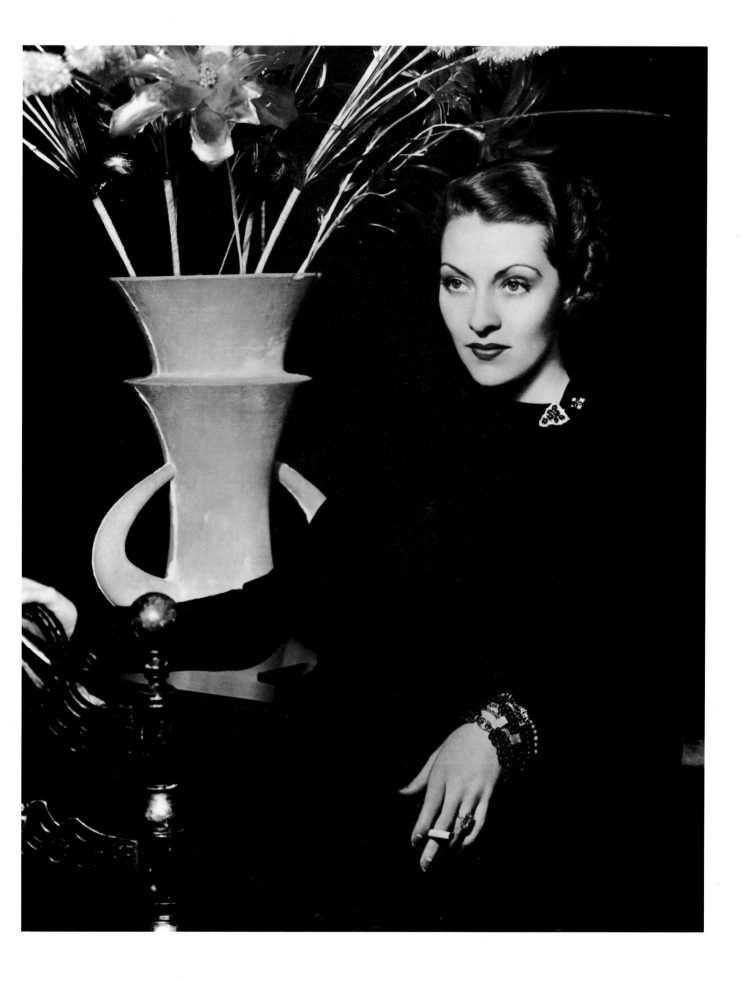

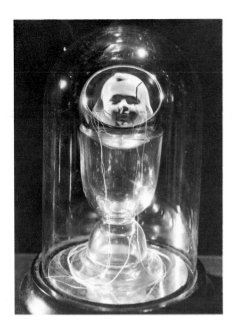

Object by Joseph Cornell. New York, 1933. (Lee Miller)

This association helped to fill Lee's diary with portrait clients from the social and intellectual elite of New York. Being photographed by Lee Miller became quite the thing to mention at a cocktail party, especially if it could be dropped into a conversation with someone who had not been able to make an appointment. Donald Friede the publisher, Lewis Galantiere the literary critic and Chic Austin, director of the Wadsworth Athenaeum, sat for portraits that were both true and flattering. Countless society women appeared, demanding that their limp stares be converted into an arresting image, but it was Helena Rubinstein who was the supreme test. Nothing seemed to bring any grace to her heavy Russian face. The session went very badly and she complained about everything, but Lee refused to be intimidated and after a while won her over. They parted friends, though the portrait never saw the light of day.

Lee did not neglect to photograph those who intrigued her, whether or not they could afford the fee. Joseph Cornell, the Surrealist artist, was regarded by most people as a pitiful little lunatic from Brooklyn. He would appear in the studio every two or three weeks with his latest creation – often some sinister arrangement of parts from broken dolls beautifully mounted under a glass dome. Seeing his art with appreciative and understanding eyes, Lee encouraged him and frequently photographed him with his objects.

All this activity intrigued the press. 'Miss Miller's technique is interesting,' wrote one reporter,

She takes one sitting a day. Never more. . . . Every sitting takes several hours. If her client hasn't eaten and is hungry, Miss Miller has luncheon served. If tired she lets her subject recline on a chaise-longue, with low tables holding beverages, cigarettes, sandwiches. She dislikes having any friend come along with her clients because, she explains, 'they always give a person an "audience complex", or make him or her wear a "gallery smile", and both are unnatural.' 'Children with their mamas are the worst of all clients,' Miss Miller said. 'It is the unusual mother who doesn't make a child self conscious by asking him to do this or that, "the cute way you did yesterday".' 'It takes time to do a good portrait,' Miss Miller went on. 'I must talk to the sitter, find out what idea of himself or herself he has in mind. Also if it is a picture for a grandmother or a husband or wife.' 'Young men never know whether they want to look like a pugilist or Clark Gable,' she said. 'Older men often want you to catch the twinkle in their eyes, a certain angle of their profiles or their "Mussolini jaw" that some woman has told him she loves. Men are much more self-conscious than women. Women are used to being looked at.' Miss Miller thinks photography perfectly suited to women as a profession. . . . 'It seems to me that women have a bigger chance at success in photography than men,' she told me. 'Women are quicker and more adaptable than men. And I think they have an intuition that helps them understand personalities more quickly than men . . . And a good photograph of course is just that, to catch a person not when he is unaware of it but when he is his most natural self.'[7]

Lee's and Erik's first excursion into the realms of colour photography using three separation negatives nearly defeated them. They used a 10″ × 8″ camera, their intention being to use black and white film to make three separate exposures with the film carefully locked into register and to alternate between a yellow, red and blue filter in front of the lens. The negatives would then have the different grey tones required for making the colour separation negatives. This was standard practice for colour photography at that time but was usually undertaken by a team of specialists using a rostrum camera.

The problem for Lee and Erik was not the technique but the subject – a perfume advertisement. The bottles were placed on the surface of a mirror with a frame of about eighteen inches square, which was surrounded by real gardenias. Under the fierce heat of the lights, the tips of the leaves and petals quickly started to wilt and move, throwing the image out of register between the successive exposures. Erik recalled:

Fortunately we did not have an art director there. If we had we would be still trying it now. We were on our own, and this was the kind of thing where Lee would really buckle down. Lee could be intolerably lazy when she wanted, but when the chips were down, she just would not quit. We worked for almost twenty-four hours straight, hardly stopping to eat or go to the john. We ended up rushing the gardenias straight from the refrigerator, spraying them and then gently placing them on the mirror so that there would not be any water spots. The film would be all ready, so we would hit the lights, make the first exposure, then bing, bing, change the film and the filter for the second and third time. Well, finally we did it, and it was a very, very successful picture.[8]

Joseph Cornell, the Surrealist artist, combined with one of his objects. New York, 1933. (Lee Miller)

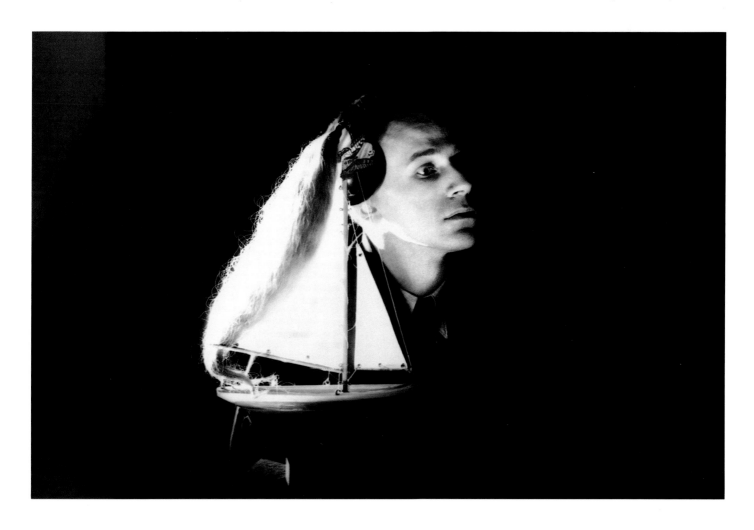

Despite their close working association, Lee and Erik never mixed socially, and this was characteristic of the way Lee compartmentalized her life. In the evening she would resume her social life: the demonic games of poker, visits to the theatre and films or wild parties that never included Erik. He would trudge off to his gloomy bachelor room in a cheap hotel a few blocks away and while away the evenings making model aeroplanes or going to the Radio City Music Hall. This was a prudent move on his part because not many people could stand Lee's frenetic pace and work effectively as well. Besides, Erik had other things on his mind, and on 22 August 1933 he and Mafy were married.

Accommodation in Manhattan was far too expensive for Erik and his bride so they were forced to live out in Flushing, Long Island, which involved Erik in an hour's journey on the subway, morning and evening. Compensating for the discomfort and long hours was the satisfaction of being established at the beginning of a satisfying career.

The prospects of the studio seemed set fair, when a quiet, gentlemanly Egyptian arrived in New York to negotiate the purchase of equipment for the Egyptian State Railways. To the family, Aziz seemed like just another of Lee's many friends. It was true that his arrival had triggered off a dieting jag that had shut Lee away on a health farm for a week, but that was not unusual. Neither was there anything remarkable in the fact that Lee took him to visit her parents at Kingwood Park, and accompanied him on long rambles over the farm. She did that all the time with John Rodell, and others, too. So they were not prepared for the surprise in store for them when one afternoon Lee telephoned her mother and inquired, 'Did you like Aziz?' Florence replied, 'I hardly know him but he seems all right – yes – I do like him.' 'That's good,' said Lee, 'I married him this morning.' The first formality had been at a Manhattan registry office, where the presiding official took it upon himself to caution Lee about the inadvisability of marrying a black man, and a foreigner to boot. Lee delivered a tirade that left the wretched man completely taken aback, and the papers were swiftly produced. The couple were better received at the Royal Egyptian Consulate in New York City where they were married under Mohammedan law on 19 July 1934.

Committed to a new life in Cairo, Lee cabled Man Ray to ask him if he wanted to take over the studio. 'PULL YOUR OWN CHESTNUTS OUT OF THE FIRE,' came the reply. Erik sorrowfully packed up Lee Miller Studios in the blistering heat of the New York summer. Business had been good in spite of the Depression and had every prospect of going from strength to strength. Erik and Mafy had staked much of their own future on the enterprise, and now, with Erik too inexperienced and lacking in contacts to start on his own, things looked bleak for them. To make matters worse, there was an acute shortage of work in the world outside, away from the shelter of an established reputation and well-disposed friends in high places. How could Lee, with total disregard for all those who had committed so much to help her, have jettisoned all her achievement and potential at one stroke? The answer lies at the core of Lee's character: for Lee, travelling was always more important than arriving.

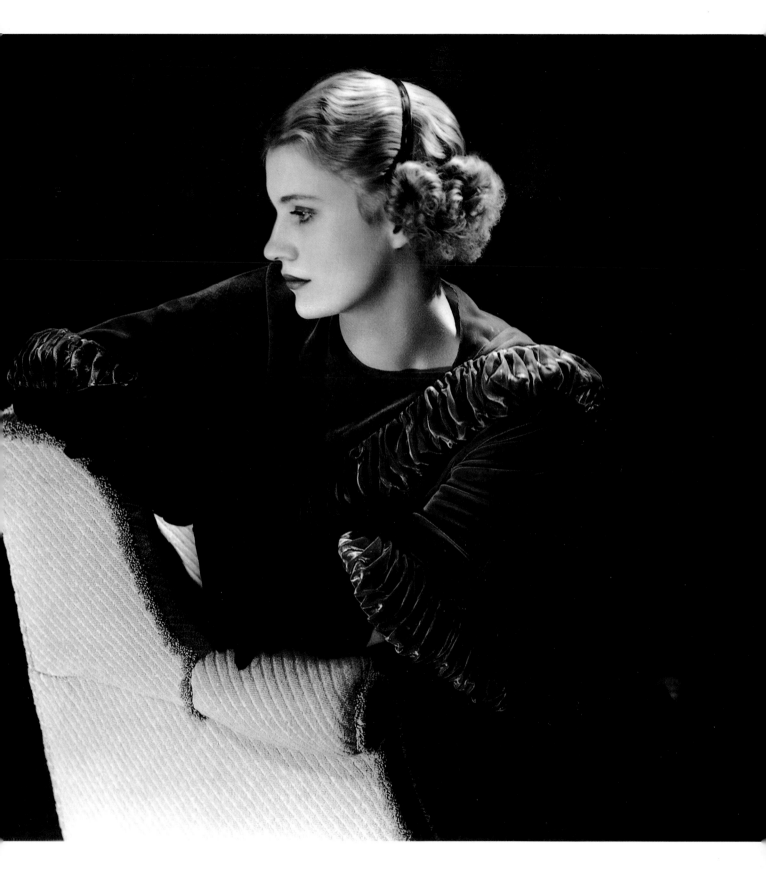

Self-portrait, for a fashion article on
hairbands. New York, 1932. (Lee
Miller)

Embarking on a new project was the excitement. All the while plans were coming together, while she was learning, building and breaking new ground, she was wholly absorbed. Change – the self-replacing objective – and the mastery of new techniques were her stimulants. When the studio was set up and running, there were no more frontiers to cross; the idea that just staying in business and being a successful photographer could be a great achievement had no appeal for her. In a slack period or when confronted by a dull assignment she sulked in her bed for days at a time. She always made her boldest decisions by blind instinct, not calculation. Her desire for self-determination was a deep underlying drive. For a woman, the constraints of the period made this nearly impossible. Basically she wanted adventure, excitement and freedom from responsibility and routine. She wanted to take pictures and to travel, and being born neither rich nor a man she could achieve this only through others, such as Aziz.

The honeymoon was at Niagara Falls. Lee photographed towering formations of clouds that roll, tumble and seem to roar with more force than the plummeting water beneath them. Did these images of turbulence on a deistic scale reflect some of Lee's innermost thoughts as she pondered on how her latest gut reaction had caused her to reject her friends, family and professional achievements to go to the other end of the world with a man she hardly knew?

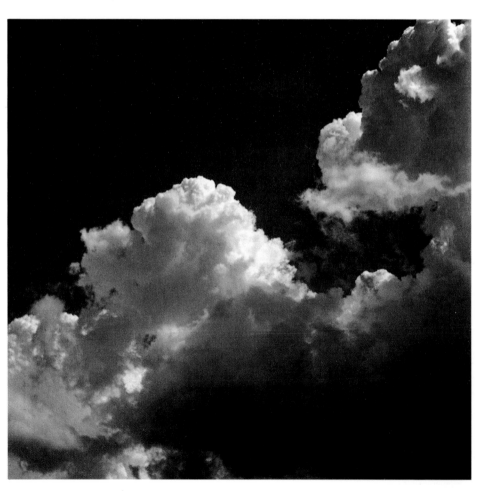

Turbulent clouds photographed by Lee on her honeymoon at Niagara Falls. July 1934. (Lee Miller)

Opposite: Lee. Egypt, 1935. (Photographer unknown)

Chapter Four

Egypt and First Marriage
1934–1937

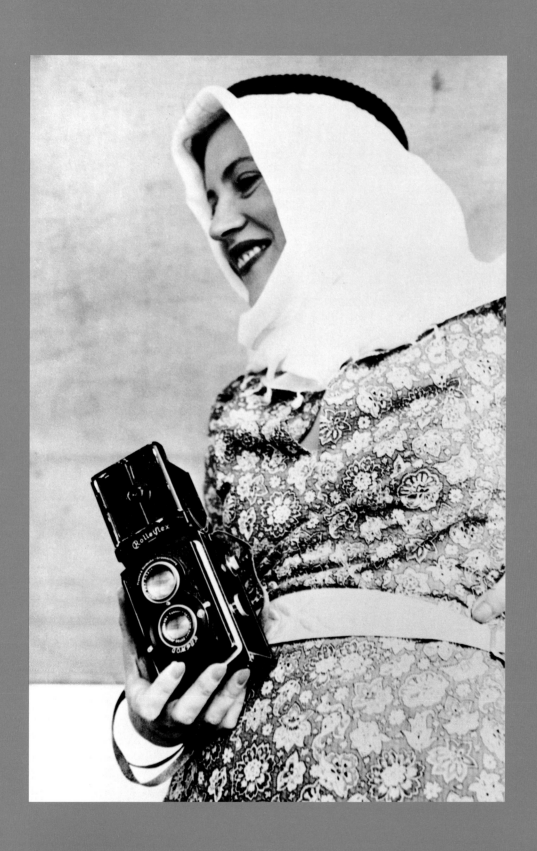

Cabinet
du
Directeur Général   *Le Caire*

My two little dears. I am still shy to call you Mother and Dad. The principal reason is that Mother is so young and Dad despite his serious countenance drives at night just as madly as a road hog. One does not take risks when one has to look after a large family, composed of an aviator with a wild reputation, a young boy ready to fight life, a girl in a distant land, a wife with a regime.

Will you please, Dad, drive on the right side of the road specially round curves. I have enough worries as it is.

But let me tell you first how Lee feels. First we had a terrific flood. The highest in recorded years. Fortunately we had no breakage in the Nile banks but in some places large areas were under water. The result was an invasion of mosquitoes. Their breeding was helped by the perfect weather, no wind, just an even temperature all the way thru. The sewage of Cairo also broke down by an abnormal pressure. So I took Lee over to Alexandria where some friends asked her to stay with them. She had a good time there. Every person she met liked her and made her feel at home. She was rather lazy and took only two sea baths, although every day we conscientiously took our clothes and went to spend the day on the beach where our friend has a marvellous cabin. Lunch was brought there every day and life was soft and easy as usual over here.

We would lunch for instance at 3 o'clock or later. Then play bridge or poker until we sleep on the table. If I suggested a sea bath everybody would jump and say, 'No, we must lunch right now.' Right now was usually two hours. Then of course after eating you could not bathe. Then during the game no one dared say anything but call a handful of cards. Then we would be off to a night club but eventually reaching another house and start a dance or another game for a change.

We decided to go back though Cairo was dull, everybody being absent. Then Lee had to take typhoid injections that disturbed her. The reaction was comparatively mild. About two days of fever and uncomfortable feeling. The first time when she was sick I wanted to take an injection myself to keep her company but my devotion was limited only to the desire.

Last week we were invited to a dinner party when she met several friends back from the holidays. They all liked Lee, and no wonder. If I could see her with cold scrutinising eyes I'd pick her up in the center of a crowd as a distinct bright feature, as if the other people are handicapped to a disadvantage and I only see them as a negligible quantity at the side.

I have a great possibility of becoming Under Secretary of State which is my next step, and that would create another burst of speeches. It could not be worse than my appointment here. My position being reached only after 20 years of satisfactory work.

I thought of showing Lee a typical country house. So we went to a cotton farm about 100 miles away. A party of course to enable us to have a game of cards instead of seeing the plantations. My friend there gave us a nice room with a private bath, and we were very comfortable. We ate so much that we must have gained at least a pound in the weekend. Lee took pictures of camels and sacks of cotton and hundreds of thousands of pigeons bred for manure. We had a marvellous time except for an attack of mosquitoes which made Lee very miserable. This combined with a 100-mile motor car ride nearly ruined our beautiful friendship. Any one of the two things was enough to drive her crazy. Egypt is not America, and we could not stop every 20 miles and find a nice hotel to sleep in. Nor had we any device to kill mosquitoes and enjoy the sight. All we can do is to sleep under a mosquito net or when driving insult all the other road users as we go by.

We shall have to move to our house at Giza next month. Lee likes it although she was horrified when she saw how the tenant treated the walls and woodwork. He drove a nail in every square yard of the walls and even in the oak panelling to hang pictures. The house needs a lot of repairs, but we are not at ease in spending money just now. We must move because Lee has to invite friends this winter. She was invited already more than twenty times and this will continue all the year round.

Lee wants to buy a horse, so I am on the lookout for a lamb. When I find one we will have some riding in the desert. I will ride a donkey or a camel to keep pace with her and will send you a photograph of the procession.

Lee is happy. Naturally it is not easy to settle down smoothly considering her much troubled soul. Certain reactions are bound to happen. Only small things like being bored suddenly. You see she does not work any more and her brain must work to occupy Lee's time. Such reactions are scarce, and last a very short time. When she is rested from the strenuous life of New York she will be much better. I will take care of her always.

I am so sorry for Erik. It breaks my heart to have caused his being out of work. I will try and find something for him here. Ask him if he agrees on principle. It may be in the cement factory or agent for an air cooling firm.

I will write to you regularly. All of my love and affection.

Aziz[1]

In the summer of 1935, with the temperature in Cairo a humid 100° in the shade, Lee and Aziz decided to give the Egyptian summer the slip by heading for Saint Moritz and then by car to London. In Saint Moritz they discovered that the drop in temperature brought its own problems.

VILLA NIMET
ST. MORITZ   6.8.35

Dear Dad,
We have been perched up here for two weeks. It is a plateau so that we cannot see the height which is well over six thousand feet. Still we can feel it. Any attempt to walk uphill makes us pant for breath, whilst all the time we are shivering from cold.

Lee decided she should give a show of sensitiveness considering the sudden change of weather. For a week she made a display of mysterious pains in the back. The German doctor talking as if he had a sponge in his mouth said something about kidney trouble and we are waiting for an analysis.

In the meantime the pain disappeared as suddenly as it came. She was suffering terribly one evening and I gave her an aspirin. Fifteen minutes later she was playing bezique with me. The next day the pain made a fresh attempt to annoy her whereupon I gave her another aspirin. This proved too much and really mean, so the pain decided to move into more peaceful grounds. The nearest was myself, which amused Lee for a day or two only, for in between a brief interval of two rains, I played golf which put me right.

By now we are physically fit but boring ourselves stiff. The extreme high cost of living has banned this place from visitors. Those who filter through a web of money sinking wells are few and usually very old and acid. To annoy them we decided to show ourselves in the streets walking only downhill, so that we do not pant for breath. We hide ourselves going uphill, or we take the car. We look at home which makes most people feel even more prejudiced against this cold, rainy inhospitable dump.

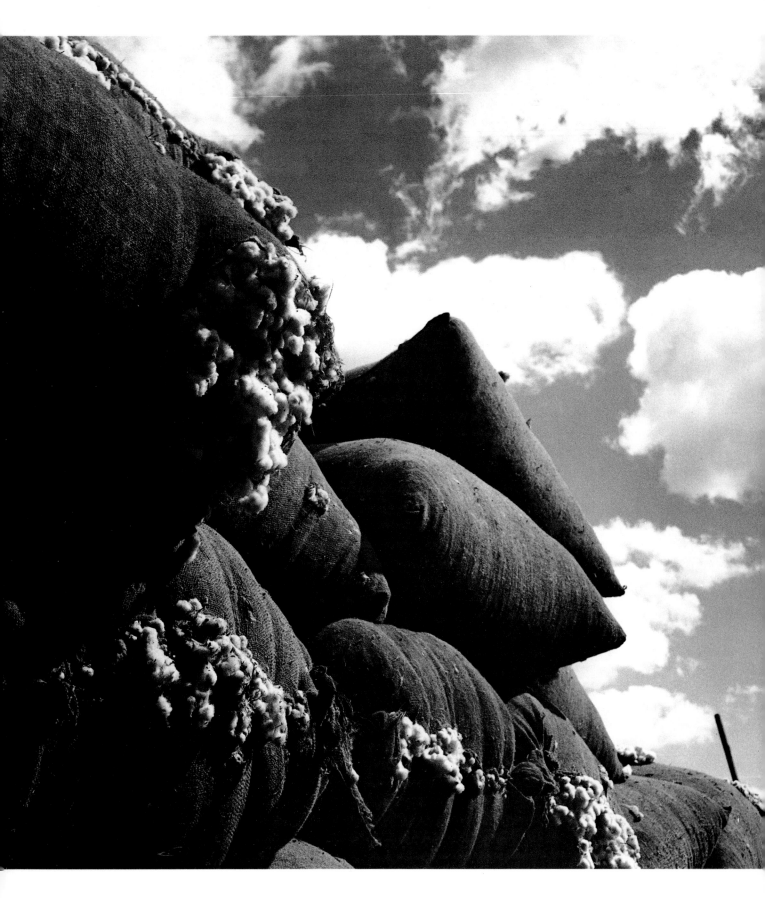

Cotton sacks. Asyut, *c.* 1936. (Lee
Miller)

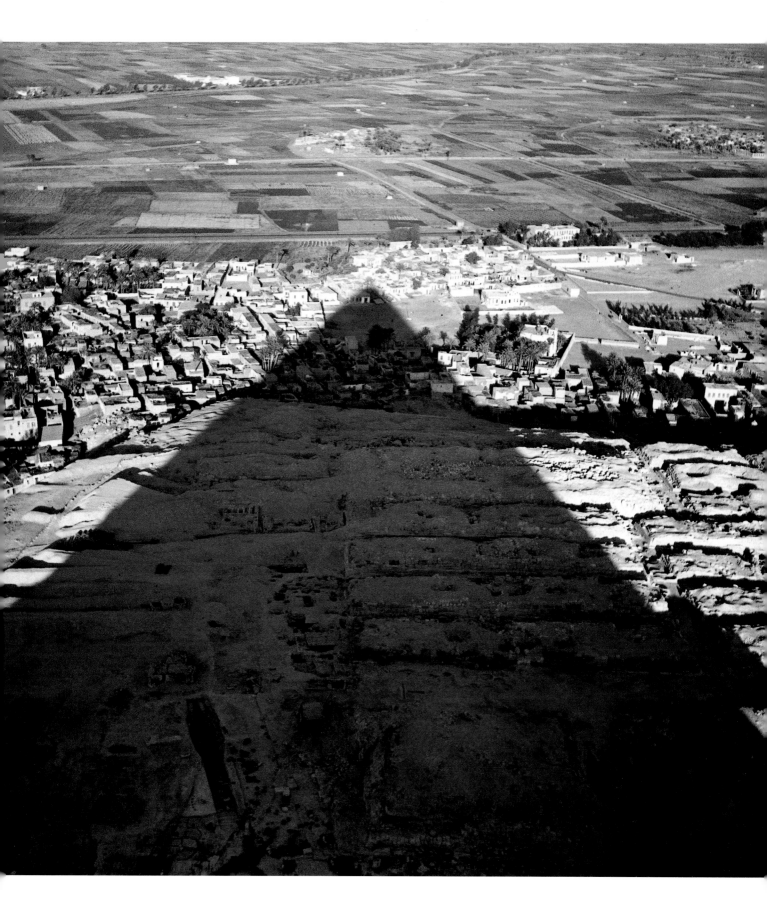

From the top of the Great Pyramid.
Egypt, *c.* 1938. (Lee Miller)

This country is in a serious plight. Just think: I will not speak of a cabbage, which in our country we give to the donkeys, if only to see their faces when they smell it, and which here costs 60 cents for a tiny one like a melon – or beans which do not exist because there is not one millionaire left, or a cup of chocolate which costs one dollar. I will just mention that coal costs 30 dollars a ton up here, whilst wood should be exposed in shop windows as something valuable. When you think that in the summer 50 degrees F is considered warm, you can imagine the deep concern of the government for the people. It appears that the majority in the government are hotel-keepers. These fat-headed people would rather die than give a room for 3 or 4 dollars. We want to go trout fishing but that is out of the question. The fly costs 2 dollars because of the high cost of transport.

I have one idea now. Sell this house here and kiss them goodbye for ever. Last year I had to pay 3,000 dollars without living in it, to keep it going. It makes me think our government is an angel when I see others over here.

We will be staying until the end of this month. Then we go to Berlin. Maybe we can do something about our houses there. We will leave the car at Basle and go by train. After that we go to London. We shall stay there at least 10 days. All my love to Mother and yourself. Where are Erik and Mafy? And John who seems like Kemal, always in the air.

Aziz

Postscript from Lee:

I'm very stiff, lame and old, on account I played nine holes of golf for the first time in my life.

Love and kisses – Lee

This postscript amounted to the sum total of Lee's correspondence with her family until she got started a few months later with this letter to Erik from Cairo.

Dear Erik –

I sit around and read rotten detective stories instead of writing you a letter which is really 'urgent since a week – and socially important since several years.

I've spent an extremely happy and healthy year, my time being occupied between studying chemistry six morning hours a week at the American University, and three afternoon hours a week of Arabic. Also a great deal of poker and bridge. I am lousy at house-keeping, I just don't bother, and when everything goes wrong as it is sure to, I get as much of a laugh as anyone.

Aziz changed jobs and quit the railways to become chief technical adviser to the Misr Bank's Industries which is a swell job and interesting albeit much overworked. On the side, we in the family, that is Aziz and his brother Kemal, have formed a company to do air-conditioning – it is an affiliation of the Carrier Company in New Jersey. It looks like a swell proposition as already the movie studios, the new bank and the Royal Automobile Club have been done. There is one engineer here, and we will need more staff. Aziz and I have had the brainwave of proposing you for the job. Every year Carrier train 6 or 8 engineers, and if it interests you to take the training you have the offer of a job here in Cairo with our company. We have had you in our minds ever since we came here, and although there have been several jobs that you could have done fine – they none of them had a future like this one, and I haven't wanted to give you the opportunity to become just another rolling stone.

As for life in Egypt – I think it would suit you both perfectly – an apartment in the middle of the town costs about 5 pounds and a servant about 3 pounds. Food is much cheaper than in America, and the foreign colony of any given country is so enormous that any number of congenial friends should be available. Mine for instance are all gambling, Aziz's are all sport. It never rains – so there is permanently tennis, golf – swimming – sailing – squash and even cricket – god help us! – as well as duck shooting – snipe in winter – fishing in Suez and desert expeditions to make. The language is no difficulty because no foreigner learns more Arabic than the first ten days and English is spoken generally. Our so-called threats of war are rather a joke, and as for the revolution it is not as bad as the New York taxi strike, and even that's finished.

I don't know whether you are still interested in photography – or got the same loathing for it I had had. Ask Mafy what she thinks of this proposition as compared to with how it feels to be a photographer's wife – I know how it feels to be a photographer and it's hell. Did my office affairs ever clear up?

Until Xmas time this year I hadn't taken even a roll of film – about three exposures I didn't bother to develop. But then I went to Jerusalem for a day and got sort of inspired and did about ten swell ones. The rest is just muck. I've found a small shop to do my developing and printing to my satisfaction, so I'm taking an interest again. There is a very nice American boy who is here to organise the new Kodachrome processing plant for the Middle East. He and I went out to a village to take some pictures – unfortunately I ran over a man or something – you see if you hit anyone here in the country, you are expected to beat it – in fact the Consulates always say HIT AND RUN – and report afterwards – so it spoiled the trip and Aziz won't let me go again unless I have a sort of guide with me – but the pictures are swell.

Since writing the preceeding thousand pages or so I've been out and played a game of poker quite successfully – except that I sat in such a draught that I couldn't go to the ball at the Greek Legation last night and I am staying in bed today – I feel simply lousy and even wouldn't play bridge if someone asked me.

I think I'll go to sleep again for a while and then write a letter to Mother – believe it or not.

Love Lee

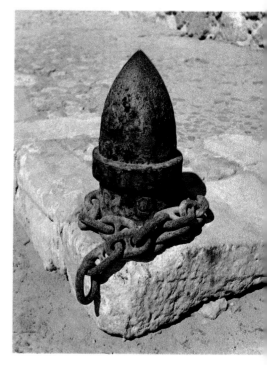

Bollard. Alexandria, 1936. (Lee Miller)

The perfunctory start to this letter from Lee to her parents may be due to there being a page missing. It was probably written in early December of 1935.

To be sent by post – NOW –

1. – a couple of Cape Cod lighters for the fire-places.
2. – a great deal of popcorn – for popping – (not planting) and one of the wire boxes to do it in – don't bother with the wooden handle as it's difficult to ship and easy to replace.
3. – Lots and lots of Golden Bantam sweet corn seed – the last I got from London was expensive and not very well selected.
4. – a bottle of Buttermilk tablets.
Please enclose all invoices or receipted bills for customs.

Mafy, please learn how to roast peanuts like 'Planters' – I think they are fried in oil or deep fat and salted – but how do they get the reddish skins off?

I've been and gone to Jerusalem. I had spent two months in bed – not very sick but certainly sulking and just too damn tired to bother with anyone or anything – you remember how I felt in N.Y.? So I hied myself off to Dr Zoudek in the Holy Land and he is certainly marvellous. I have the whole treatment with me and either Aziz, Dr Chorbagni or my sweet self give me the injections – it consists of once-a-week Cortigen – Prolan – and Ovex. I take all of it and then go back in eight weeks to see if it's long enough. Everyone here sort of pooh-poohed the idea of a gland specialist or bio-chemist – they never heard of glands – and reckoned

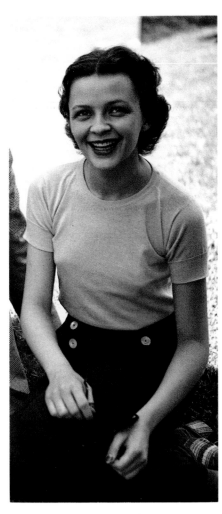

Mafy Miller. Cairo, 1937. (Lee Miller)

that a change of air was all I needed or one of those lousy European 'cures' – whereupon I went anyway and came back such a different person that now I suppose there will be a caravan going there.

I can't begin to describe or even discuss Palestine with a letter – I get so bitter when I even think of it – all the money my good Jewish friends have sunk into it – and how wrong they were. You only have to take a good look at the blasted place to be completely floored as to why everyone from the time of Moses has been screaming for that rotten country.

Erik was extremely rude in his last letter to Aziz – and I hope he feels properly contrite as in the meantime he has received about 14 pages from me. They seem to be going to delay coming – and I'm very annoyed because now they won't get here for the freezing cold weather and of course won't believe me until it happens again next year. Please imagine living in a country where the people fondly kid themselves that it is warm in winter when it was 0 degrees centigrade last night and the warmest you can get a room is 15 degrees – and that is *our* house with its fire-places and little oil stoves. Everyone seems to think it is quite normal to have the grippe twice a year and a permanent cold in between and chronic lumbago.

If this sort of letter makes you any happier O.K. – but I should think you would rather hear nothing at all than my grumbling ramblings.

Give my love to Uncle Maynard and also to all the other Millers. I suppose my two nieces are a damned nuisance, and it serves mother right as she was always saying that she wanted a grandchild – and expected me to hold the bag. On the other hand – please answer this – if I should by accident or the design of god or man produce an infant could I park it in America? – for several years – as it's a hell of a place here for small babies – besides it would bore me stiff – for the first five years – anyway the event isn't very likely.

Love Lee

Boredom was starting to creep in to Lee's life, like an enemy infiltrator, working unseen to foment her discontent. Lee had underestimated her own need to be stimulated and to stretch her formidable mental powers in a creative and self-satisfying manner. Throughout her life she seemed unable to create her own objectives. Once she had started a project, she was able to tap a vast source of self-motivation, but it was always the first step that was the most agonizing. When the initial spark failed to ignite, depression would creep insidiously into her soul.

When Erik's training at the Carrier Company was completed, he and Mafy embarked on an American liner bound for Alexandria, via the Azores. In the ship's hold was a Chevrolet sedan that they had purchased on behalf of Aziz. Following Aziz's instructions to the letter, Erik had also bought about $300 worth of shotgun shells of different gauges, which he had concealed under the back seat of the car. This act caused Erik and Mafy much anxiety, as smuggling contraband ammunition into a country that had only recently been racked by revolution and riots could easily be seen to be the height of folly. Adding to their suffering was the fact that an appalling gale sprung up the moment the ship left New York. All passengers were confined to their cabins for the first four days as the vessel plunged and reared, water sloshing over the floors and luggage breaking loose from lashings to batter around the sodden cabins. The scheduled call at the Azores was cancelled, and the ship docked at Alexandria on 4 March 1937.

Aziz had promised to be at the pier to welcome them and speed the car through customs, but there was no sign of him. Erik and Mafy hung over the rail watching all the other passengers disembark and filter away through the immigration formalities. The car was slung in a big net and craned up from the hold to be deposited among a circle of admirers on the pierside. Erik wished it would evaporate in the heat as the wait dragged on. Amid his sense of rising anger and frustration, dark pictures of life in an Egyptian jail formed in his mind.

Several hours later Aziz nonchalantly strolled up, with no word of apology for the delay. Erik and Mafy were too overcome with relief to bawl him out and willingly went with him to the customs. All three of them sat down in the office of a fat Egyptian official and over the inevitable tiny cup of gritty, highly sweetened coffee they exchanged prolonged pleasantries. Then Aziz rose to his feet, pulled a few notes from his wallet, handed them to the official, and they were on their way to Cairo.

The road had been built by the British forces of occupation and lay just a few miles west of the Nile on the edge of the desert. The vastness was impressive even to these well-travelled Americans, who marvelled at the dryness and the smells, the pungent smoke from the cattle-dung fires, the aroma of exotic cooking, the mules and camels, the verdant richness of the Delta and the stark beauty of the desert. Reaching Cairo, they drove across a huge low masonry bridge over the Nile onto the island of Giza and meandered down the road about half a mile. There, in this colony of widely separated houses concealed behind huge hedges, stood Aziz's mansion. There, of course, was Lee, with her blond hair and her blue eyes and her arms tight around them, crying and carrying on and then all of a sudden very calm, glad they were there.[2]

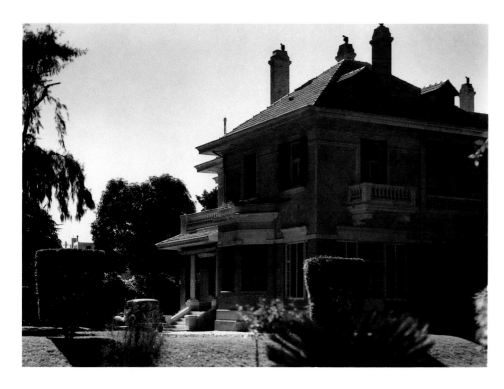

Aziz's house. Island of Giza, Cairo.
(Lee Miller)

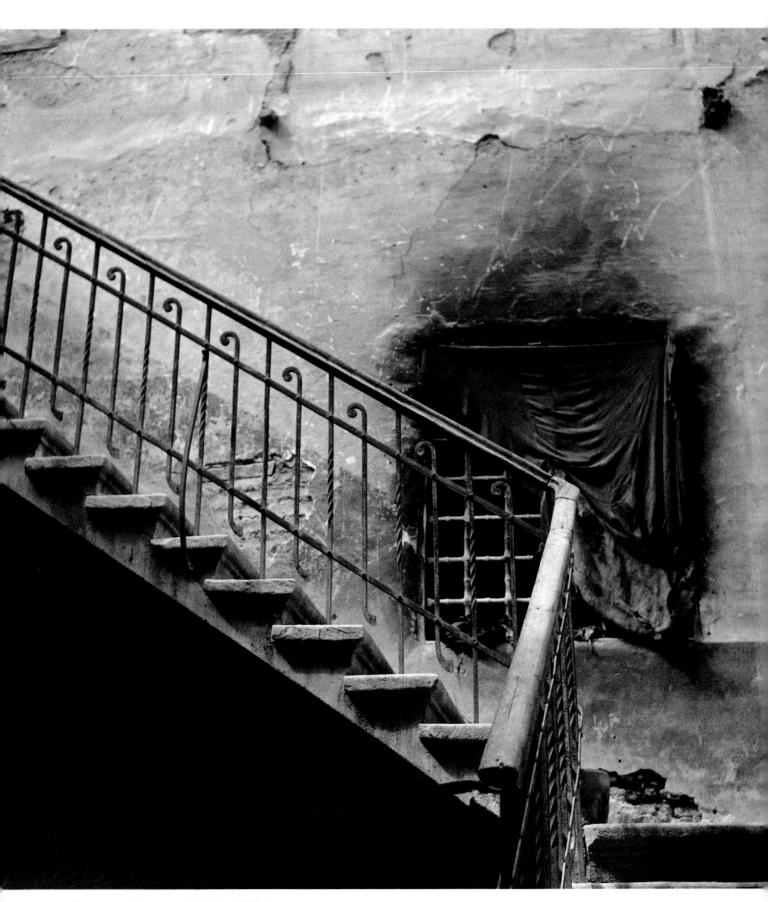

Stairway. Cairo, *c.* 1936. (Lee Miller)

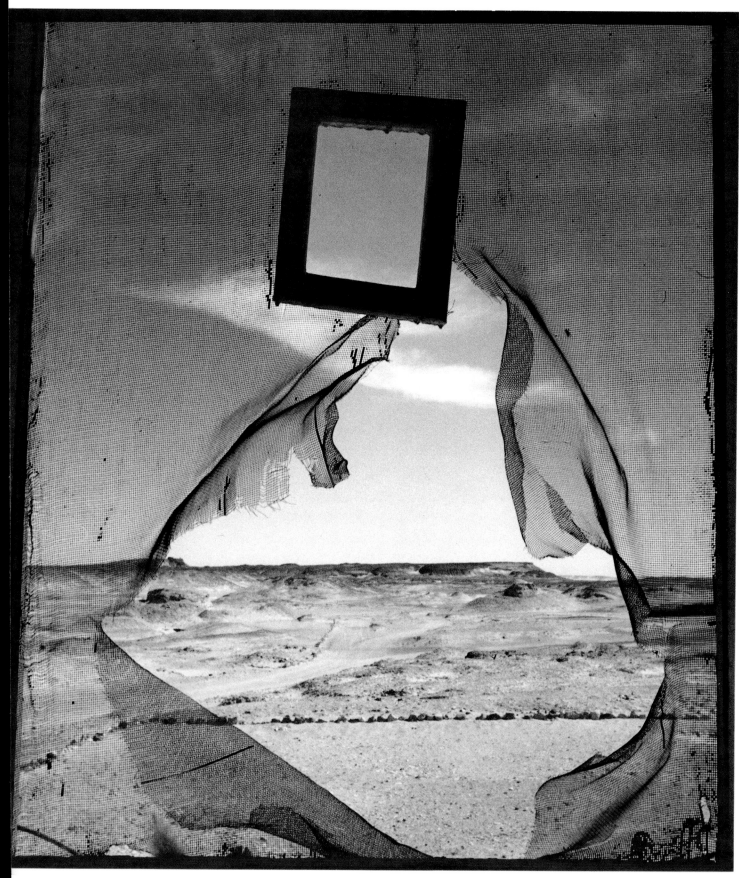

'Portrait of Space'. Near Siwa, 1937.
Magritte saw this photograph in
London in 1938 and it is thought to
have inspired his painting *Le Baiser*.
(Lee Miller)

The house would have fitted comfortably into a smart London suburb, with its marble floors, oak panelling, and spacious rooms. There were several servants. Lee had her own personal maid, Elda, a woman of Yugoslav origin whom Lee regarded as more of a friend than an employee. In the kitchen presided an Arab chef with Italian training who cooked a great variety of food. His Koran was an Arabic translation of that great French cookbook by Ali-Bab. He was attracted by the name, not realizing it was the *nom de plume* of a Frenchman.

Erik started work straight away, as the Carrier Company was installing the air-conditioning in the House of Parliament and the inauguration ceremony presided over by King Farouk was drawing dangerously close. Failure to complete in time would have ruined the company. With a team of Egyptian mechanics headed by Peter Grey, a Scottish engineer, Erik had to work the kind of hours that left him no time for socializing and attending the never-ending round of parties. Aziz remained detached from the struggle, to the point where he disappeared to Alexandria completely, forgetting to make arrangements for Erik's salary to be paid. After a couple of penniless months, Lee had to intervene and demand that things be sorted out.

As soon as the pay cheques started to come through, Erik and Mafy set up home in a bachelor apartment in the centre of Cairo rented from the Comte de Lavoisin. Lee's housewarming gift was a servant called Mohammed, a young man from Upper Egypt whose previous position with some English officers had given him a grave formality that belied his kindly nature. Immediately, Mafy was struck down by severe dysentery and haemorrhaging and remained bedridden for a month, cared for tenderly by Mohammed.

The short excursions with Aziz, like the trip to the cotton farm that had been such an ordeal, had given Lee an unexpected taste for desert travel and she wanted to make longer and more adventurous trips. Desert travel is an art that takes many years to perfect, but the thought of adventure had broken Lee's despondent mood and she set about planning with enthusiasm. A guide was hired, a Sudanese soldier who had his own vehicle fitted with a sun compass, and Lee organized a group of friends who had four other vehicles. Each member of the party had to provide some portion of the food and it fell to Lee to supply the water and drinks.

The expedition set off, heading for the monasteries of Saint Antonius and Saint Paul on the hinterland of the Red Sea. By the afternoon of the first day the party was well into the desert and at about four o'clock they halted to make camp while the guide went ahead to scout the route. By this time they had all used up the contents of their personal water bottles, so they turned to Lee for replenishment. The huge insulated container that she unpacked looked promising enough and there were hoots of laughter when it was found to be full to the brim with iced Martini cocktail. Good-naturedly, they sipped their drinks and waited for the guide to return. The hours stretched by at a slower and slower pace as the effects of alcohol increased their dehydration, and they were all practically raving with thirst by the time a plume of dust announced the

Sand tracks. Red Sea, *c.* 1936. (Lee Miller)

70

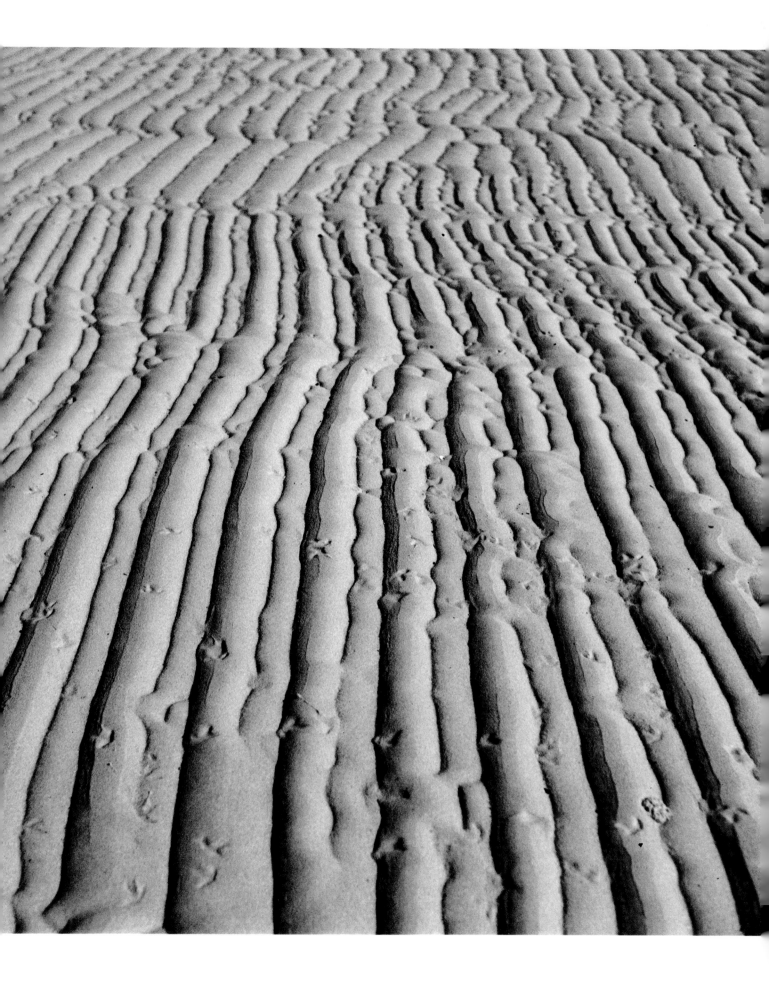

approach of the guide's truck. In the back were his emergency supplies: two jerry cans full of water that had not been touched for months. With some difficulty they hammered open the lids and fell on the rusty, stale water with more delight than if it had been Mouton Rothschild.

The introductory disaster did not deter Lee in the slightest, and her desert trips became more ambitious, though they were usually undertaken with fewer fellow-travellers. Some journeys lasted just a couple of days, others were for several weeks' duration, ranging to far-off oases, desert ruins or secluded swimming spots on the Red Sea. Lee's journeys were not made quite in the spirit of Freya Stark or with the daring of Wilfred Thesiger, but they were highly enterprising, and contained a large enough element of risk to make both the planning and the trip exciting.

Diverting though they were, these adventures never fully satisfied Lee; the call of Europe was growing too strong. At unexpected moments a longing for Paris would surface and overwhelm her like the nausea of homesickness. Sometimes this was more than she could bear and she was plunged into a depression that not even Aziz's most solicitous tenderness could dispel. There seemed to be only one answer to this Arabian dream that had turned into a nightmare. With Aziz's indulgent blessing and his generous financial support Lee left Egypt in the early summer of 1937 on a steamer bound for Marseilles. From there she caught the train to Paris.

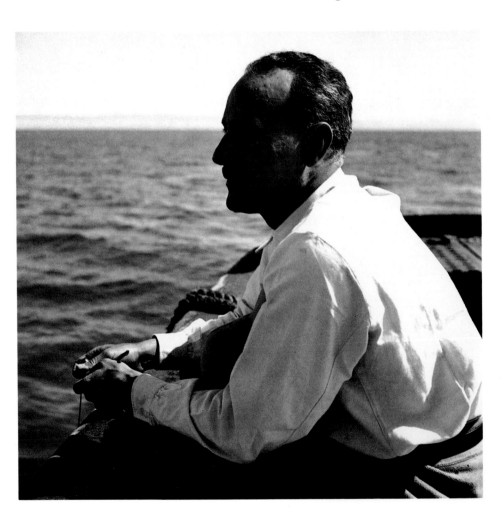

Aziz, fishing. Egypt, *c.* 1935. (Lee Miller)

Opposite: Lee. Alexandria, 1938. (Bernard Burrows)

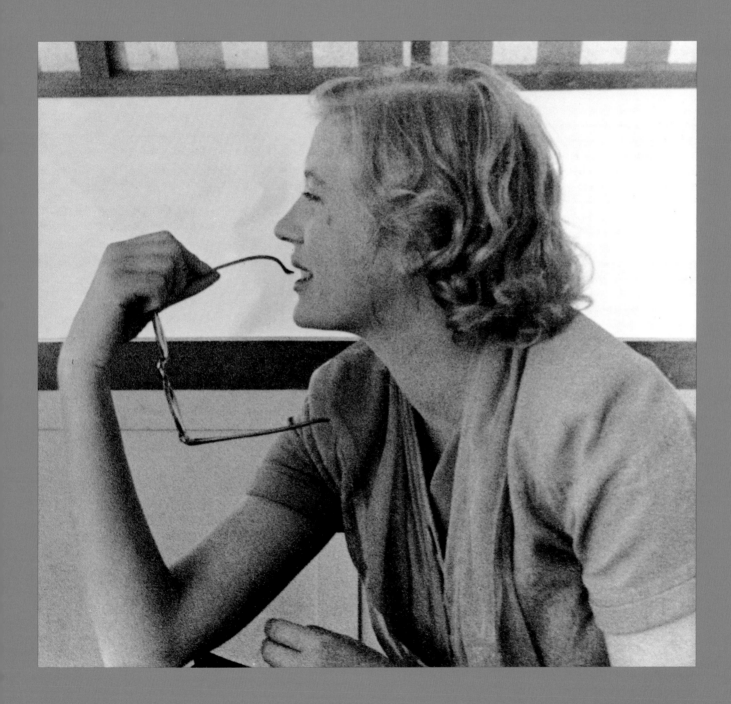

Arriving in Paris accompanied by her maid Elda, Lee checked in at the Hôtel Prince de Galles and telephoned a few of her old friends. That night there was to be a Surrealist costume ball given by the Rochas sisters, the elegant daughters of an important businessman, and Lee was immediately invited. Among the Surrealists, *tout Paris* was there. Max Ernst, clad in beggar's clothes, had dyed his hair blue; Man Ray, Paul Eluard, and Michel Leiris all wore outlandish attire. The girls had used much cunning and often little material to adorn themselves provocatively. Amid this scene, Lee was the only person dressed conventionally in a long dark blue robe. Everyone was delighted to see her, falling on her with cries of delight and rebuking her for being away for so long. It was her first contact with Man Ray for nearly five years and in the uproar of the party they buried the hatchet and became friends again.

As so often happens when contact is renewed after a long absence, once the excitement of welcome dies down, one finds oneself in limbo. Lee was standing beside the ornate mantelpiece watching the company with an air of detachment when Julien Levy appeared, accompanied by a beggar in paint-encrusted trousers. He introduced this appalling creature, whose horrific appearance was accentuated by his having his right hand and left foot dyed bright blue. Lean, with blue eyes, black hair and all the bright eagerness of that period, he was unmistakably English. It was Roland Penrose, who wrote of his first meeting with Lee:

Blond, blue-eyed and responsive, she seemed to enjoy the abysmal contrast between her elegance and my own slumlike horror. And so it was for the second time that the *coup de foudre* struck. As the party broke up owing to the return from New York in the early morning of Monsieur Rochas, who disapproved categorically of entertaining Surrealist artists in his house, I asked Max if he knew a fabulous beauty called Lee Miller. 'Of course,' answered Max, 'let's ask her to dinner tomorrow.'[1]

The dinner party at Max's studio was an amazing success. Lee's beauty and vitality fired the evening. Her outrageous Surrealist wit, strange tales from Egypt and reminiscences of Paris in the 1920s entertained everyone far into the night. There was a great deal of laughter and the wine bottle passed round again and again in the lamplight. Late the next morning Lee awoke in Roland's arms in his small room at the Hôtel de la Paix. Gesticulating unsteadily as he was shaving, Roland nicked her hand with his cut-throat razor. The cut bled profusely and needed a stitch, but Lee laughed it off, claiming that they were now blood-brothers. In the next few weeks, Lee returned to her hotel only occasionally to take a nap and change her clothes before going off on the next jaunt with Roland. Exhibitions, plays, Surrealist meetings, parties; for Lee it was like finding a spring of clear cool water in the desert.

Lee stayed on in Paris while Roland and Max Ernst left for England to arrange Max's exhibition at the Mayor Gallery. Then, after about two weeks, leaving Elda in Paris, she set out with Man Ray and Ady, his Martiniquaise girlfriend. They took a ship to Southampton, and then the train to Plymouth where Roland met them and whisked them away in his Ford V8. Beyond Truro their route lay through narrow Cornish lanes with granite drystone walls on either side that cut off the view. After about ten miles they swung through a farm gate and followed a track across a rolling pasture. Truro was just visible in the distance, and in the foreground they were confronted by the broad sweep of the Truro River. Concealed among tall beech trees, and clinging hard to the side of the steep hill at the water's edge as if to prevent the tide from wetting its feet stood Lamb Creek.

This beautiful Georgian house, which seemed to come straight from the pages of a romantic novel, belonged to Roland's brother Becus, who was away, travelling the Labrador coast as third mate on a sailing ship. In his absence, Roland had leased the house for a month. Paul and Nusch Eluard were already there with Max Ernst and Leonora Carrington and in the weeks that followed the Surrealist invasion forces grew with the arrival of Herbert Read, E.L.T. Mesens, Eileen Agar and Joseph Bard. Surrealist arguments raged, interspersed with sight-seeing jaunts to Land's End, remote creeks and logan stones, the fascinating delights of Cornish pubs, and ardent lovemaking. Lee's hedonism can seldom have been more fully indulged and completely satisfied, as Aziz sensed when he wrote:

AERO CLUB D'EGYPTE

Sweetheart,
Your letter makes me think of a thoroughbred who has been kept in stables too long. The moment he steps out he jumps on all fours.

Somehow I don't think you will care long for this hectic life with this funny list of names. To me this list of which I know only a few seems to be the subtitles in a film given in the *Cinema Agriculteurs*.

I am rather glad you left Paris, with that hotel. What a place for money! And only to sleep! Now you have no more need of Elda, you had better write to her and tell her to come back here. She can go to her parents on the way if she wants to. Don't worry about sending her any money, I will send her a cheque tomorrow. She will be better off here as I want to take a flat in Alexandria. I was thinking that it may be better for me not to join you, and wait here for your return. I will send you the money I would have needed for my trip which is better for you seeing that you have already spent the biggest part of £200. You see we are very busy and somehow I don't think I will be able to leave the office with three installations in hand and another big one in Alexandria coming at the Cinema Royal. You can stay till August and come back to Alexandria, when we can have a lot of fun with the speed-boat. The Hopkinsons will be there too, so we can amuse ourselves. Incidentally I am going to write our names down for the sailing club.

Amuse yourself darling, but not too much. . . . Cairo is pretty boring as you can imagine, which makes me support the idea that you should be away for your own sake even though it makes me feel lonesome and dejected to be without you.
I adore you,
Aziz

The month at Lamb Creek came to an end and everyone dispersed, to reassemble a few weeks later at the Hôtel Vaste Horizon at Mougins in the South of France. Here the focus of attention was Picasso, who had arrived a few days earlier with Dora Maar. Before leaving Paris he had completed *Guernica* and, spoken or unspoken, the tragedy of the Spanish Civil War provided a fierce counterpoint to the revelries at Mougins.

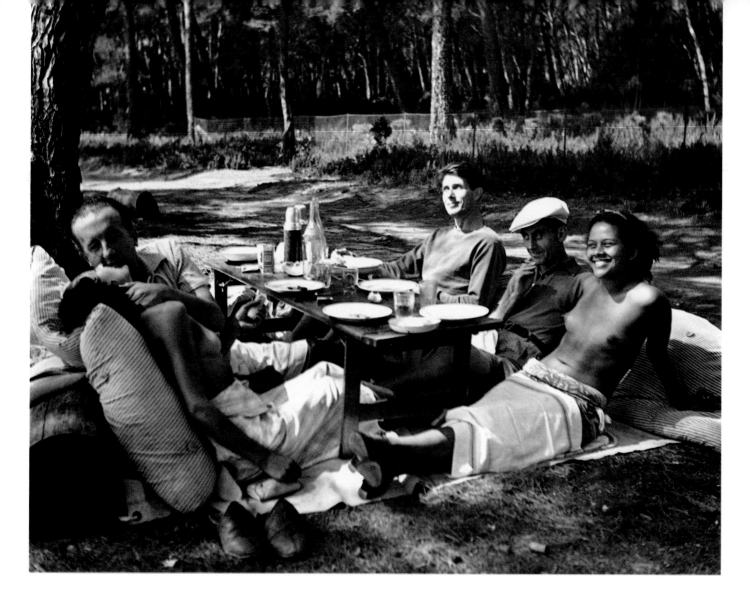

Left to right: Nusch and Paul Eluard, Roland Penrose, Man Ray and Ady. Mougins, France, Summer 1937. (Lee Miller)

Picasso was unable to live without working, and most days he would paint during the morning.

Although he made drawings from life, chiefly of Nusch and Dora, most of the paintings were made without a sitter. One day it had been Paul Eluard dressed as an Arlesienne and unexpectedly giving suck to a cat. Next he announced he had made a portrait of Lee Miller. On a bright pink background Lee appeared in profile, her face a brilliant yellow like the sun with no modelling. Two smiling eyes and a green mouth were placed on the same side of the face and her breasts seemed like the sails of ships filled with a joyous breeze. It was an astonishing likeness. An agglomeration of Lee's qualities of exuberant vitality and vivid beauty put together in such a way that it was undoubtedly her but with none of the conventional attributes of a portrait.[2]

Roland bought the portrait for £50 and gave it to Lee. A few weeks later her parole was over. With great resolution she packed the painting among her baggage and boarded a ship at Marseilles bound for Alexandria. To Roland it was *au revoir*, because they had many half dreamed and hazily sketched plans for further travels together.

Overjoyed at having her home, Aziz threw a party for more than a hundred friends, including of course Erik and Mafy. The Picasso portrait was hung on a wall in the hall where everyone entering would have to pass by it. Lee stationed Mafy near the painting with strict instructions to eavesdrop on the guests' comments. Word had got round before the party that Lee had sat for a famous artist, and it was naturally assumed that the result would be a conventional portrait. The guests were astonished. As the drinks took effect the current of the conversation was dominated by many of them claiming they could easily do a better likeness with their eyes shut. Lee had anticipated this and, choosing her moment, flung open the doors to another room where paints, paper and brushes were all laid out. 'OK!' she challenged, 'Let's see how you make out.' The party was a memorable success with all the guests ruining their evening clothes by daubing away with abandon.

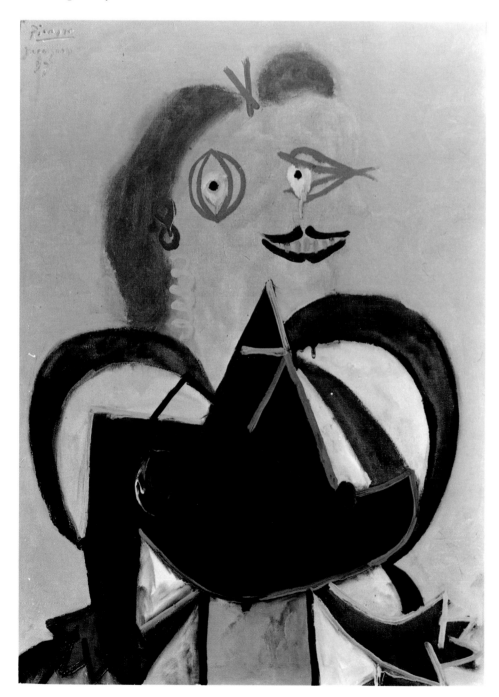

Portrait of Lee Miller, by Picasso. Mougins, France, 1937.

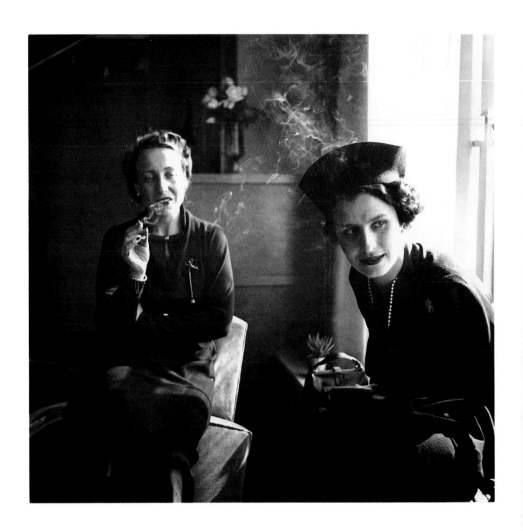

'Black Satin and Pearls Set'. Cairo, *c.* 1935. (Lee Miller)

Opposite: Eileen Agar, Brighton Pavilion, England, 1937. Part of the bulge in the silhouette is caused by Agar's Rolleiflex. Picasso asked for a copy of this photo; he liked the notion of Eileen Agar being pregnant with a camera. (Lee Miller)

After the months of freedom and gaiety, the social life of Cairo – the 'black satin and pearls set', as Lee described it – was anathema to her. Parties with puerile games of telepathy and clairvoyance and days spent lounging round the pool at the Gezira Sporting Club were now even more insufferable than before her trip abroad. The privilege of being an American brought more relief than Lee probably appreciated, because it gave her – unlike other women from foreign nations – the social freedom to enter places like Tommy's bar at Shepheards Hotel. Lee and Mafy were known as the 'two American girls' and their freedom was often envied. 'It's all right for you two,' others grumbled jealously, 'you're American; nobody thinks anything of what you do!'

It was hardly surprising that Lee had begun to attract the attention of the more malicious gossips. Since she delighted in being outrageous, she herself was never disturbed by salacious tattle, but the hurt inflicted on Aziz and her close friends wounded her. Sometimes she managed to turn the tables by means of the same gossip channels. There was a young serviceman, for example, who had a predilection for tying up and beating unsuspecting girlfriends as a prelude to sex, and during one of his sessions he became excessively enthusiastic, severely hurting the girl, who was a friend of Lee's. Lee and two willing helpers inveigled him to an assignation at a beach house in Alexandria. There they tied him up and thrashed him

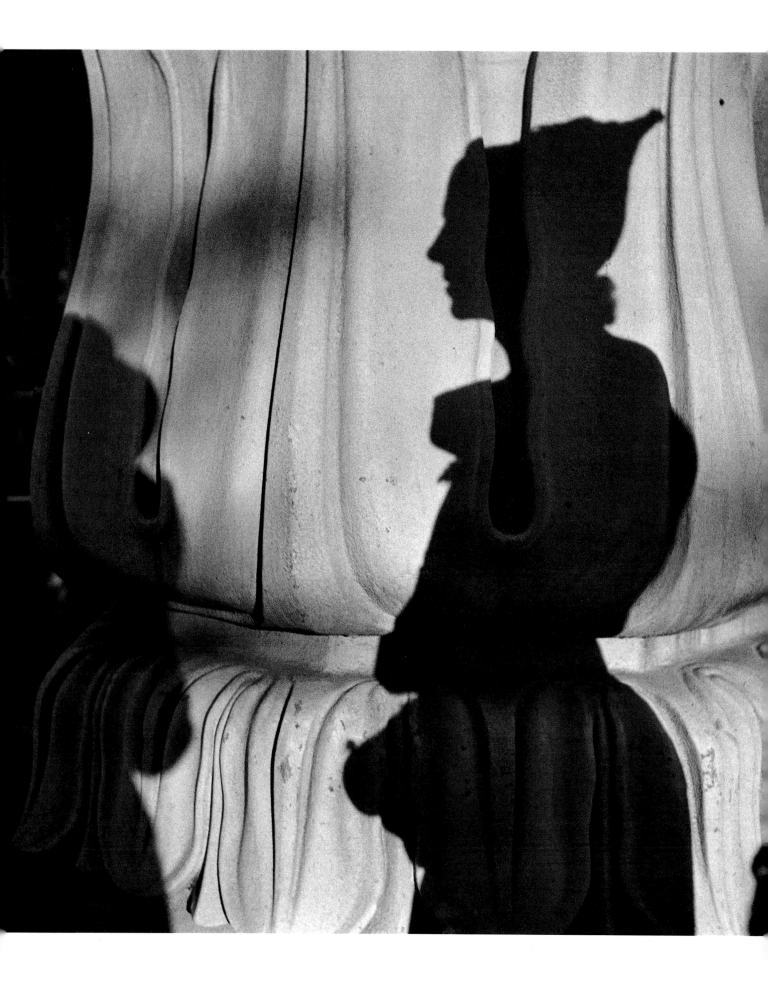

until he was black and blue. Then, to ensure that he received plenty of sympathetic inquiries about his condition, they put the rumour about that he had been wounded by unknown assailants. He applied for a transfer to a safer posting.

Desert trips were the only real escape from the social round. Aziz seldom accompanied her; he preferred fishing and, besides, the pressures of his work were mounting. Lee now had her own car, a powerful Packard convertible rugged enough to stand the punishment of roadless motoring. The travelling parties were composed of carefully chosen friends like Guy Pereira, a merchant, and his wife Diane; Henry and Alice Hopkinson from the British Embassy; and Giles Vandaleur, a captain with the Irish Guards. They were all not only good travellers but also discreet; desert travel is strangely liberating and it was no good enjoying this sense of freedom only to have its effects reported all over Cairo. Giles in particular became close to Lee. She loved his subtle Irish wit, which he used to tease her mercilessly, as well as his capacity for turning everything into a joke.

On one journey to Luxor the party encountered a snake charmer. Hopkinson, who could speak fluent Arabic, discovered that the man's special talent was tempting snakes to come out of their hiding places among the rocks. Hopkinson and the other men in the party took the snake charmer behind some boulders and made him strip to his underwear to prove that he did not have any snakes concealed in his clothes. Then they selected an area where they were certain that there were no snakes. The man played a droning melody on his pipe and within minutes snakes were slithering out from everywhere. Lee was fascinated, and demanded to learn the secret. In true native fashion the snake charmer told her it would take years to learn, but as an interim measure he made her take a solemn vow never to hurt a snake. Then, to prove the mutual efficacy of this charm, he scooped up a large cobra and draped it round Lee's shoulders where it rested contentedly.

On another trip to the hot springs on the Red Sea coast, the party was caught in a fierce sandstorm. They made for an army post where they sheltered in a miserable fly-blown hut while the storm howled around them. In the middle of the night Hopkinson was taken violently ill, racked with quaking chills. No medicine seemed to have the slightest effect, and all they could do was pack Evian bottles filled with hot water around him in an attempt to keep him warm. At first light the storm had abated enough for them to drive to Suez in cars that had had their paint stripped to the bare, bright metal by the flying sand. The hospital diagnosed Hopkinson's ailment as pleurisy and confined him to bed for many weeks.

Perhaps it was Egypt's contrast to the green of England, or perhaps the stimulation of Lee's recently renewed contact with the Surrealists; whatever the cause, Lee started taking photographs again. Many of these were little more than snapshots of friends loafing around on boats or by swimming pools. There are very few candid pictures of native Egyptians, perhaps because they had a marked reluctance to be photographed and Lee respected privacy. Overall it is the landscapes and buildings that dominate this period. These photographs are not just the gawpings of a

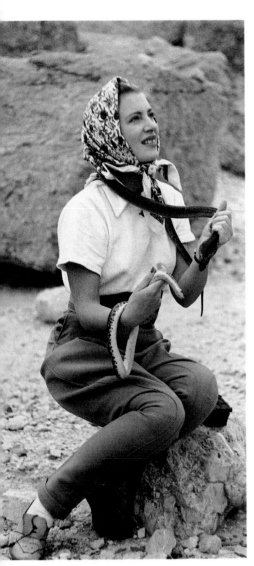

Lee's introductory lesson in snake-charming. Egypt, 1938. (Guy Taylor)

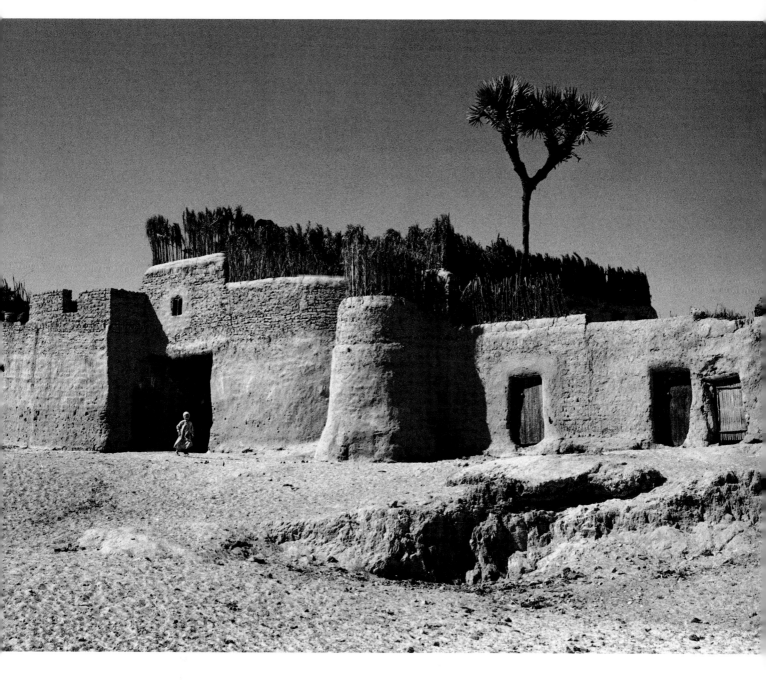

tourist; time after time a picture contains some quirky juxtaposition or observation that gives the image a second perspective. Ever present is the oblique poetry of the Surrealist eye that turn plants growing on the roofs of a mud village into hair above a face, or makes the white domes of Wadi Natrun monastery more sensuous than breasts, with the added irony of the celibate monks within them. Even those photographs which at first seem little more than perfectly composed architectural shots reveal a heightened perception and symbolism. A wind eroded rock rears up as a ragged phallus, and with similar sexual symbolism doorways of temples are jammed tight with piles of rocks. The contents of the cotton bales become compressed clouds straining against their tight bonds, a few wisps escaping to rejoin their fellows in the sky beyond.

Oasis village. Egypt, *c.* 1939. (Lee Miller)

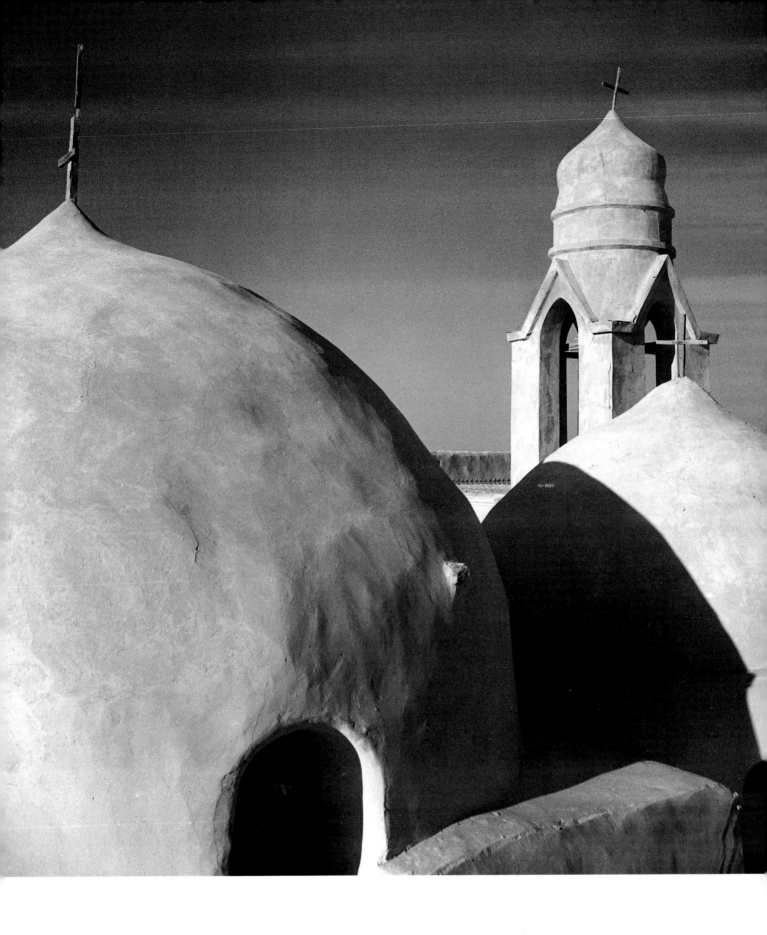

Monastery of Wadi Natrun. Egypt,
c. 1935. (Lee Miller)

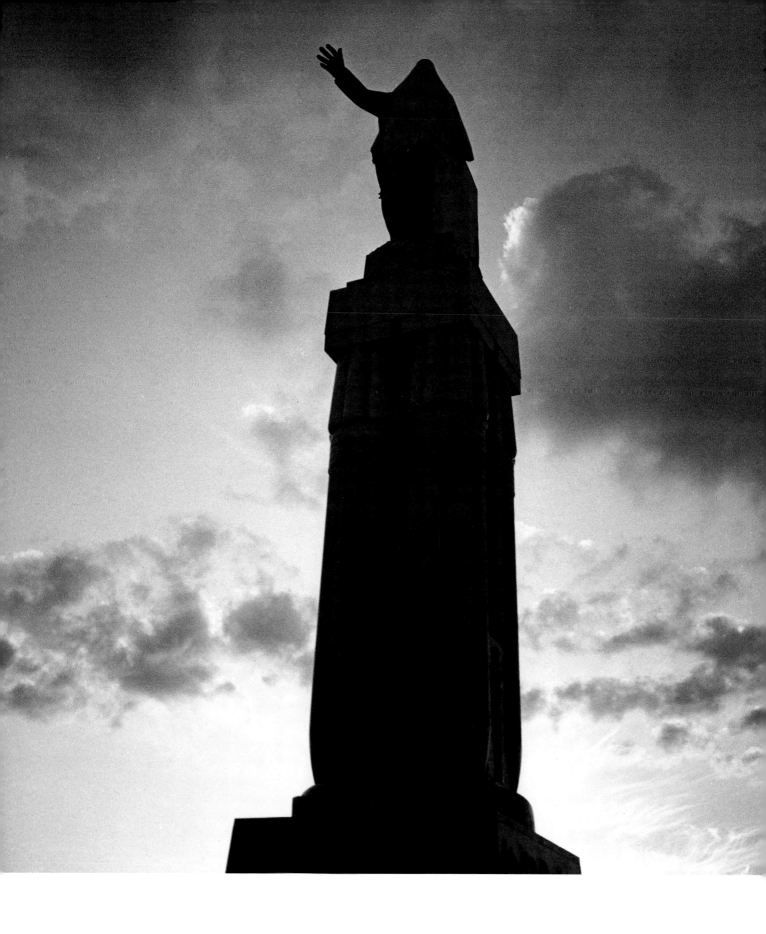

Statue beside the Suez Canal. Egypt,
c. 1938. (Lee Miller)

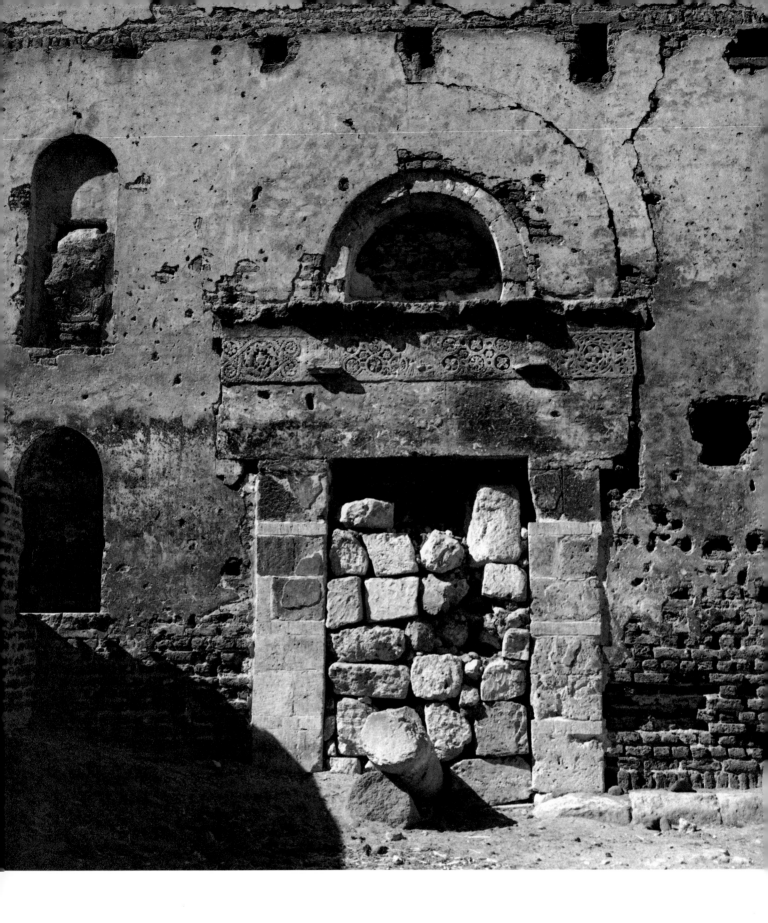

Blocked doorway. Syria, 1938.
(Lee Miller)

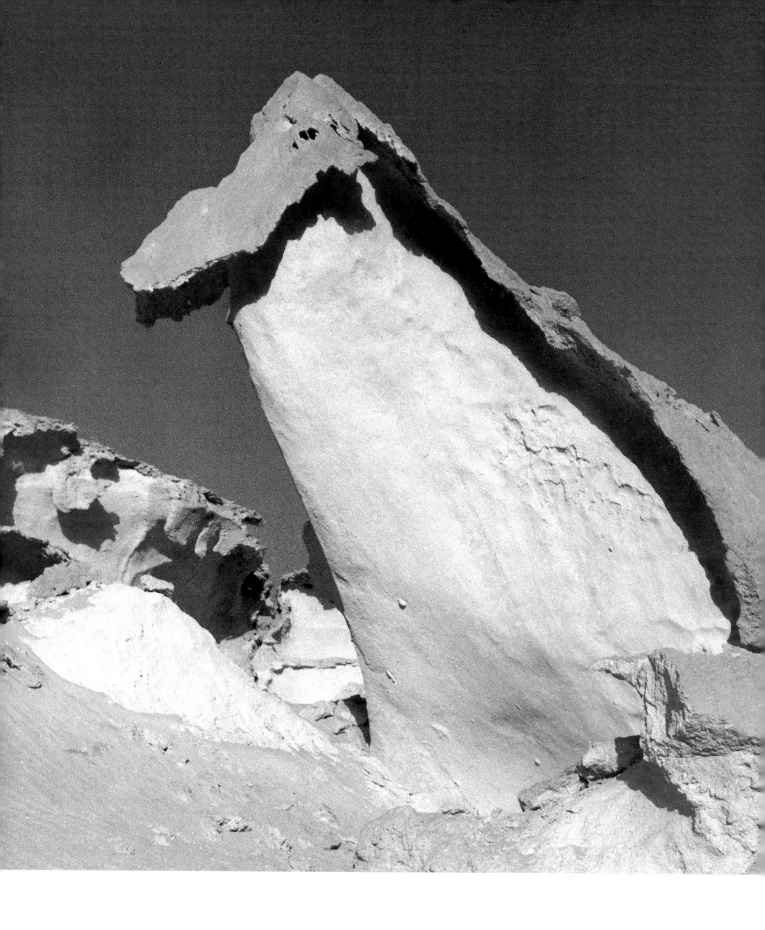

'Cock Rock'. Near Siwa, Egypt, 1939.
(Lee Miller)

Lee's new exuberance of spirit was buoyed up by letters from Roland, confirming their *rendezvous* in Athens in the spring of 1938. When the time came, Lee had the Packard loaded onto a ship at the port of Alexandria, and she boarded in the company of Gerti Wissa and her brother. The Wissas — an old-established Coptic Christian family from Asyut — were cotton growers and old friends of Aziz. Gerti, a sparkling girl of nineteen, was on her way to the International Bridge Tournament in Budapest as captain of the Egyptian team. Aziz affectionately waved goodbye from the shore and the ship began to slip her cables. The last line had hardly been let go when, wholly unexpectedly, Giles Vandaleur, with whom Lee had been having an affair, popped up from a place of concealment. He had heard that she was on the ship and, having some leave due, had decided to go along for the ride. From that moment on, the four-day voyage was one riotous party.

In Athens Lee and Giles checked into the Hôtel Grand Bretagne in a scorching heatwave. A few days later a cable from Roland announced his imminent arrival on a Greek trader from Marseilles and Giles obligingly moved out.

In his book *The Road Is Wider Than Long*, which he described as 'An Image Diary from the Balkans', Roland wrote:

After a brief taste of the wonders and the excitement of ancient and modern Greece we left the tavernas, the enchanted islands and the beaches to steer inland towards the north enjoying along our route remote villages, mountains, vineyards, olive groves. We camped in lonely places and stopped in the shade of great trees to refresh ourselves with the cool sour milk made by shepherds from their flocks.

After visiting the groves of Thassos we crossed Bulgaria and on reaching Roumania we were first entertained by the decaying sophistication of Bucharest where tea houses sold caviar and every horse cab had a violinist perched up beside the driver. . . . Sadly for me all these roads came to an abrupt end when I was obliged to leave Lee in Bucharest and take the Orient Express back home. On the way a sudden reminder of political reality awaited me in Munich. The vault of the main station was decorated along its entire length with thousands of Nazi flags in honour of Chamberlain's appeasement visit to Hitler.

After Roland had left, Lee stayed on in Bucharest. She continues the narrative in the following unpublished manuscript which she probably wrote in 1946.

Pagan customs in some areas are quite normally mixed with Christian rites . . . the priest turns his back while a mourning mother places a penny for Charon in the mouth of her child . . . and ties him into his coffin so he can't return to haunt her. For three days she must lament over the body . . . extemporaneous verse is a native talent of most peasants and the pleas that the child should not leave the world alternate with phrases begging him not to return as a ghost.

All these things I knew in 1938 from wandering the country with Harry Brauner who is now Professor of Musical History in the University and director of the folklore research institute of Rumania. I'd arrived in Bucharest rather vaguely from Greece, via Bulgaria, and really on my way to Warsaw, armed with a frightening packet of introduction letters. Royalty and dictators and blackmarket exchange dealers. . . . smart black satin and pearl society and massive landowners. There was a letter from Surrealist painter friend in Paris

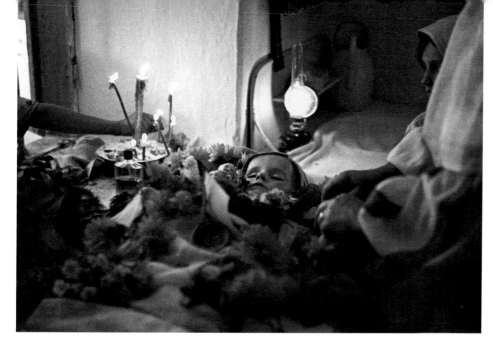

Dead child. Romania, 1938.
(Lee Miller)

Victor Brauner to his brother. With the greatest of luck I drew it from the grab bag. I never used the others. Harry, his brother, was a musician and researcher, busy packing his bag to go on a three month tour of his country with an artist named Lena and a recording gramophone and a crotchety fascist-minded old professor. They were going to travel by infrequent trains, hitchhiking and feet. I had my once super-sleek grey Packard, Arabella, and nothing to do. We followed the gypsies, camp by camp . . . we scooted across the whole country for a wedding party . . . we stayed days while witchcraft was being performed or devils exorcised from a barn . . . when I'd get cramp from driving all night to catch a piece of magic to be performed at dawn in an ex-Roman settlement we'd limp from the car and dance like scalp hunting American Indians in the headlights of the car . . . chanting 'Of, mor mor . . . aulimika dor dor dor . . .' or an old Macedonian song, 'Tun Bey', with choral responses. We slept in peasant beds piled high with feather quilts on handwoven sheets which filed the skin off at every roll. Fleas did jumping exercises on the coverlet and girdled our ankles and middles with rosettes of bites. We drank quantities of hard liquor and gallons of Lapte Batute buttermilk for re-hydration. We made documentary photographs of all the frescoes painted on the outside of the ravishing steep-steepled churches of the Budkovina province, and accepted for the institute the under-glass ikons which the churches might not destroy but were discarding in favour of chromos, oleos and plaster statues of saints *en grande série* from mail order catalogues. Troubles came in well defined geographical areas . . . all four tires punctured several times, once the canvas top was razored open for a pilfering arm . . . there was no food, no place to sleep, no petrol, the telephone switchboard was dead, no hospitality or good will.

Music, festival dancing, and the ritual of weddings or funerals, magic to bring on rain or to fertilise the bride or the fields are traditional to very small areas, but may be totally unknown across the river or the other side of a forest. In the gypsy rites to produce rainfall, a boy and a girl are dressed in leaves arranged like Hawaiian skirts. They prance around singing a primitive prayer ditty while the adults throw buckets of water over them. The peasants' ritual harks back to a ceremony as ancient as the oldest of Greek literature. The pure children (under the age of 10) fashion a moist clay doll in relief on a board. Gentians make blue eyes, and a scarlet petal the mouth. The sex is well defined. The offering is trimmed with blossom, laden with fruits and carried by child pall-bearers to the nearest remaining water on the parched plains. Bearing lit candles and suitable prayers the sacrifice, symbolic of one of themselves, is placed on the water where it floats away to death by drowning.

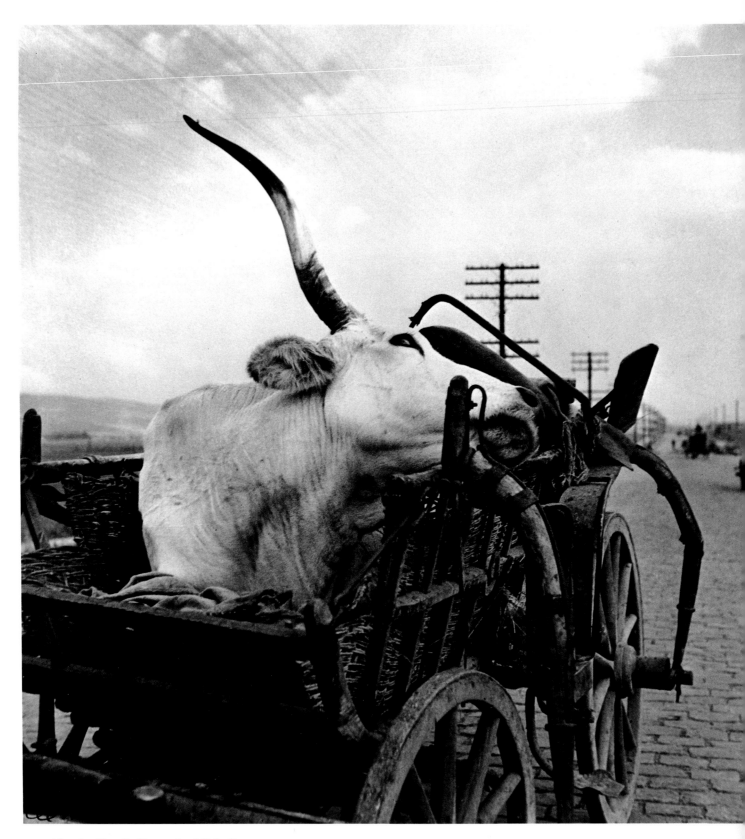

'On the Road'. Romania, 1938. (Lee Miller)

Opposite: Tree crosses in a cemetery. Romania, 1938. (Lee Miller)

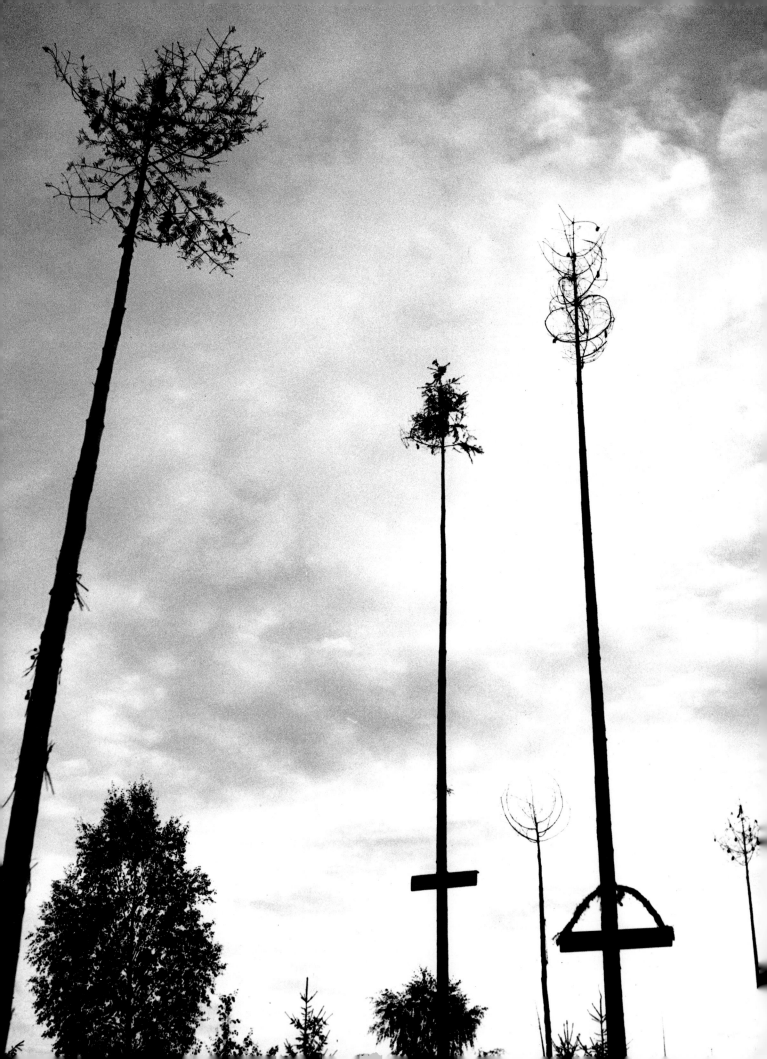

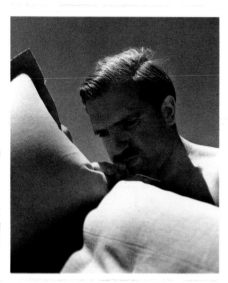

Bernard Burrows inflating an airbed.
Red Sea, 1938. (Lee Miller)

Before returning to Cairo, Lee had already planned her next trip. On this occasion her companion was Bernard Burrows, the Third Secretary at the British Embassy. Lee had met him earlier in the year and they had taken some trips to the Red Sea together, but this adventure was to be far more ambitious. Arabella the Packard was ill-disposed after the Balkans so they shipped Bernard's Ford up the Levantine coast to Beirut. It was a difficult time to be travelling because the Arab revolt in Palestine had caused many restrictions to be placed on civilian movement. Their route took them southwest into Syria as far as Damascus and then north across the desert to the ruins of Palmyra, returning to Beirut by way of Aleppo for a few days skiing.

Bernard had been a classics scholar and his passionate interest in antiquity brought the ancient cities and ruins to life. Relating history like an adventure story, he filled the desolate landscape with battles, sieges and civilizations that had vanished, swallowed whole by the desert. All the other qualities of an excellent travelling companion came easily to him, experienced as he was at planning and navigating, and well versed in diplomatic ways of handling intransigent officials. He was fun to be with, and he was in love with Lee. The journey, however, was a limited success for Lee because she had a sudden attack of conscience.

HOTEL NEW ROYAL
BEIRUT

Le 17 -Novembre 1938

Dear Aziz – :
Here I am – after several ridiculous days skiing – snow – freezing cold – & fun. There have been as many changes of scenery and weather here as there are kinds of religions and races of people. The desert – the cultivation and the mountains – comforts and discomforts – fun and boredom. And all of them vaguely disappointing because of my own state of mind – I can't attack or appreciate anything directly because I'm so torn and shredded in my own self that my sub-conscious tic-tocs and irritates all my waking and sleeping moments, and I can't think of anything satisfactory to do about it. I can't just stuff my ears the way I used to for the dogs in Giza – or your fancy new clock or the gardener clipping the lawn – there is no further way of escaping – no way of pretending there isn't a problem – & worst of all I am such a coward that I'd rather solve it from a distance and let the details take care of themselves. It ought to be much easier from here for me to say and know about coming back. And it ought to be easier for you to say if you want me – and why – and how – its too 'shymaking' to talk about it face to face and inclined to get buried in tears or my hysterics, – or shingled under by some petty quarrel (about friends or hours for lunch) but it isn't simple to know what one wants – I feel that you want most of all to be excused from further trouble for and about me and of course to feel absolved in all good conscience, free of responsibility and preoccupation with me. But either from tenderheartedness or misplaced faith in my possible reform you are blinding yourself to my worthlessness as your wife – and even as a companion.

As for me, I frankly don't know what I want, unless it is to 'have my cake and eat it'. I want the Utopian combination of security and freedom and emotionally I need to be completely absorbed in some work or in a man I love. I think the first thing for me to do is to take or make freedom – which will give me the opportunity to become concentrated again, and just hope that some sort of security follows – even if it doesn't the struggle will keep me awake and alive.

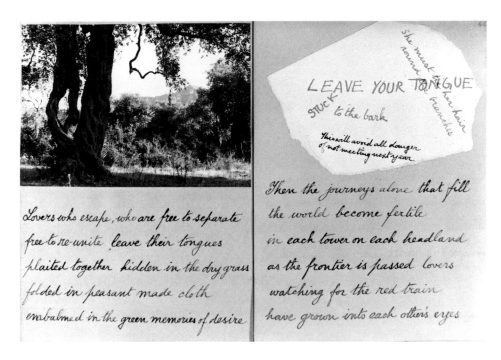

Lovers who escape, who are free to separate free to re-unite leave their tongues plaited together hidden in the dry grass folded in peasant made cloth embalmed in the green memories of desire

Then the journeys alone that fill the world become fertile in each tower on each headland as the frontier is passed lovers watching for the red train have grown into each other's eyes

LEAVE YOUR TONGUE STUCK to the bark this will avoid all danger of not meeting next year She must round her hair branches

From the original manuscript of *The Road Is Wider Than Long*, by Roland Penrose. 1938. (Antony Penrose)

For the moment I've come back to Beirut to make another start at solving the impasse of visas and identity. – in case you would like me to come back to Egypt to really and truly talk over yours, or my or our plans for the future – otherwise I'll go to America or Europe . . .

Goodbye darling – and good luck until I return and even if I don't.

Love Lee

Lee did return to Aziz. Kind, gentle and affectionate, he welcomed her back although it was obvious by now that there could be no hope of salvaging the marriage. He never allowed his exasperation to show as time and time again he tried to find a solution to Lee's inner restlessness. No indulgence seemed capable of quelling her disquiet; it was too deep-seated and fundamental to her nature.

Lee tried to absorb herself again in the social round. The lavish dinner parties at the home of Baron Emphain and his beautiful young American wife Goldie were some distraction. The guests were drawn from all the different nationalities of Cairo, with some of the world's big names, such as Barbara Hutton, drifting through from time to time. The dining room, with its excessively ornate decor, looked like a movie set. The place settings were gold and a liveried footman stood behind each chair. After dinner, which always followed lavish cocktails, Baron Emphain would blow a French hunting-horn – the signal for all the guests to pile into cars and go off to a night-club.

In the early spring of 1939 Lee was staying with the Wissa family in Asyut, when Roland Penrose appeared, bearing as a gift a pair of gold handcuffs and the manuscript of *The Road Is Wider Than Long*. He had arrived in Egypt on the pretext of accompanying the Egyptologist Belle de Zout as her photographer while she was making a study of Egyptian folk dance.

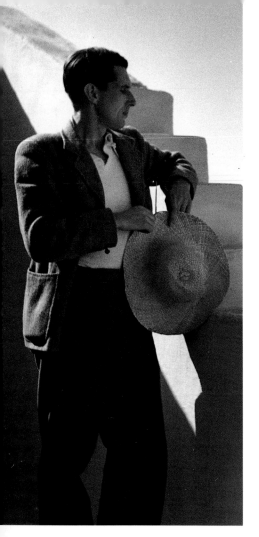

Roland Penrose in Egypt, 1939. (Lee Miller)

With the help of Aziz, an expedition in Lee's powerful Packard was planned. In company with Mafy, Lee's sister-in-law, and an old friend, George Hoyningen-Huene, the photographer, Lee and I set off for Siwa, a strange isolated oasis some five hundred miles west of Cairo. Following an ill-defined track past cliffs splendidly eroded by the wind, the fantastic buildings of Siwa in one massive block appeared above an extensive grove of date palms. Before returning to the amiable Aziz, two days were spent bathing in the warm ebullient turquoise water of the springs and drinking sweet tea with the authorities, all friends of Aziz and therefore friends of Lee.[3]

Even in the remoteness of Siwa the clouds of war were gathering. Parties of Italians disguised as Arabs were reputed to be mapping the desert and the Egyptian government was under pressure from the British to restrict the travel of foreigners. The 'help from Aziz' that Roland Penrose mentioned actually meant the sum total of his influence which was necessary before the authorities would allow Hoyningen-Huene to go on the expedition.

Siwa was something more than a mere oasis town. The isolation of the community had given it a unique culture. The indigenous Sanussi tribe had blue eyes and red hair. It was not uncommon, and entirely legitimate, for men to marry men. Boys had a patch shaven on their heads to denote when they were eligible for marriage, and girls were considered marriageable at thirteen and signalled this by wearing a silver medallion.

Lee's party stayed at a government rest-house. As there was an artesian hot spring nearby, Lee and Mafy borrowed shorts from the men and jumped in topless. Far from being outraged, the local officials were

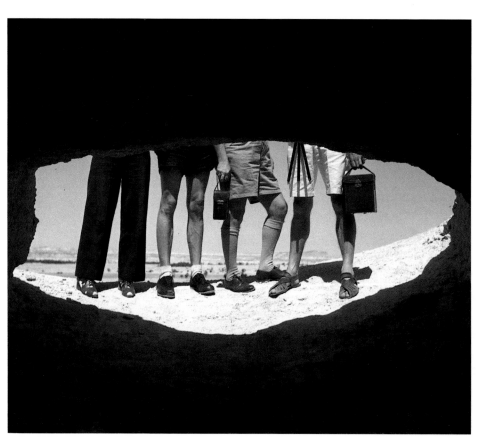

Left to right: Mafy Miller, unknown, George Hoyningen-Huene, Roland Penrose. Near Siwa, 1939. (Lee Miller)

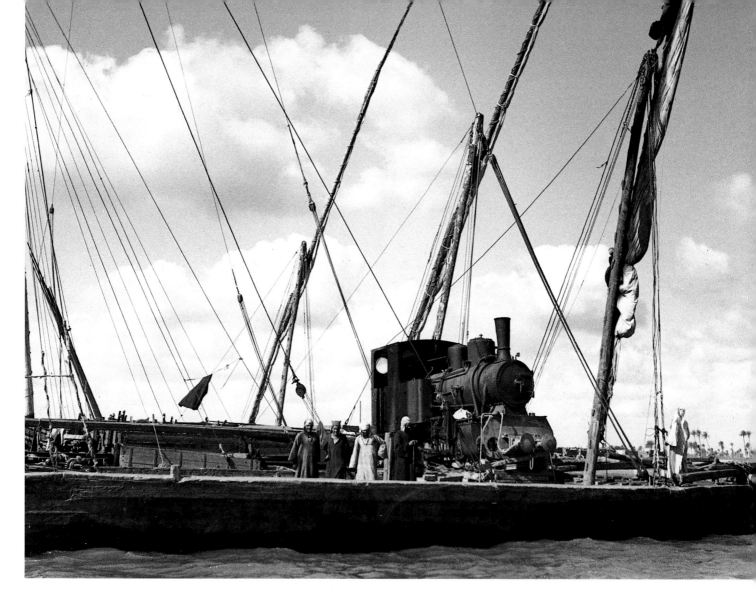

'Steam Dhow'. Egypt, c. 1936. (Lee Miller)

enchanted, and offered generous hospitality throughout the stay. On the last night, by way of a celebration honouring their guests, they issued a permit for the general distribution of date wine. This rare event was met with delight, but what was intended as a farewell party degenerated into a hysterical brawl in the course of which the distinguished visitors barricaded themselves in their rooms.

After Roland had returned to England, Lee sought further respite in more desert journeys with Bernard. They completed an ambitious 900-mile round trip taking in the oases of Farafra, Bahariya and Dakhla, as well as the Great Oasis – El Kharga. Another journey took them down the coast of the Red Sea to Bur Safaga, and back inland to return along the Nile. But such journeys no longer brought Lee any lasting satisfaction. Her travelling 'jag' was finally played out.

By June she had decided to leave Egypt for an indefinite period. Aziz had given her a large portfolio of investments to ensure her some financial security. He was still deeply in love with her but far too realistic to imagine that he could ever make her happy. With unlimited generosity he had never stood in the way of demands which would have made most men go berserk. Now, on the 2nd of June, he went to Port Said to bid her a dignified farewell as she boarded the S.S. *Otranto* for Southampton.

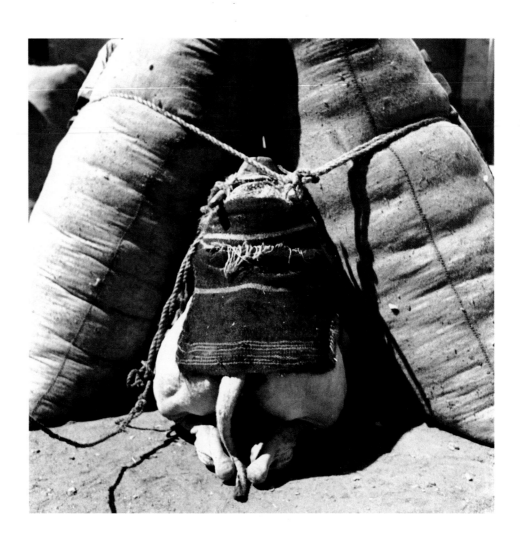

Rear view of camel. Egypt, c. 1938.
(Lee Miller)

The parting caused Lee little grief. She had been keeping up a passionate correspondence with Roland Penrose ever since the Siwa trip and it was to him she was now running.

Extracts from Lee's diary:

It's pretty typical that I should start my journal nearly a week late and during the minutes allotted to the dissolving of a glycerine suppository in my backside – a nervous-making procedure designed to remove food – also from last week, – so this starts as a general purging.

1st day – arrival:

First saw land at the Needles thru bursts of rain, and felt most uneasy and nervous, – quite unexpectedly Roland loomed up at the bar table, and we looked longingly at each other during the endless fiddling. Went shiny-eyed thru the customs and was very impressed by the world's oldest and biggest Rolls acting as a taxi on the quay. Wonder if Roland really did tell the policeman I was ill. Sandwiches in a pub and a long drive to London – feeling rather dried up from too much brandy all day. – dinner immediately at the Etiole with Man Ray – talked mostly to Mesens, who is very stimulating. – All went back to Hampstead – where Man was also spending the night. – Love – sleep and breakfast led to the Picasso show at the London Gallery, lunch and Man's airplane departure from the Dorchester where the W.C. woman is simply like a duchess – as compared to the French ones who seem to be ex-bordel keepers or whores – always fat, jolly and chummy. Was very damned cold and damp but saw Roland's show at

Freddy Mayor's – renewed acquaintance with Freddy and various reminiscences. –

Extracts from a copy of a letter to Bernard Burrows, dated 21 June:

Darling: – It's practically only dawn and I'm already back from a lion hunt. After two hectic days seeing old friends in London – dinner with Man Ray who had stayed over a day for me – 4 painting shows the following morning – then dashed down to Cornwall thru moist lusciousness and sailed, played snooker and talked, talked, talked.

We dashed off by car to Malpas and went out chug chugging in a small boat – thru very low mud flats – and lunched stuck on a bank surrounded by birds and swans looking like prehistoric monsters. On up the estuary which was mostly pushing, ploughing and waiting until the tide raised us off the bottom. I managed to sleep, drink, piss and amuse myself at everybody's efforts but mine. Such a parallel to desert travel and me doing all the work and worry. How nervous and high strung I've always been about organising those trips – and wonder if my guests were always as happy-go-lucky as I was yesterday.

On the way down we passed Stonehenge and realised we'd be returning on the longest day – you know, Druids, sun rays on the altar and devil worship. So we spent the night at Amesbury in a pub so close to the main road that the devil worshippers from London whistling past on high-powered broomsticks sounded more and more excitingly sinister. Up in the pale blue pre-dawn – slightly dripping – to find several thousand people waiting – sheepishly wrapped in feather quilts, motoring goggles – jodhpurs – mink, and me in my Holy Land coat comfortably gloating at the lot. There were a great many people who looked like professional devil worshippers – some in the pay of the little men – witches who had hacked there, and one wonderful descendant of Merlin in leather kit, long gray hair, and slightly stubbly beard (a female!). There was no sunrise. Forlorn and frustrated folklorists sought the shelter of their cars with shawls dragging in the mud, and twenty young hearties formed in circles etc to the harmonica music – breaking into Old English folkdancing as if it were quite natural to be flinging around in what was almost sleet.

As for me, I had breakfast, eventually, in a dainty café called Dolly Vernon with all the lorry drivers who had quit London early for traffic considerations – a tiny cottage surrounded by England's biggest lorries and patronised by the toughest men. From their swathed shapes some of the trucks were carrying unicorns – and shooting galleries – and there was one with a trailer which was most certainly carrying the upper and visible loops of the Loch Ness monster – in pieces – ready to be set up on the south coast.

They've placed black silk umbrellas over each rose tree in my neighbour's garden and I find that so inspiring that I shall contribute to the community one live bright green cat – thirty hand painted snails and a pair of chinese doves with whistles in their tails. I've already dropped balls of chewing gum on the Rev. Neighbour's Angora eunuch but will perpetrate all my other un-British humane deeds on the same day so that the S.P.C.A. [sic] can only have me up once.

I'm not very convinced about Federal Union [Bernard had written enthusiastically about this movement which was based on the proposal of a Federal Union of Atlantic countries to counter dictatorships and prevent war. It was attracting a following in the United States and Great Britain] as altho' these nice idealistic societies have to try and try again – and you seem to have urges of noble responsibility for what your friends' grandchildren are going to enjoy – this particular one is getting off to a very unexalted start – fled into by threat of war and fright of a couple of gangsters [Hitler and Mussolini]. . . . I don't think it's good enough for you to be professional champion of lost causes – permanent secretary of that curious sect: – 'peace lovers'.

But if you leap – sink or swim it would be a bog of your own choosing instead of your spider's net of diplomacy – a web of counterfeit good intentions and contemptible muddling. I'm being denigrating and depressing – and perhaps attacking too savagely but I feel you're gazing at a landscape from Juliet's balcony, and your Juliet is a faithless hussy who doesn't like holding hands or looking at vistas anyway.

You see darling, I don't want to do anything 'all for love' as I can't be depended on for anything. In fact I have every intention of being completely irresponsible.

Tell me more about the whys and wheres and whats of the job – and if I see the light I'll become the opposition – or the telephone operator or shall I just be a tired politician's despair?

Your Lee

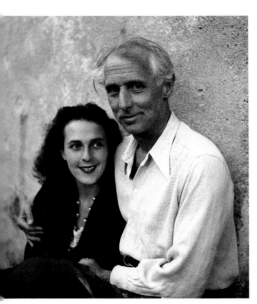

Leonora Carrington and Max Ernst at Saint-Martin-d'Ardèche. Summer 1939. (Lee Miller)

Lee and Roland's travels to the remote parts of Greece and Romania had been partly motivated by the desire to see and record a way of life before it was destroyed by the inexorable march of the motor car and so-called civilization. Now, similarly prompted by the threat of war, they sought one last contact with their European friends. They crossed the Channel with Roland's Ford V8 and headed south to stay for a few days with Max Ernst and Leonora Carrington in their old farmhouse at Saint-Martin-d'Ardèche. In a futile attempt to fend off the approaching disaster, Max had decorated the walls with concrete sculptures of guardian monsters, but to no avail; a few weeks later he was taken to an internment camp for enemy aliens. Leonora, after enduring terrible miseries, including incarceration in a lunatic asylum, escaped through Spain to Mexico.

Roland and Lee found Picasso and Dora Maar at Antibes and spent a few days enjoying the beaches and cafés. Then the blow fell. Hitler had invaded Poland, a reality that gave pause for thought to even the most committed hedonist. There were many options open to Lee, the most obvious being to go back to the United States, but she decided to return to England with Roland. Using the back roads, they travelled crosscountry through villages where church bells were ringing the tocsin and the roads were blocked by peasants taking their horses to army requisition camps.

At Saint Malo they had to abandon the car to the care of the A.A. and take the passenger ferry to Southampton, then a train, which arrived in London to the wail of air-raid sirens. Barrage balloons floated in the sky above Roland's house in Downshire Hill, Hampstead, and in the mail awaiting them was a strongly worded letter from the US Embassy. It instructed Lee that unless she boarded the next ship to the United States, they would no longer be responsible for her safety. Lee tore up the letter, certain that this next adventure was going to be too good to miss.

Opposite: Lee at *Vogue.* London, 1944. (Dave Scherman)

Chapter Six

'Grim Glory': Wartime London
1939–1944

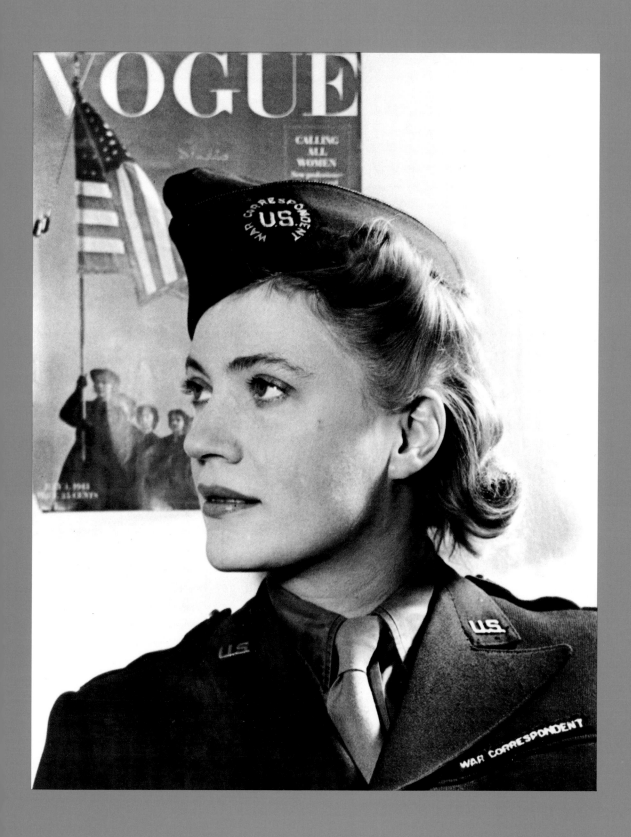

Lee wasted little time in getting round to *Vogue* studios and offering her services as a photographer. To begin with, she was given the cold shoulder. Her professional work had lapsed by five years and the studio headed by *Vogue*'s star-turn, Cecil Beaton, was well enough staffed not to require any additional help. If anything, the rebuff fuelled Lee's persistence, and she turned up day after day without pay, making herself useful in any way she could. Despite the natural resentment from some of the established staffers, she made friends with most people, notably the studio boss, Sylvia Redding. By January 1940, with staff members leaving to serve in the forces, a space had been cleared for her. Harry Yoxall, *Vogue*'s managing editor, applied to the Home Office Aliens Department for her work permit, and at £8 per week she was put on the staff. A few weeks later this somewhat patronizing cable came from New York:

WESTERN UNION
CABLEGRAM

LEE MILLER VOGUE
1 NEWBOND STREET LONDON =
DELIGHTED YOUR WANTING TO JOIN US STOP YOUR INTELLIGENCE FUNDAMENTAL TASTE SENSITIVENESS ART VALUES MUST ULTIMATELY MAKE YOU GOOD PHOTOGRAPHER STOP SENDING CRITICISMS YOUR TRIAL PHOTOGRAPHS =

NAST.

The first year's assignments were very plain fare. There was the occasional celebrity portrait, or pictures of Mrs Rex Harrison and Mrs Michael Redgrave, chosen for their exemplary style of dressing, but more often it was some tedious series of shots of handbags and accessories called 'Choice Of The Month', tied in with an advertising promotion. Fashion was restricted to less glamorous features such as maternity wear and children's clothes. It was uninspired but honest toil, made easier to bear by Roland Haupt, an Anglo-Indian who was frequently the butt of Beaton's contempt. He had joined *Vogue* as a darkroom technician – a 'hypo-bender' – and became known as a talented photographic printer, an art that Lee particularly appreciated. He escaped call-up because he suffered from a form of leukemia. Lee enjoyed fostering his talent and used to pass him the dull study assignments that she herself did not want. By the time she went to Europe, Haupt was shooting fashion and he eventually became a photographer in his own right, winning some assignments from *Picture Post*.

Back issues of wartime British *Vogue* (generally known as *Brogue*) have a strange incongruity with the violence of the period. Scant reference is made to the war at all. The well-bred and elegantly dressed ladies on the pages are aloof from the terrors of the blitz. Even the wrecking of the *Vogue* offices in October 1940 did not rate a mention, perhaps because the staff, with typical British *sang froid*, never allowed production to be halted. The bombing that obliterated the *Vogue* pattern house could not be similarly ignored and Lee was sent round to photograph the ruins.

Because of rationing, publishing companies were allotted a quota of paper based on a percentage of their 1938 usage. This was adjusted according to the amount of paper available and at one point was as low as 18 percent. As a result, articles were savagely edited and there was a limited production run of each issue. *Vogue* was sold by subscription and since every copy was bespoke, it did not find its way on to a news-stand for the next eight years. In fact, the circulation department had a waiting list of hopefuls whose only chance lay in a subscriber's death.

Life at Downshire Hill suited Lee well. The house was comfortable and kept in order by the elderly Scottish housekeeper Annie Clements, who was amazingly tolerant of the constant ebb and flow of people. Lee had always been fascinated by history, and particularly by books about medieval sieges. In the early days of the war, when it came to preparing for the inevitable shortages, she knew just what to do. Shunning the queues for sugar and flour, she headed straight for Fortnum and Mason's spice counter. No amount of persuasion would convince her that the huge basket that overflowed with exotic herbs and spices was only for display. Summoning the manager, she implored him to sell it to her, complete. 'In all the great sieges, the defenders eat rats, and if I have to eat rats, they are going to be well spiced!' she explained. Everything at Downshire Hill was well spiced for ever after. Annie Clements' traditional poached haddock was never the same again.

Roland Penrose, in addition to his duties as a lecturer on camouflage, was also doing his stint as an air-raid warden. One evening, early in the blitz, Lee joined him on his rounds. It was a beautiful moonlit night and the docks were taking a fearful pounding. From Hampstead the criss-crossing searchlights, bursting flak and the glow from the fires presented an astonishing panorama, made more awesome by the skull-splitting din of guns and aircraft. During a particularly ferocious moment as spent ammunition clattered around them, Lee grabbed Roland's arm and spun him round to face her. Eyes blazing with ecstasy, she gasped, 'Oh darling, aren't you excited?'

Roland was less thrilled. In the front garden of the house he dug a small air-raid shelter, decorating the interior in pink and blue. From the outside, presumably for camouflage, it was made to resemble a small tumulus, and was entered via a hatch and down narrow wooden steps. Its efficacy as a refuge was questionable but it gave a certain peace of mind. During air raids, Lee, Roland, and whoever happened to be staying, crammed into the shelter. Since sleep was impossible, endless card games were alternated with Scrabble and Lee's universal panacea – crossword puzzles. During one particularly severe bombardment Lee's cat Taxi (so named because it never came when called in the blackout) hurtled in through the partly open hatch door. The poor creature landed on the card table rigid with fright, its back arched, its tail like a bottle brush. Immediately behind it on the top step, perfectly illuminated by the explosive flashes, was its pursuer, a tiny mouse.

One of the first visitors to Downshire Hill was Roland Penrose's estranged wife Valentine, a Surrealist poet and author. She had tried to

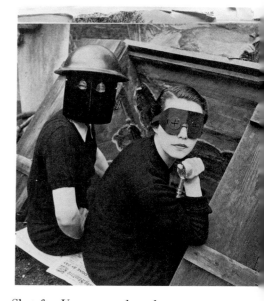

Shot for *Vogue*, posed at the entrance to the air-raid shelter at 21 Downshire Hill, showing mask and eye-shield worn as protection from incendiary bombs. The woman at the right holds an air-raid warden's whistle. 1940. By courtesy of Condé Nast Publications. (Lee Miller)

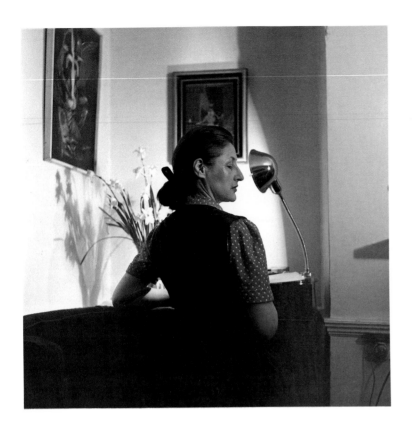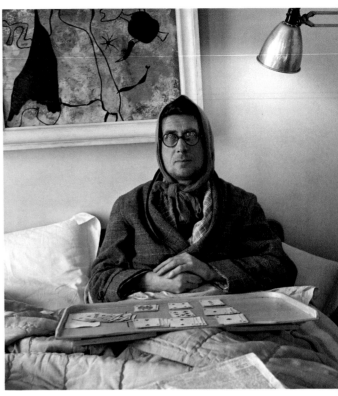

Left: Roland Penrose's first wife, Valentine, at 21 Downshire Hill, Hampstead. 1940. (Lee Miller)

Right: Roland Penrose suffering from mumps. Hampstead, 1941. (Lee Miller)

return from the Himalayas to her parents in Gascony, but the war intervened, stranding her in London. Roland had made no secret of his relationship with Lee so she was apprehensive about meeting her. A rendezvous was arranged at a pub near the house called The Freemason's Arms. As Roland's arrival was delayed, Lee went along and recognizing Valentine from her portrait managed to start a conversation with her. When Roland arrived,

Valentine leapt to her feet, saying how glad she was that I had turned up at last as she had heard that Lee Miller, who of course she did not want to meet, might be arriving at any minute. 'But,' I exclaimed, 'that's Lee you were talking to', in answer to which came Valentine's spontaneous exclamation: 'Oh! but she's wonderful!' This auspicious accident, which could never have happened with such candour had it been planned, was the beginning of a close and lasting friendship which astonished me and brought great pleasure.[1]

In truth, this friendship was nowhere near as close as Roland so fondly imagined it to be. Because he loved both these women so passionately, it never occurred to him that they should not love each other. The relationship between Lee and Valentine was more of an armed truce than a friendship. Lee was unfailingly generous towards Valentine, who maintained an air of distant politeness in return.

When Valentine's hotel was bombed Lee insisted that she should move into the spare room at the top of the house in Downshire Hill. There she remained through the worst of the bombing, imperturbably writing her Surrealist poetry. It was more than a year before she left to become a *soldat de troisième classe* in the Free French Army and to serve in Algiers.

One night Lee and another guest, the journalist Kathleen McColgan, were alone in the house. They had gone to bed happily drunk and were awakened by a scraping noise on the roof. Lee flung back the blackout curtain to see what was going on. Attempting to look out into the inky blackness, she suddenly found the darkness was palpable as a soft, billowing mass flooded into the room. Surrealist dreams became reality in the form of a barrage balloon that had come down and neatly straddled the house. Everyone spent the rest of the night helping the balloon operators get the thing under control and down into the garden. At dawn a procession of weary people filed out through the front door clutching the rolled up balloon like a giant snake. The bizarre sight made no impression on the neighbours. By now wild parties and strange goings on at No 21 had made such events seem commonplace.

Roland Penrose came from a strict Quaker background where extremely formal manners were an essential social grace, but he was delighted with the way Lee dramatically altered his household. Most evenings, regardless of the blitz and the neighbours' complaints, groups of friends gathered from an enormous cross-section of society, added to as the war continued by more of Lee's fellow-countrymen, like the photographer Dave Scherman.

I was assigned immediately to join the beleaguered *Life* London bureau and soon met the already legendary Lee Miller. Twenty-five years old and a brash and

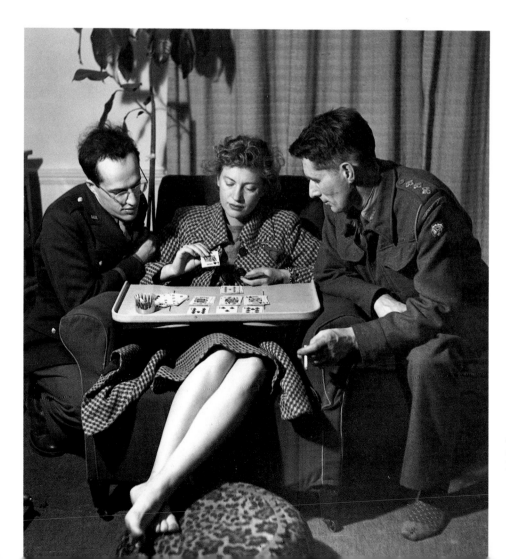

Left to right: Dave Scherman, Lee, and Roland Penrose. Hampstead, 1942. (Dave Scherman)

101

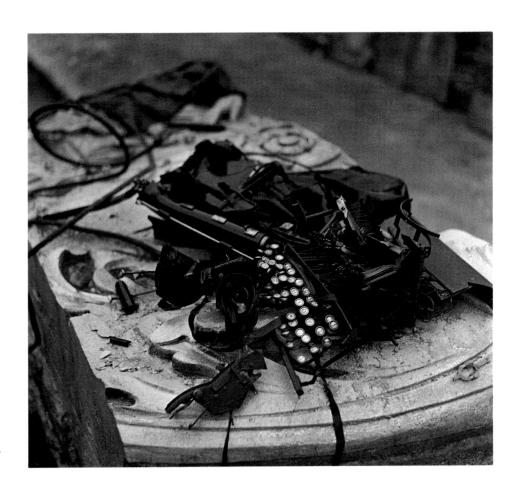

'Remington Silent'. From *Grim Glory*, 1940. (Lee Miller)

bumptious squirt, I had the eternal good fortune to be invited by Roland to visit his house in Hampstead. Its walls were completely covered with what I thought were absolutely first-rate copies of the works of Picasso, Braque, Miró, Tanguy, de Chirico, Brancusi, Giacometti, Tunnard, Max Ernst, René Magritte and a dozen by Roland himself. Only they were not copies, Lee explained to me patiently. They were originals, and what's more they were merely the ones Roland wanted to keep near him – the main body of his collection was hidden away safely out of the blitz in Devon.

The house was mind-boggling and so were Roland and Lee's regular soirées, the guest-lists of which read like a *Who's Who* of modern art, journalism, British politics, music and even espionage, though we did not know about the latter until years later. Communists, Liberals and Tories drank and jostled one another in an amicable *mélange* that will never be seen again.[2]

As a counterpoint to her succession of dull assignments, Lee started collaborating with two fellow Americans on a book. *Grim Glory: pictures of Britain under fire* was aimed at the US general public with the intention of demonstrating the sufferings of the blitz. The editor was Ernestine Carter and the preface was written by the American broadcaster Ed Murrow:

These are pictures of a nation at war. They are honest pictures – routine scenes to those of us who have reported Britain's ordeal by fire and high explosive. These Englishmen have bought survival with their tender-roofed old buildings; with their bodies and their nerves. This little book offers you a glimpse of their battle. Somehow they are able to fight down their fears each night; to go to work each morning.

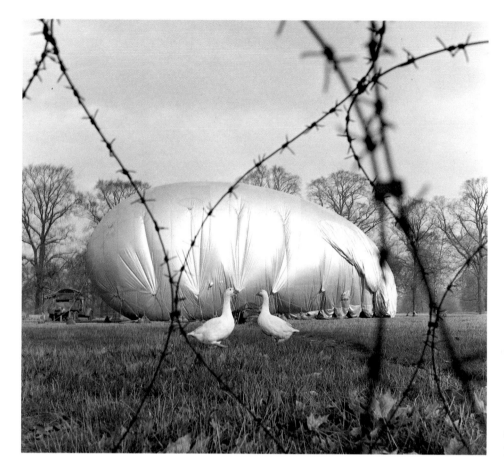

'Eggceptional Achievement'. London, 1940. (Lee Miller)

The pictures are selected with great discrimination. I would have shown you the open graves of Coventry – broken bodies covered with brown dust looking like rag dolls cast away by some petulant child, being lifted in tender hands from the basements of homes. This book spares you the more gruesome sights of living and dying in Britain to-day.[3]

The publisher's note states, 'Miss Lee Miller's photographs were all especially taken for this book,' but in fact it was the pictures that came first and inspired the book. This was one of Lee's most creative periods. Not since the early thirties in Paris and New York had she taken photographs with this degree of perception. Her eye was Surrealist and poetic, seeing in each image a statement that could be interpreted at many levels. Superficially the picture titled 'Remington Silent' may be of a bashed-up typewriter; subliminally the shattered machine taps out an eloquent essay about the war's assault on culture. The simplest shots are often the most eloquent; they are the photographs carrying a truth that cannot be articulated in any other way. In these images anger burns deep. But there is also wit, as Lee shouts at the devil, in her photographs of the congregation of bricks tumbling out of the door of the wrecked Nonconformist Chapel; the mannequins, naked but for their top hats, trying to hail a taxi in an empty street; and the two ineffably proud geese posing in front of a colossal silver egg, an adopted barrage balloon. If *Grim Glory* had not been published, it is hard to imagine how some of these photographs would have found their way into the public eye, as their idiom was far in advance of the current style. The book was widely acclaimed and a hardcover version published simultaneously in New York by Scribners. The press on both sides of the Atlantic gave rapturous reviews. One photograph in particular, 'Revenge on Culture', the fallen beauty whose throat is cut by a bar of iron and whose breast is bruised by a brick, caught the attention of the press throughout the world. It was reproduced countless times, even on the front page of an Arabic newspaper.

Lee was often dissatisfied with the text presented with her pictures. She felt that the cloying pap produced by some of the copywriters reduced the impact of the photographs and compromised her ideals of honesty and accessibility. Worst of all, it lacked intimacy, failed to flow, and made laborious reading. Lee had always devoured books. She had the facility, which used to make her friends furious, of skimming through a book or an article as though she had hardly noticed it, and then discussing it with unshakable conviction. She filed away in her memory facts, figures and opinions which could be instantly recalled and fired with deadly accuracy into the heart of a raging argument. Among her favourite writers were Steinbeck, Hemingway and James Joyce, but she read anything and everything from 'Penny Dreadfuls' upwards. What she looked for was the ability to communicate clearly but with flair and imagination.

'Nonconformist Chapel', Camden Town. From *Grim Glory*, 1940. (Lee Miller)

Opposite: 'Bridge of Sighs', Lowndes Street, Knightsbridge. From *Grim Glory*, 1940. (Lee Miller)

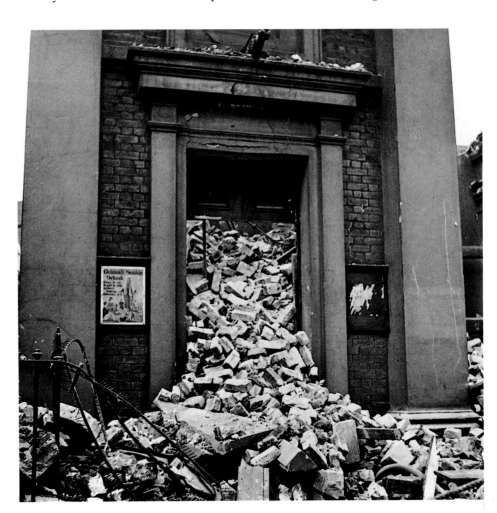

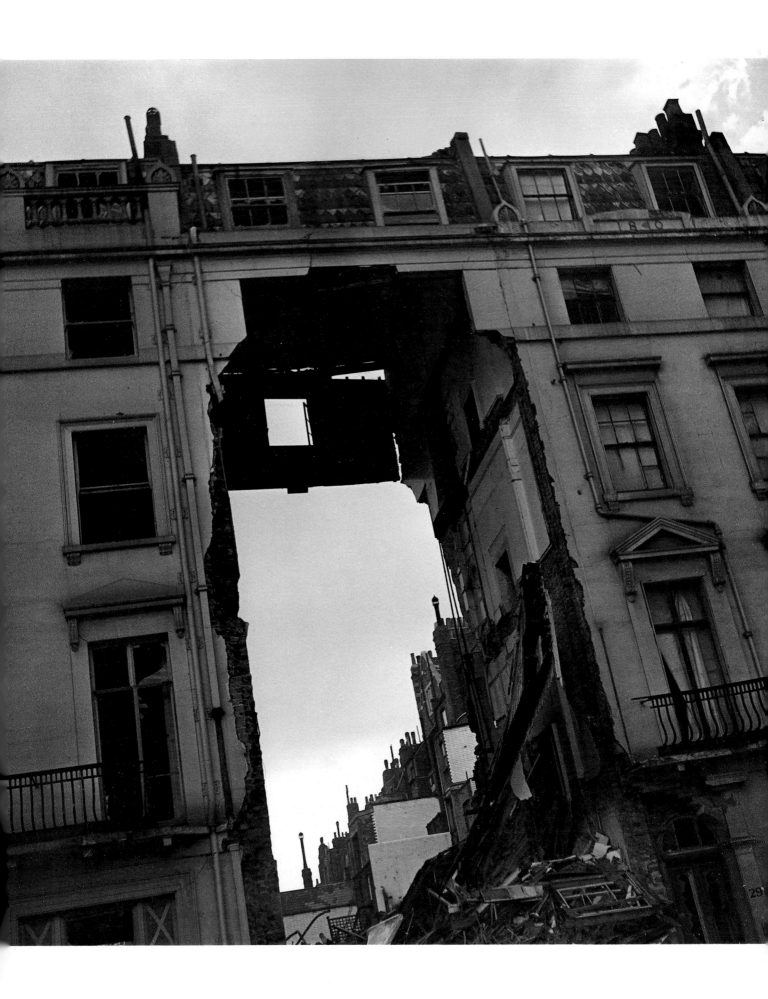

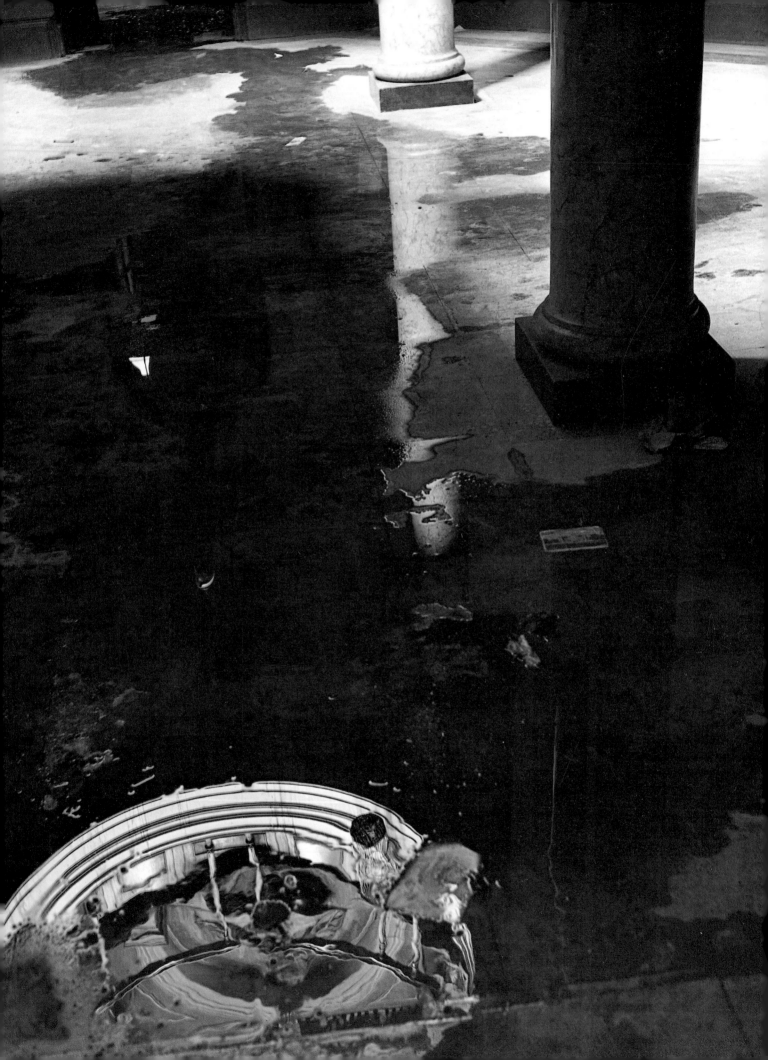

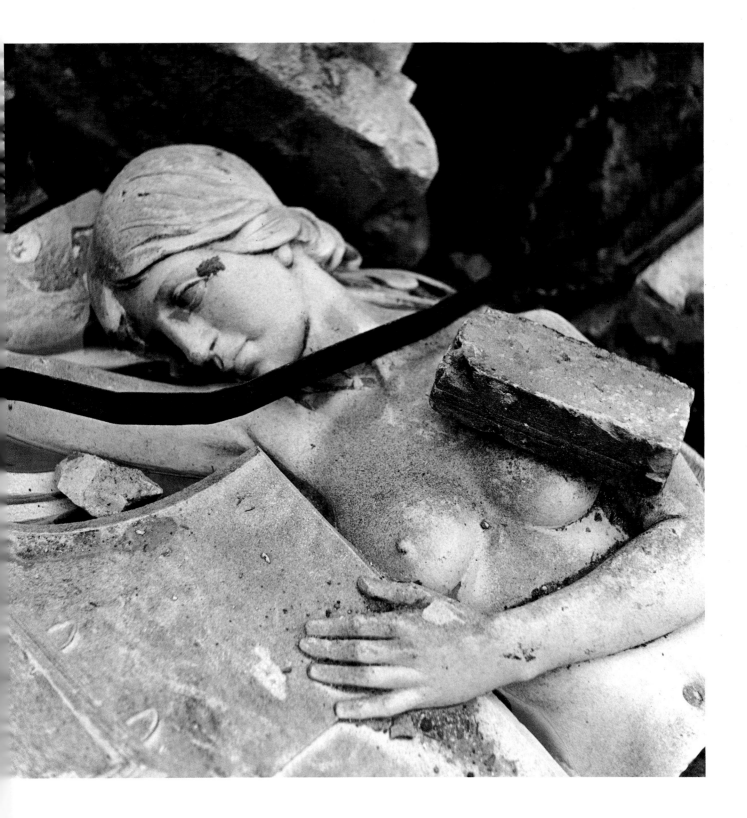

'Revenge on Culture'. From *Grim Glory*, 1940. (Lee Miller)

Opposite: The shattered roof of University College, London, reflected in a pool of rainwater. From *Grim Glory*, 1940. (Lee Miller)

Lee's letters always had a direct narrative style, from which her first articles stemmed. This is from a letter to her parents:

We've been having the most extraordinary lull in the blitz since before Xmas – it's given us all a chance to catch up on being human a bit – instead of just hanging on to the edge of the precipice – with nerves and tiredness – frustration and worry. At the time, I might have written you an adequate description of it all – each time some superstition or feeling of futility stopped me, as if by the time you received it things would have caught up with me too, or it wouldn't be true any more or something – and the few letters or bits of writing I did attempt at the time were hopelessly false – and just the reflection of a very temporary mood of fright, bravado, indifference, anger or as often as not just plain drunk and sentimental.

After the first few days of Sept. – feeling like a soft-shelled crab – before we had any barrage working, there was the exaltation of winning the big daytime air battles – it wasn't quite as pep-making as it might have been as we were all into the strain of what became three months of solid hell at night – and harrowing by day to get to work by some crazy route – to count noses to see if everyone had really lived thru it – it became a matter of pride that work went on – the studio never missed a day – bombed once and fired twice – working with the neighbouring building still smouldering – the horrid smell of wet charred wood – the stink of cordite – the fire hoses still up the staircases and we had to wade barefoot to get in – little restaurants producing food on a primus stove – carrying

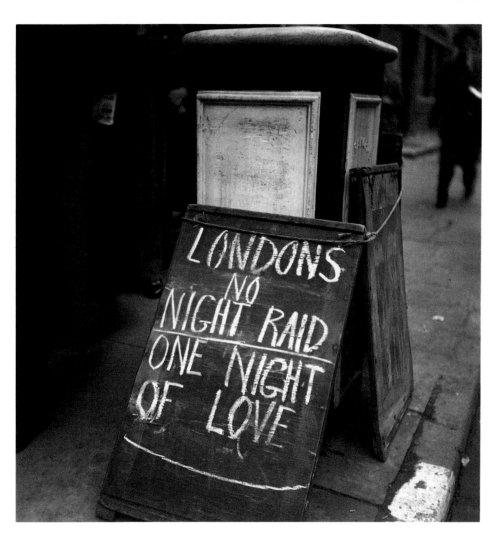

'One Night of Love'. From *Grim Glory*, 1940. (Lee Miller)

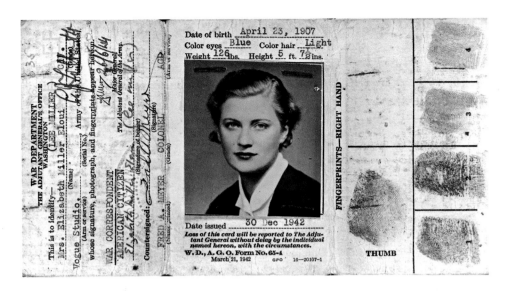

Lee's identity card.

water to flush toilets and whoever could taking the prints and negs home to do at night if they happened to have the sacred combination of gas, electricity and water, in fact we slept on the floor of the kitchen corridor and sometimes had ten or more friends, either bombed out of their own flats – or isolated by the presence of a time bomb – or just thinking that Hampstead [was safer].

Then much later she recalled in a letter to Erik and Mafy:

I'll never forget wonderful Edna Chase [Editor of American *Vogue*], the doyeness – the goddess – the former of taste, discretion and elegance – sending a memo to us in the bombing, that she noticed we weren't wearing hats and she didn't approve that we dyed our legs and made lines up the backs to simulate stockings – (Britain had no nylons until the US Air Force brought them in as rich presents) – and I happened to be in charge of the office that day though it was none of my affair to answer the boss, I sent a cable in my own name: WE HAVE NO RATION COUPONS AND NO NYLON STOCKINGS ANYWAY. The next week every member of the staff was sent three pairs.

The winter of 1941–42 brought an influx of Americans:

Lee saw her insufferable compatriots rolling in cigarettes, canned goods, Scotch, Kleenex and goodies that the harassed British had not seen for years. Her new-found American journalist friends had signed on as war correspondents with the US Army, Navy and Air Force. They bought new uniforms in Savile Row and shopped at the American Army post-exchanges (PXs) that put to shame the yet-to-be-invented supermarket. They were also preparing, not so secretly, for what was obviously to be a re-invasion of the European mainland. The two phenomena, no-Kleenex-in-the-midst-of-plenty and the threat of being left out of the biggest story of the decade, almost drove poor Lee Miller mad until one of us suggested that she too, a perfectly bona fide Yank from Poughkeepsie, apply for accreditation to the US forces as a war correspondent. She was an expatriate of twenty years and the thought had never occurred to her.[4]

Despite the weight of prejudice against allowing women to do tasks that might encroach on the male domain, Lee was a successful applicant. The routine studio work still had to be done, but now, as well as Kleenex and Camels, Lee had the scope and incentive to find her own stories. The AGO

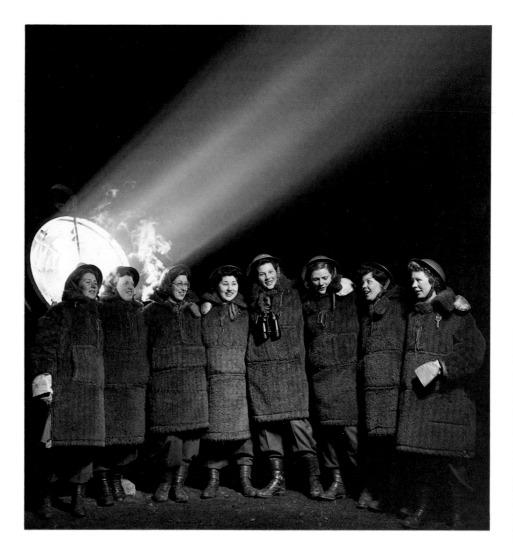

Opposite: Henry Moore, sketching in Holborn underground station in London during the Blitz. He was being filmed for *Out of Chaos*, by Jill Craigie, which showed war artists at work. 1940. (Lee Miller)

ATS searchlight operators in north London, 1943. Their faces are lit by a mirror held by Dave Scherman. Minutes later, the battery was called to action and came under fire from the air. (Lee Miller)

ATS searchlight operators on the target, 1943. (Lee Miller)

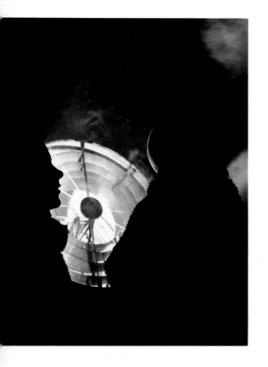

card was a magic key that gave her access to the forbidden areas where the excitement was. Her first story as a photo-journalist was about US army nurses, an appreciative account that took the trouble to consider the nurses' feelings about their role. Later, teaming up with Dave Scherman, she found that they could help each other with their assignments. He travelled with her to Scotland and helped with the photographs of WRENS in training and at work for 'Seaworthy and Semi Seagoing', published as a four-page spread in *Vogue* with text by Lesley Blanch. The photographs were later published by Hollis and Carter as a successful book called *Wrens In Camera*.

The next story that Lee and Dave covered together was a feature about ATS (Auxiliary Territorial Service) women operating a searchlight battery in north London. Using a mirror, Lee and Dave were diverting a small part of the searchlight beam to spotlight the women when suddenly the alert sounded and they all got more excitement than they bargained for. The battery was called to action and enemy fire from the air gunners whipped across the emplacement. The article appeared in both British and American *Vogue* as an impressive double-page spread, the beam of the

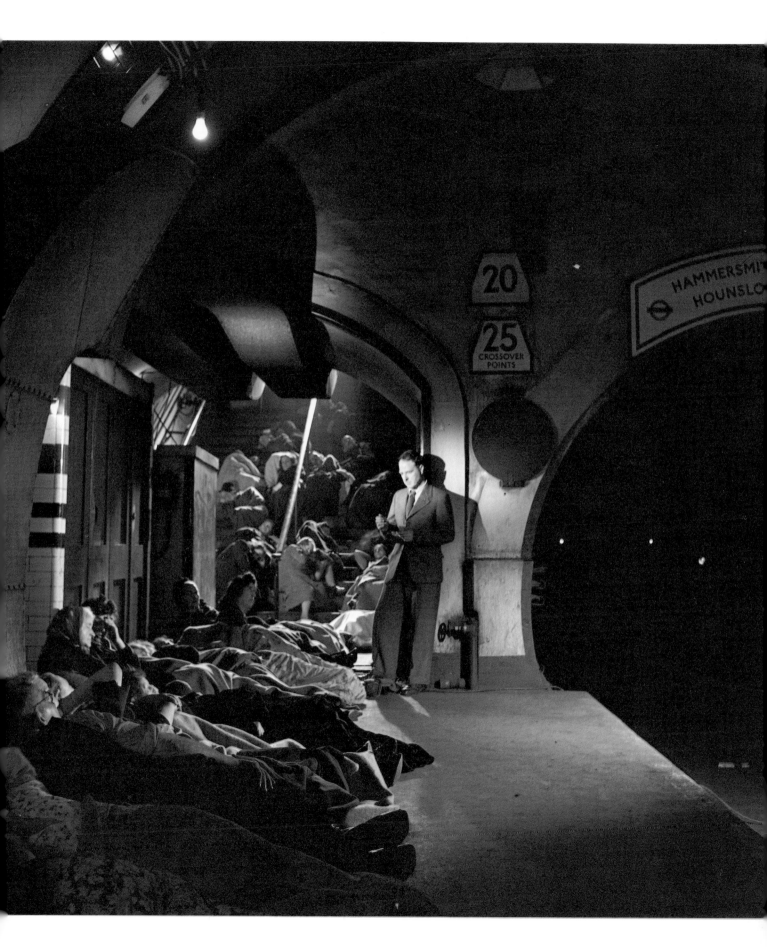

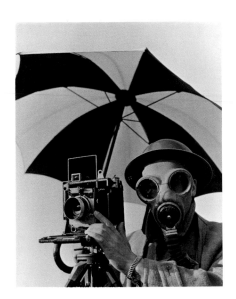

Life photographer Dave Scherman, suitably equipped for the war in Britain. 1942. (Lee Miller)

searchlight slashing diagonally across the black background which was dotted with vignetted night scenes from the battery. Lee liked the layout, by Alex Kroll, but took issue with Audrey Withers, the editor of British *Vogue*:

Saw the 'Night Life' spread in N.Y. *Vogue* and think I might have had more than the usual hidden signature – after all it was me who (a) thought it up (b) stayed up all nite for a month doing it (c) didn't kick when my London credit was so small (d) would appreciate the N.Y. office knowing that their little War Correspondent *did* a war story – on acc't of what they might even like to assign a few similar jobs.

Lee and Dave were also annoyed by *Vogue*'s treatment of a lengthy and difficult story they had covered, featuring Henry Moore at work as a war artist in the London Underground air-raid shelters and at his studio in Much Hadham in Hertfordshire. It was on the occasion of the making of a film by Two Cities production company called *Out of Chaos*. Directed by Jill Craigie, the film covered the work of war artists and included Stanley Spencer, Graham Sutherland and Paul Nash, who were also photographed by Lee. The pictures got too little space too late and were coupled with an ineffectual text. In the same note to Audrey Withers Lee stormed on: '. . . is it worth spending five working days, to say nothing of travel, discomfort and material, the risk of having gangsters do my jobs in London in my absence – and my pictures sent to the engravers without my initials to have Mme X [Lesley Blanch] report on a film? I'm all for group journalism if it is group journalism – but not when I pay for it, *me*.'

Lee's worries about 'gangsters' doing her jobs while she was away probably had no basis in reality. The assignments were in fact carefully regulated by Audrey Withers and there were only just enough photographers to cover all the work. The leading photographer was Norman Parkinson who posed no threat as his attention was divided between his work and his small farm in the Cotswolds.

It was a different matter with Cecil Beaton. Lee loathed him and found his conceit, his technical incompetence and the flaunting of his antisemitic feelings repugnant. In a fury one evening, fuelled by copious quantities of whisky, she made a wax model of him and thrust pins into it. The next day news came that a Dakota with Beaton on board had crashed on take-off from Land's End. The report stated that there were no survivors. Lee, stricken with remorse, sobbed that she had only wanted to wound him a bit, not kill him outright. When he turned up a few weeks later completely unscathed, she was almost glad to see him.

Other colleagues at *Vogue*, Audrey Withers included, became friends for life. In particular Lee had a special affection for Timmie O'Brien, the Managing Editor. They first met when *Life*'s Eliot Elisofon and US Sgt. Jimmy Dugan bamboozled Timmie into letting them use her flat to hold a party, since they had been chucked out of the Savoy. The occasion was to celebrate the liberation of a vast *Leberwurst* that Elisofon had stolen while on an assignment to Finland. Lee and Roland were among the many guests who packed into the tiny mews flat for what turned out to be a blockbuster of a party. Most people got drunk and Lee made a better than average job of it, to the point where she disappeared. On discovering her being sick in the tiny downstairs toilet, Timmie immediately gave her a drink. 'I like you,' said Lee with carefully considered approval as she made herself comfortable on the floor. 'Most people would have offered me coffee, but you're different!' Next morning the *Leberwurst* did more damage than the hangovers. Slightly the worse for its travels, it gave everybody who ate it a short but violent dose of diarrhoea.

The bold, realistic images in the pages of *Life* magazine were providing photographers with a strong stimulus to break away from the posed studio style shot. The means of escape from the heavy studio camera had arrived in the form of the Rolleiflex and the so-called miniature camera, the 35mm Leica. Faster lenses and higher film speeds made action shots easier and the shortage of studio space was the final nudge. Fashion photography took to the streets, Lee and Toni Frissell setting the pace.

Backgrounds both mundane and profane appear suddenly in the pages of *Vogue* in Spring 1941 as legitimate settings for clothes. In the context of today's fashion photography, where virtually all combinations of images are commonplace and few frontiers remain, it is easy to overlook the impact of this quantum leap from studio to location. By now Lee knew her way around London well enough to pick good places for her shots. With equal skill she used railway stations, the Albert Hall, elegant streets, friends' gardens, and on many occasions both the outside and inside of 21 Downshire Hill, where paintings from Roland's collection add an unexpected touch. The photographs are an excellent compromise, realistic and informal, but at the same time a perfect foil for the fashions, and full of the excitement of a new trend.

In the United States the circumstances forcing this change of style were less pressing, but Condé Nast, despite his life-long championing of studio photography, did not fail to recognize a useful trend. One of the last letters he ever wrote was to Lee, after she had sent him some recent samples of her work. It was dated 17 August 1942, a month before he died, and reads, 'The photographs are much more alive now, the backgrounds more interesting, the lighting more dramatic and real. You managed to handle some of the deadliest studio situations in the manner of a spontaneous outdoor snapshot.'[5]

By 1944 Lee was getting a major share of the photographic work and each month *Vogue* carried five or six features illustrated with her photographs. They were mostly refined fashion shots and fashion-oriented portraits of Margot Fonteyn, music-hall star Sid Field, James Mason, Robert Newton, Bob Hope and Adolphe Menjou, actress Françoise Rosay or old friends like Humphrey Jennings, shown filming *Lili Marlene* at the London docks. But Lee was still far from satisfied. The artificiality of contributing photographs of beautiful clothes to a magazine for the soigné elite gnawed away at her. Fashion seemed utterly trivial at a time when she suspected that many of her friends in Paris were risking their lives every day in support of the resistance.

The bombs had stopped raining down on Britain, and though it was evident there was to be an invasion of Europe, no one could guess with certainty when or how it would happen. In place of the adrenalin and the clarity of purpose that the blitz provided, the run-up to the invasion seemed like a vacuum. To fill this void Lee found another challenge: the adding of her own words to her pictures. The subject of her first picture/ story was her old friend Ed Murrow. She visited him at home one morning to photograph him at his desk and, insisting on authentic action as a foil to the pose, asked him to type something. This is what he wrote:

This is Lee Miller . . who is taking pictures . . the whole thing is a fake and it should be that I am working in my office instead of playing about with such things . . But at least this provides us with the opportunity to have a drink in the morning . . a good old southern custom . . or maybe it's Irish . . for up there they wake you up with half a water glass of Irish whiskey . . . Janet [Murrow] might press her black suit . . . thinks she might wear it for lunch . . . I wish I didn't have to go to that picture tonight . . Lee has a boyfriend . . they have been celebrating . . . Lee says there is a difference between theory and practice . . . When Lee comes to take pictures she also straightens out the wiring . . . must ask her if she brought her pliers . . Now Lee and Janet are gossiping . . soon they will be deciding who it is that they like least . . . Lee doesn't like butter and egg men . . she would like to see them all powdered . . . . . I can still see Lee but can Lee see mee . . whoopeee . . and the bards they all sing of an English king who lived long years ago . . . . . . Golf balls on the table . . whiskey in the stomach, who could ask for anything more . . . I didn't know Lee was a cook . . .

Having badgered Audrey Withers into assigning her the text, Lee found writing to be a far more agonizing and solitary process than she had supposed. The following passage, full of false starts, distractions and blind alleys, comes from the second draft of her original manuscript.

Very few people here have heard of Ed Murrow. We have heard of him – we know him, like him, respect him. He is a star in our journalist constellation. He is constantly quoted, and referred to by people who know people with short wave sets – or cable quoted back from New York to the press here as an authority – yet he lives in London.

Somehow he seems to put things together differently than other people – and I don't mean he draws startling or genial conclusions – but just that his facts are not axe-grindings and he's never tried to fool anyone and therefore they are emphasised and stabilised in their proper proportions.

He seems to be entirely unworried about being biased or prejudiced – hates to contemplate the idea of such a person in fact. He is unfrightened of making a corny quote or going for instance to an air base and describing it in his own words conscious of the fact that someone did that yesterday – as since he had never done it or said it before, it became valid by that fact alone and since he only wrote what he saw, or understood, or knew, or experienced, and in his own words, which were not a search for bigger and better phrases, but just a simple explanation of what went on – it became valid as no one else except himself could possibly have been him.

He doesn't raise his voice, or scream, or talk faster – he has none of the tricks of a story-teller or the hesitations and speed gears of the actor – there's no crescendo, diminuendo, largo or pizzicato marked in on his script. There is no more than his honestly writing what he honestly wanted to say – and his speaking it with the honesty which endeared him to all of you.

He suggested that it was a sort of elaborate game, like a treasure hunt to read in to and interpret the speeches of the great. That when he was put in to comment

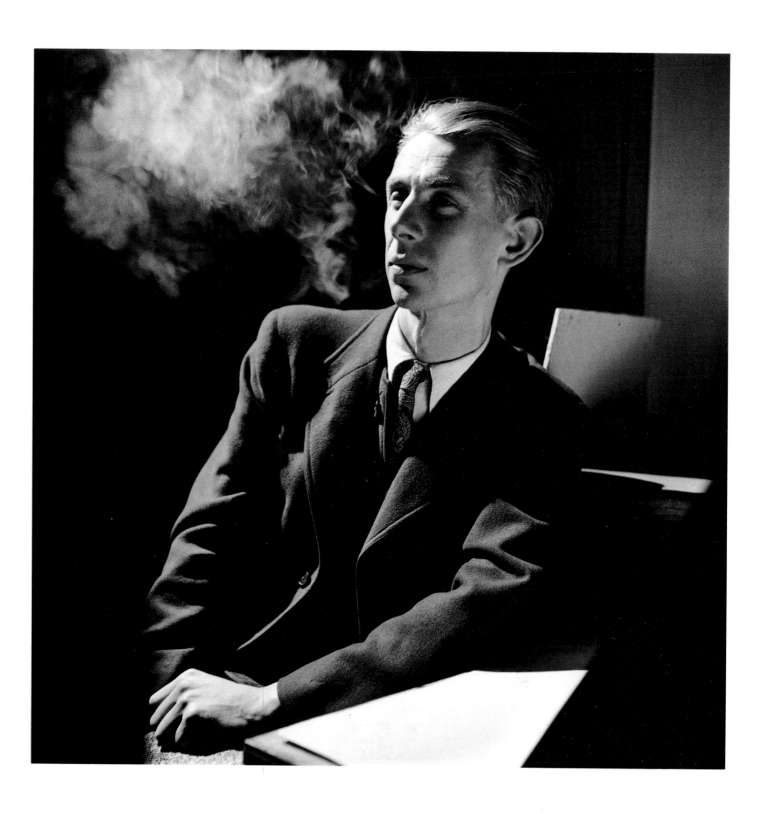

Humphrey Jennings, Surrealist
painter, poet and film-maker, known
for his brilliant conversation – an
attribute easily forgotten as words
disappear like smoke. London, 1941.
(Lee Miller)

on a speech of the Prime Minister's, for instance, it became like an elaborate treasure hunt – not to merely pick one or more phrases which themselves were headlines, but to choose the one that carried the back-ground and the implications all in one. or what the hell did he say? something of this sort, I made up the treasure hunt, just now – maybe he was against it.

Incidentally, I knew just enough about broadcasting to know when to turn it off, and there is a ghost in this god damn building, and I'm irritated as hell about it as I spend five minutes in every ten getting up to see who is walking around back of me – add to list of never agains along with writing, – staying in this office.

The qualities Lee admires in Murrow's reporting are those she is aiming for herself and which she eventually achieved. The final draft was a witty, well-crafted 750 words, the whimsy slashed out and the whole rearranged as a smooth flow of sharply observed fact that runs with the genuine intimacy of a friendly conversation. The self-confidence behind this adroit performance was paper-thin as can be seen from the letter she enclosed with the final draft.

Dear Audrey,
This was all a big mistake – after all, I've spent fifteen or so years of my life learning how to take a picture – you know, the thing that is worth ten thousand words, and here I am cutting my own throat and imitating these people, writers who I've been pretending are *démodé*.

My surprise and grief is not that I find words a technique all alone – I already knew this – but that I should have been naive and idiotic enough to accept such an assignment, and have the temerity to attack it in the face of knowing better has subjected me to many hours of frustration and anguish over written organisation of the facts and ideas I had the luck to have handed to me on a platter by Ed Murrow.

I will hereby append what I have written, and also what other notes I have. I abandon them to your mercy – a disagreeable task for a writer, to put together someone else's interview with someone else . . . but I am afraid that it will not now be possible for anyone else to catch hold of Ed or Janet . . . I've buggered all our sources. As I've already used up all the time and trouble they could decently be asked to spare . . . even if they had large quantities of vanity.

Love Lee

Lee's fascination with technology led her at this time to renew her interest in colour photography. The catalyst was Planskoi, the Russian colour expert and physicist with whom she became friendly when he visited London in the winter of 1943–44. The colour reversal process was in its early stages and Planskoi was one of the leaders in the field. His connections with Kodak gave him access to seemingly unlimited quantities of film stock and chemicals which Lee shamelessly made use of to improve her technique, while also plundering his knowledge.

Most months, the magazine carried a prestigious full-page colour shot which became Lee's regular assignment and the June 1944 issue used one of Lee's colour pictures on its cover. The pose and lighting are entirely conventional; no hint of even a touch of quirkiness. The dictates of the format had suppressed those imaginative zigzag leaps that gave *Grim Glory* its richness. As if to compensate for this hindrance of photographic expression, her ability as a writer was now poised, fully primed and ready to go.

Lee, Normandy 1944. Lee had her helmet cut away and fitted with a visor to facilitate the use of a camera. Roland Penrose painted the eye slits on the visor. (Photographer unknown)

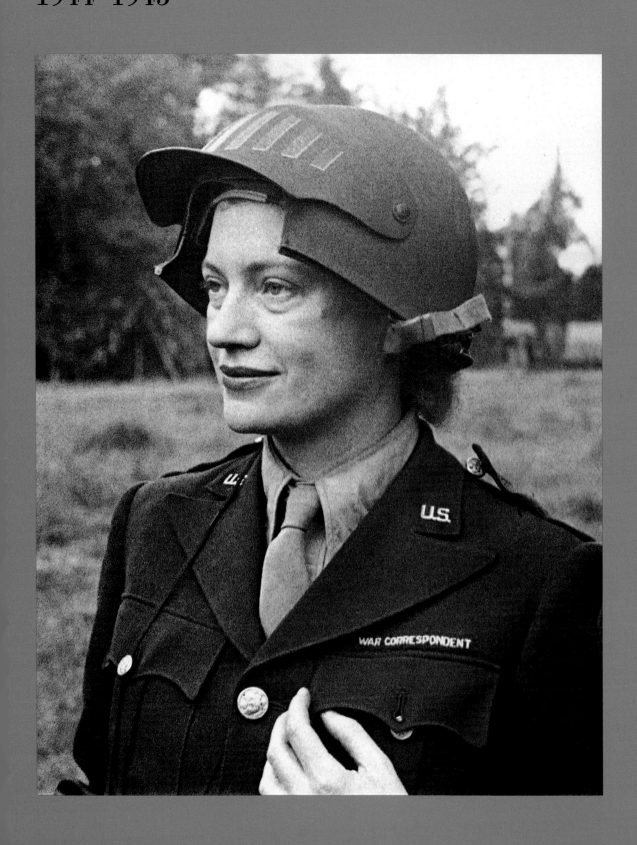

D-Day came and went and six weeks later, at the end of July, Lee was on board a Dakota heading for the US Army field hospitals in Normandy. The assignment was to do a quiet picture story about nurses working in an evacuation hospital where the wounded from the front line were being treated. When Lee returned to England after five days, she had covered two tent hospitals and a front line casualty clearing station. Along with about thirty-five rolls of film she filed nearly ten thousand words of the kind of reporting that established her domination of the major features of *Vogue* for the next year and a half.

I grabbed a pocket full of flash bulbs and film, and clambered into a command car which was going to take us up to a field hospital about 6 miles nearer the front. A field hospital is the nearest completely equipped unit to the fighting lines. The desperately wounded who can't travel the 6 more miles to the evacuation hospital arrive here. Every case is life or death, and ambulances come in with one or two men instead of waiting for a full load. They are transferred from the pre-ops tent, the X-ray tent or laboratories to the surgeon's table with plasma bottles carried above – like a silent, dark convoy ship floating a balloon.

In the bluey dusk, the artillery flashes were like summer heat-lightning, and the rumbling was an accompaniment to the sense of strain and urgency. The tempo was quicker than at the Evac. – the doctors and nurses even more tired, and they knew that during the night they were going to run out of blood. . . .

The wounded were not 'knights in shining armour' but dirty, disheveled stricken figures – uncomprehending. They arrived from the frontline Battalion Aid Station in lightly laid-on field dressings, tourniquets, blood-soaked slings – some exhausted and lifeless.

The doctor with the Raphael-like face turned to a man on a litter which had been placed on upended trunks. Plasma had already been attached to the man's outstretched left arm – his face was shrunken and pallid under the dirt – by the time his pierced left elbow was in its sling, his opaque eyes were clearing and he was aware enough to grimace as his leg splint was bandaged into place.

The *Vogue* editors were astonished. They ran the full story and fourteen pictures in two double-page spreads in the September issue, which also carried four of Lee's civilian assignments, including some beautiful portraits of Margot Fonteyn. Lee's contribution had given both British and American *Vogue* an involvement with the war and was dispelling somewhat the guilt and frustration among the staff that arose from their seemingly frivolous work. Audrey Withers described it as 'the most exciting journalistic experience of my war. We were the last people one could conceive having this type of article, it seemed so incongruous in our pages of glossy fashion.'

Something had unfettered Lee's talent, and all her previous experiences were now channelled into one direction. Her former hypochondria vanished without trace, proving it to have been the product of her dissatisfaction. Gone was the *soigné* appearance and the refined taste in food and wine; now she wore crumpled battle dress and ate K rations or worse. Playing cards, 'chewing the fat', taking pictures, doing crossword puzzles, writing letters, foreign travel, insatiable desire for excitement, social mutability, iron-hard resolution, and natural ebullience coalesced into one huge creative output. For Lee there was only one thought in her mind at this moment: getting back to the action.

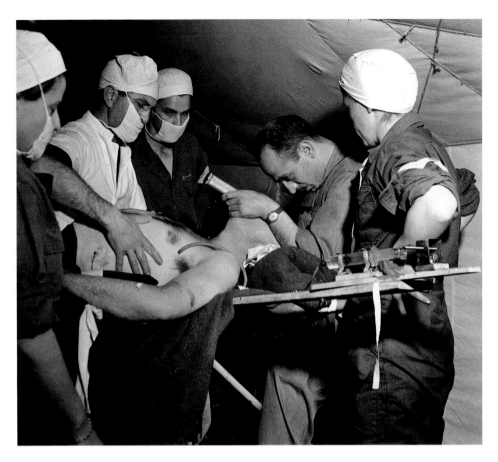

Field hospital in Normandy.
Emergency surgery for a patient with
chest wounds. 1944. (Lee Miller)

After struggling through the August holiday and refugee crowds from
London, Lee boarded US Navy Tank Landing Ship Number 371 for a
night crossing to France. She was on an assignment for the US Army
Public Relations Office to go to Saint Malo and cover the Civil Affairs
team which had moved in after the fighting to speed the return to civilian
life. In mid-Channel the convoy was rerouted from Utah Beach to Omaha
Beach where it ran aground at high tide to unload. The crew lined the rail
to cheer as Lee was carried ashore in the arms of a sailor.

Hitching a ride into the town, she found that, contrary to official
information, the war in Saint Malo was far from over. The German
commander, Colonel von Aulock, was convinced that reinforcements were
arriving which would push the Americans back into the sea. He vowed
that his garrison would defend the citadel Forte de la Cité to the death,
and with the impregnable fortifications dug into solid rock flanked by the
other smaller fortresses of Cezambre, Grand Bey and Saint Servan, it
could only be a bloody struggle for the attackers – the 83rd Division of the
US Army.

Lee was quick to appreciate that she was the only reporter for miles
around and now had her own private war. The Civil Affairs team, who
were overwhelmed coping with refugees, gave Lee a corner of their billet to
store her equipment and from this base she made her sorties to the action.
Sometimes she put aside her cameras to help with the floods of wounded,
hysterical civilians, or prisoners released by the Germans.

At critical moments during the fighting, Lee climbed up to an observation post in the honeymoon suite of a hotel. In the first draft of an article for *Vogue* she describes an air attack:

. . . the boy at the phone said, 'They hear airplanes.' We waited, then we heard them swelling the air like I've heard them vibrating over England on some such mission. This time they were bringing their bombs to the crouching stone work 700 yards away. They were on time – bombs away – a sickly death rattle as they straightened themselves out and plunged into the citadel – deadly hit – for a moment I could see where and how – then it was swallowed up in smoke – belching, mushrooming and columning – towering up, black and white. Our house shuddered and stuff flew in at the window – more bombs crashing, thundering, flashing – like Vesuvius – the smoke rolling away in a sloping trail. A third lot! The town reeled in the blast – a large breach had been made – and we waited for the next attack.

This was one of the first times the new secret weapon, napalm, was used. When Lee's photographs were processed at *Vogue*, the British censor grabbed the rolls showing the napalm strike and eliminated all the shots that might be revealing.

A horrendous and futile infantry assault stormed up the steep exposed rock faces that girdled the fort.

The building we were in and all the others which faced the fort were being spat at now – ping, bang – hitting above our window – into the next – breaking on the balcony below – fast queer noise – impact before the gun noise itself – following the same sound pattern – hundreds of rounds – crossing and recrossing where we were.

Machine gun fire belched from the end pillbox – the men fell flat – stumbling and crawling into the shelter of shell holes – some crept on, others sweeping back to the left of the guns' angle, one man reaching the top. He was enormous. A square-shouldered silhouette, black against the sky between the pillbox and the fort. He raised his arm. The gesture of a cavalry officer with sabre waving the others on. He was waving to death, and he fell with his hand against the fort.

The picturesque town of Saint Malo which had stood securely on its small promontory was turned to rubble by the fire from the citadel guns.

Tall chimneys standing alone gave off smoke from the burning remnants of their buildings at their feet. Stricken lonely cats prowled. A swollen horse had not provided adequate shelter for the dead American behind it – flower pots stood in roomless windows. Flies and wasps made tours in and out of underground vaults which stank with death and sour misery. Gunfire brought more stone blocks down into the street. I sheltered in a kraut dugout, squatting under the ramparts. My heel ground into a dead detached hand and I cursed the Germans for the sordid ugly destruction they had conjured up in this once beautiful town. I wondered where my friends that I had known here before the war were; how many had been forced into disloyalty and degradation – how many had been shot, starved or what. I picked up the hand and hurled it across the street, and ran back the way I'd come bruising my feet and crashing in the unsteady piles of stone and slipping in blood. Christ, it was awful.[1]

After more assaults, bombing and repeated shelling day and night, Colonel von Aulock, no doubt fearing more napalm, surrendered to Major Speedie of the 83rd Division. Lee, who was by this time the Division's

Bombs bursting on the fortress of Saint Malo. 1944. (Lee Miller)

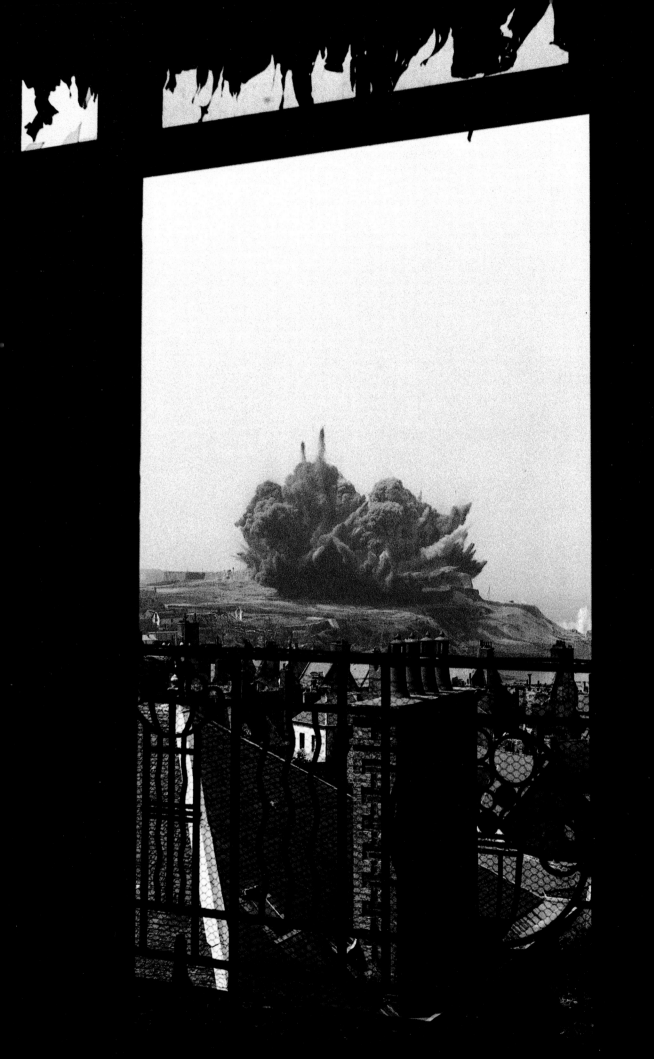

unofficial mascot, was allowed right up front and photographed von Aulock's less than dignified exit. She concluded her story:

Reporters had gathered like vultures for the kill, all the way from Rennes. French people were already trying to move back into their houses. I didn't walk around the pillbox to see the man who had waved – and I put off going to the top and walking down where I had seen the little men crawl up. I never did go. The American flag was waving on the top, and that was enough. The war left Saint Malo – and me – behind.

Soon after the surrender, Lee was picked up by an officer from the US Army Public Relations Office. She had violated the terms of her accreditation by entering a combat zone and was immediately put under house arrest in Rennes. This was a blessing in disguise. The first twenty-four hours of her detention were spent in almost unbroken sleep. Then she stirred herself and for the next three days typed non-stop. The article ran to over ten thousand words and *Vogue* printed it in the October 1944 issue with lavish picture spreads.

By the time she was ready to move, the race was on to liberate Paris. The Public Relations Office had cooled off a bit so she slipped away. Hitching rides and bluffing her way, she arrived in Paris on the day of the liberation. The avenues were packed with crowds of cheering people, waving at every vehicle and clamouring to kiss anyone in allied uniform. Tanks, troops and the Free French infantry still slugged it out with snipers and pockets of die-hard German infantry, but the occasional bursts of fire that scattered the crowds did nothing to dampen the celebrations. Paris was the fashion capital of the world, and Lee automatically switched from battles to frocks.

Everywhere in the streets were dazzling girls, cycling – crawling up tank turrets – their silhouette was very queer and fascinating to me after utility and austerity in England – full floating skirts – tiny waist lines. . . . The G.I.s gasped *en masse* – at a town full of flying pin-up houris – and thought that tales of wild women in Paris had come true – but finally settled for the evidence that good women and bad – the fast and loose and the prudes – the innocent and the wicked, they all had deliberately organised this style of dressing and living as a taunt to the huns – whose women were clumsy and serious women – dressed in grey uniforms (the German army women were known as the *Souris Gris*). If the Germans or the French government representatives wore cropped heads – they grew their hair long – if three meters of material were specified – they found fifteen for a skirt alone – saving material and labour meant help to the Germans – and it was their duty to waste instead of to save.[2]

Lee's immediate concern was to visit her old friends and her first stop was near the Place de l'Odéon where she found the painter Christian Bérard and the ballet impresario Boris Kochno. When they had stopped hugging each other she went with Kochno to Picasso's studio. They fell into each other's arms, Picasso declaring: 'This is the first allied soldier I have seen, and it's you!' Becoming a soldier, he said, had made her so different from the pink and yellow portrait he had painted seven years before in Antibes that he would have to paint her again. In the bistro next door Lee added her K rations to the lunch, which was also well boosted

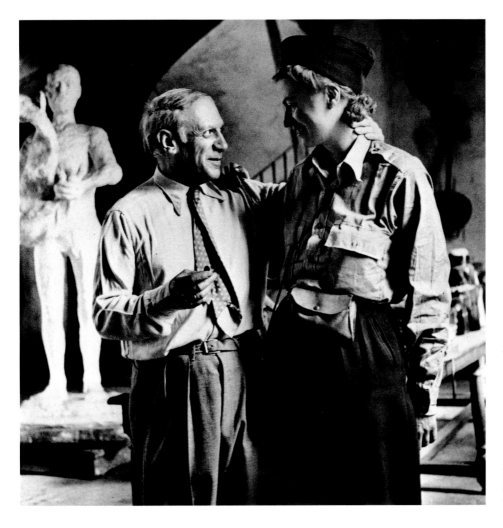

Picasso and Lee in Picasso's studio during the liberation of Paris. August 1944. (Lee Miller)

with large quantities of wine and brandy. Picasso wanted to gossip endlessly about English painters and people he had lost track of. He was particularly amused to hear that Roland Penrose was involved in camouflage, speculating that the results would be like something out of a Marx Brothers film. More meetings were to come:

I found Paul Eluard – he was talking on the telephone in the back room of a *librairie* – He didn't notice who had come into the gloomy little den, and waved for silence. Then he noticed my uniform, and froze a little. He hadn't been on sitting terms with a 'soldier' for a very long time. I just stood there quietly and watched his hand shake. He has a terrific tremble due to a pneumo-thorax operation. There was almost nothing to say to each other – stupid things about how I'd traced him – idiotic remarks about the weather – fortunately Boris Kochno had trailed along with me and he put order into the programme. We went back to the address where the concierge had denied ever having heard of the Eluards – or any other occupants of the flat. Nusch was there, a thin pale grinning Nusch, with her funny Alsatian accent and her fuzzy hair and her beautiful profile. There wasn't much left of her; so thin and delicate that her elbows were larger than her arms, her pelvis bone made sharp twin mountains in her skirt which hung slack and her blouse couldn't disguise the traces of illness and privation. There was only her big broad grin, and her big broad teeth. None of us said anything that made any sense; partly from emotion and partly because the facts weren't very sensible.[3]

A few days later Lee went back to Picasso's studio and found him occupied taking a shower. While she waited she noticed a tomato plant in a pot on the window sill. It had flowered abundantly, sprouting many luscious fruits which had been the subjects for the thirteen drawings and paintings which lay propped up round the walls.[4] Overcome by a sudden craze for fresh fruit, Lee plucked a tomato and ate it. Then another, and another until there was only one left. It was partly covered with mildew but she bit into it and was just licking her fingers when Picasso appeared. He was struck dumb. Lee watched with horrified fascination as his face first went white, then rapidly puce. He bunched his fists in a fury and turned away for a few agonizing moments before facing her. Then the anger faded as fast as it had come, and it was all hugs, kisses and bottom pinching.

The years of war had ended the feuds between Picasso, Aragon, Eluard and Cocteau, and by now they were collaborating, with Picasso illustrating the poets' work. A few weeks before the liberation, Cocteau had been beaten up and nearly blinded for refusing to salute the French flag when it was paraded by a couple of hundred Frenchmen who had joined the German 'anti-Bolshevik legion'. Lee met him at the Rochas's house, and later wrote to Audrey Withers:

We fell into each other's arms – I'm still a big girl inspite of having lost 24 pounds these last two weeks – so I could lift him off his feet. He's looking incredibly well, and younger than I thought possible – less nervous and not mournful or whining which was so much his style when I left Paris five years ago that day. . . . He felt he could only write plays and things with all the troubles going on – but after all he made a new poem, 'Leone', about 600 verses.

The Hôtel Scribe was the allied press camp, and Lee installed herself immediately in Room 412. The french windows opened onto a small balcony, the ideal place to store the dozen jerrycans of petrol which were essential to her way of life. The room itself looked like the supply dump of an assault force. Weapons and equipment of every description overflowed from the wardrobe and drawers, cases of K rations were piled up against cases of Rouyer's cognac and the whole lot buried under large cartons of flash bulbs. An absurd, dangerous and barely workable collection of lighting equipment was jumbled up in a corner. Everywhere there were heaps of loot, everything from lace to leather, Nazi insignia or ostentatious silver stamped with German military crests. The fact that most of it was entirely useless was immaterial, it could always be bartered for other things in times of need, or given to the folks at home as souvenirs.

For much of the time the bathroom was a photo-lab where Lee made attempts at developing Ansco reversal film. There was plenty of colour negative available, but it was unusable at this stage of the war because the censors would not allow it to be sent back for developing in a commercial laboratory. The Ansco film came with a do-it-yourself development kit to allow the despatch of finished film, but it was too slow and unreliable to be effective.

In the middle of all this confusion was a small table where Lee typed her despatches on her battered portable Baby Hermes. The act of writing

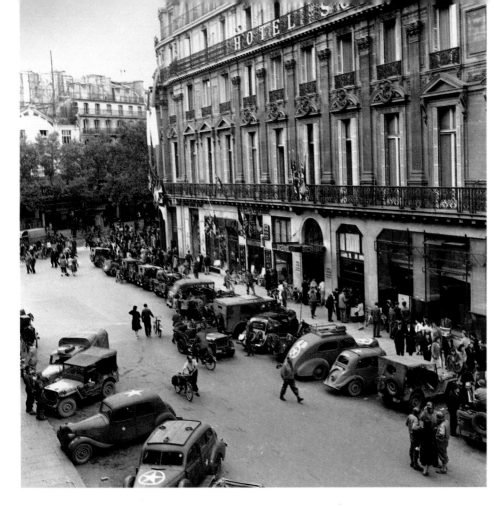

Hôtel Scribe. Paris, 1944. (Lee Miller)

never came easily. It took a monumental effort before she could concentrate her thoughts and focus her attention on the task. This took hours of what she termed 'boondoggling', when she would find any number of things except the matter in hand to occupy herself with. As the deadline approached, the many alternatives to work seemed increasingly urgent. She would make love, hang around the bar and get drunk, argue, sleep, curse and rail, cry, in fact do anything rather than make a start on the article.

She spent hours inventing mythical characters whose names were frightful bilingual puns. Ma Foi and Pa Dequoi were the heads of the family. Their cousin Nicky Tepa ('ne quittez pas') was a telephone operator, son-in-law Sammy Tegal ('ça m'est égal') was a real slob, and they were close friends with Harry Coverre ('haricot vert'), a chef. They had three cats led by Poussez Fort, who shamelessly dominated poor Cat Ildee ('qu'a-t-il dit?') and the Greek singing cat, Cat Inapaxinou ('Katina Paxinou'), but never overcame the family hound Dogui ('d'orgueil'). Then of course there had to be some Russians. Ilnya Pasdequoi and Ilnya Plusdetout always used to do a nihilistic double act, to the dismay of the overly romantic Vouki Passez-Samovar (a line from the popular song 'Vous qui passez sans me voir'). Then there had to be a press corps of eminent reporters including Brown from 'The Sun', Behind from 'The Times', Lowering of 'The Evening Standard', and finally De Bilitating of 'The Atlanta Constitution'.

This procrastination was a self-flagellation routine designed to bring the deadline so close that its pressure formed a substitute for her own lack of resolve. Then, at the very last moment, she would work non-stop through the night glued to the Hermes, fortified by gargantuan amounts of cognac. The effortless, smooth flow of words that followed belied the agony that went into their production. Witty, perceptive and full of daring and oblique imagery, it is hard to believe that they are the product of such self-torture.

Steadfastly supporting Lee through this oft-repeated procedure was Dave Scherman. She had seen him briefly at the surrender of Saint Malo and then to her delight he turned up at the Hôtel Scribe and moved into a room adjoining hers. They covered many assignments together and it was Dave who alternately comforted and badgered Lee through her worst moments of anguish. If they had not been bound by love as well as a passionate camaraderie he could never have stood the torment. He compared being present during Lee's creative process to feeding his brain slowly through a meat grinder. This in itself is one of the strange characteristics of Lee: her ability to inspire love and devotion in those whom she tormented the most.

A double-edged feature of life at the Hôtel Scribe was the excellent communications equipment installed by the previous incumbents, the German Army Press Corps. Several rooms were crammed with the latest developments in telegraph and wireless technology which the engineers wasted no time in linking up to London instead of Berlin. Although Lee was forever cabling for Audrey Withers to send her spare uniforms, extra shoes, the guide book she left at Downshire Hill or three cartons of Tampax, she soon found the return cables an infringement of her independence. *Vogue*'s editors could send her instructions and some of their demands were not always to her liking. She escaped briefly to cover twenty thousand German troops surrendering to her pals in the 83rd Division at Beaugency on the Loire. She also scooped the meeting in Louis Aragon's flat where Maurice Chevalier exonerated himself from charges of collaboration. But there was no ducking the main brief: to help Michel de Brunhoff get French *Vogue* (known as *Frogue*) back on its feet, and to cover the first post-liberation shows of the major *couturiers*.

De Brunhoff had managed a tenuous survival during the occupation of Paris though his son had been arrested and shot by the Nazis just before the liberation. In a letter to Audrey Withers, Lee wrote:

De Brunhoff voluntarily closed all his papers with the armistice [between the French and the Germans in 1940], however he managed to publish four Albums during the occupation, without help or permission of the enemy, by collecting the material here in Paris, making blocks in the suburbs – carrying them in suitcases to Monte Carlo – printing and distributing there in the non-occupied zone for infiltration back to Paris to the rage of the krauts.

Lee was quite ready to help De Brunhoff, but she resented gathering and forwarding other people's work at the expense of her own, particularly when she disagreed with their bias. It fell to her to handle the commissioned articles, chase round to find artists to make the drawings, and then cable the whole back to England. Her previous contacts were invaluable for this, and she used Bernard Blossac and her old friend Bébé

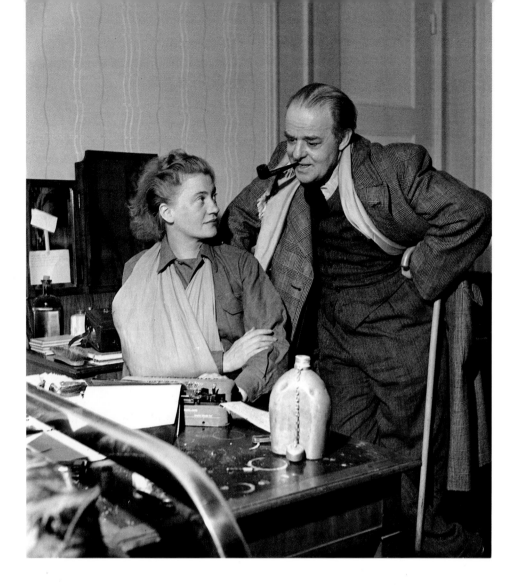

Lee with Michel de Brunhoff, editor of French *Vogue*. Paris, 1944. (Dave Scherman)

Bérard as illustrators whenever possible. While heavily occupied with this work, she suddenly discovered that Cecil Beaton had arrived in Paris. Sensing that he was missing out on something, he had wangled a *Vogue* assignment and was now operating from the newly opened British Embassy and wafting all over town like a *grand seigneur*. Lee was livid, particularly when he began to treat her like the office boy.

The pressure on fashion reporting was immense. The entire world wanted to see what the Parisian *couturiers* were going to produce now that they were free from Nazi oppression. The leaders of some fashion houses were under the deadly suspicion of having been collaborators; others, like Solange, whose husband was still a prisoner of the Nazis, were afraid of becoming too conspicuous for fear of reprisals against their loved ones.

After the Salons at the beginning of October 1944, Lee reported:

The fashion is simpler, simpler yes, but not simple. Paris is still a little mad, an unsuppressible exuberance still expressing itself in folderols, a splurge of red and a desire for oversize muffs. To be brief and explicit, after seeing most of the collections Paris *Vogue* had decided that the silhouette is slimmer. Jackets and skirts straighter. Coats less flared and flounced. The waist remains very snug and natural at its natural line. It is also interesting to note that several of the best known houses are using, both on afternoon coats and dresses, a beltless, wide, tight-fitting princess waistline.

The summary goes on for many pages, covering all aspects of the collections, and concludes:

To sum up, Paris is wakening slowly, but surely, from the nightmare slumber that this beloved 'Belle au Bois Dormant' has been plunged into for the last four years, and it is with a song in her heart and a smile on her lips that she sets to toiling and spinning to weave her cloaks of magic for hard working military and business women, who in their leisure moments can relax from their job of making this a winning war, and be for a few hours at least deceivingly frail and alluringly feminine.[5]

Lee photographed most of the collections under very difficult circumstances, and was understandably stunned by Edna Woolman Chase's reaction, relayed in a telegram from Audrey Withers: 'EDNA CRITICAL OF SNAPSHOT FASHION REPORTAGE AND ESPECIALLY CHEAP MANNEQUINS URGES MORE ELEGANCE BY STUDIO PHOTOGRAPHS + WELL BRED WOMEN AND EXCELLENT DRAWINGS STOP CANT BELIEVE PICTURES TYPICAL HIGHCLASS FRENCH FASHION.'

Lee replied to Audrey:

I find Edna very unfair – these snapshots have been taken under the most difficult and depressing conditions – in the twenty minutes a model was willing to give of her lunch hour – most of which was being taken up with further fittings

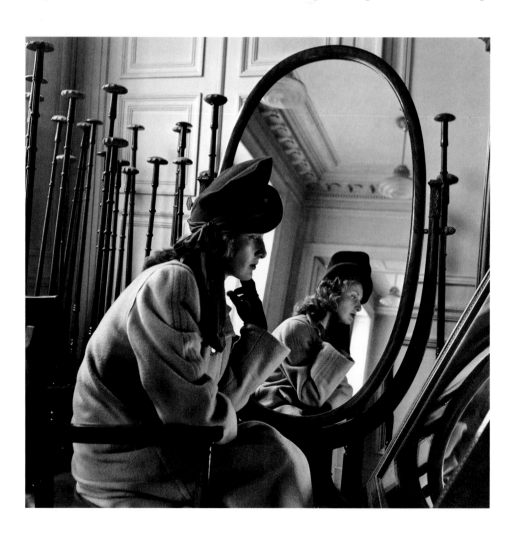

Model preparing for a millinery salon after the liberation of Paris. 1944. (Lee Miller)

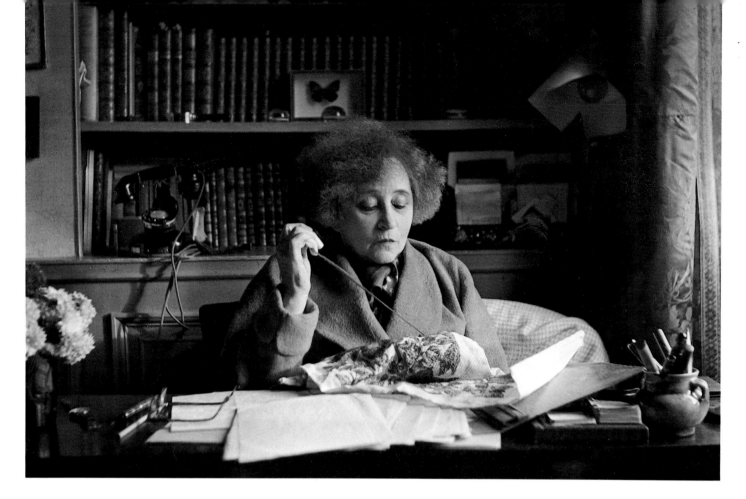

for unfinished dresses – or after five o'clock in rooms with no electricity – using the seeping daylight from a courtyard window – with a howling mob around and the amount of daylight that reaches thru the couloir to the can. Any suggestion that dames de monde could and should have been used is strictly out of this world. Edna should be told that there is a war on.

Colette, aged 71, embroidering in her apartment at 9 Rue de Beaujolais, Paris. 1944. (Lee Miller)

Such uninformed carping added to Lee's growing impatience to catch up with the 83rd Division and get back to something more real. Before this could happen she reported on the Brussels Salons and then took a trip to England for a riotous Christmas with Roland Penrose at Downshire Hill. Back in Paris the first assignment was to cover a visit to a person *Vogue* were to describe as 'France's greatest living woman writer'.

Up the darkest staircase in Paris to press a mute electricityless door-bell – to pound until knuckles are numb and Pauline, the devoted ogress slave of Colette, stumbles thru a lightless corridor to peer at and identify the visitor, and to satisfy herself that she approves as well, for if Pauline doesn't approve there is no second invitation.

Against the cold light from the tall windows Colette's fuzzy hair is a halo. The room is hot, the fur coverings of her bed tawny rich and she is almost certainly telephoning. She took off her grotesque heavy rimmed spectacles, shifted the phone and tugged my hand for me to sit on the side of the bed while she continued tutoying and gently scolding a small female voice which leaked out into the room. Finally: The typewriter would be returned, by the small voice – she would also apply for transport to Limoges and would come for tea tomorrow. A demain!

Colette turned to me and said, '*Alors, qu'est ce que vous voulez?*' Her voice was gruff but her hand had been warm and her kohl rimmed eyes matched in sparkle and clarity the myriads of crystal balls and glass bibelots which strewed the room.[6]

Audrey Withers had repeatedly asked Lee to write an article on the 'Pattern of Liberation', which she hoped would avoid the gore and violence for which Lee automatically headed. The result was a perceptive and sensitive appraisal which *Vogue* published with poignant pictures of refugees in the January 1945 issue.

The pattern of liberation is not decorative. There are the gay squiggles of wine and song. There is the beautiful overall colour of freedom, but there is ruin and destruction. There are problems and mistakes, disappointed hopes and broken promises. There is wishful thinking and inefficiency. There is grogginess as after a siesta, a 'sleeping beauty' lethargy. The prince had broken into the cobwebbed castle and planted his awakening kiss. Everyone gets up, dances a minuet, and lives happily ever after.
    The story does, but shouldn't end there. Who polished the verdigrised saucepans? Who replaced the rusted well chain? Were the shelves dusted? The cupboards clean? Who swept up the 'petits moutons' which must have gathered under the bed? There must have been a hell of a mess. Did they start their quarrels where they left off? Did they ask what the neighbours had been saying about them all this time? Had the milkman left rows of bottles on the window sill? Were there fresh lettuces and eggs in the larder? Maybe the prince solved all these problems and brought all these things, too, or was liberation enough? . . . I saw something of its workings in Luxembourg.

Lee went on to report on the rape of a country so small that it had not even had an army to defend itself. She wrote of the stupid niggling humiliations of Nazi occupation, such as not being allowed to speak French; there was a ten marks fine for simply saying *bonjour* or *merci*. French family names had to be changed to their nearest German equivalents, cafés were labelled *Rathskeller*. Intellectuals, teachers and lawyers were shot as traitors. Reprisals were taken against civilians at any opportunity and early on the Jews vanished without trace.
    This suffering was recorded by Lee with clarity and understanding, but it was not the kind of reporting she wanted to do. She always felt most at home among the infantry up at the sharp end of the action.

There was nothing I knew in advance about the city [Luxembourg], nothing I recognised except the rain until a jeep hove in sight. I recognised the numbers. In a few seconds I was in the street peering at the identification marks of all the cars and trucks which passed. I found one I knew and stuck my hand out like a traffic cop. It was Doc Berger and the Chaplain of the 329th, 83rd division. I was home again. Colonel Crabill said, 'We consider you have been absent since Beaugency.' The sergeants said 'Lady, every time you turn up, something is bound to happen.'
    The general asked what I'd found to do better than to be with them. I told him about the Paris collection – the mad-house of openings – the gorgeousness of the ersatz clothes. He looked me up and down, muddy boots, soaked hooded cloak, and said, 'It may or may not be "better", but it certainly is different. You'd best stay around with us.'
    The M.P.s said 'Stow the red scarf and put on your helmet. What do you think the General would say?'[7]

After this, Paris was too tame for Lee. However much she loved fashion, the prospect of another round of Salons was daunting, and she persuaded Audrey Withers to let her go roving again. By some strange irony, Dave

130

Scherman, who had been covering some vicious fighting at Brest, found himself assigned to cover the spring collections for *Life*. For Lee, it was off to Alsace in the snow, mud and confusion that surrounded some of the war's most bitterly contested territory. The neat, prosperous little medieval farms and villages on the alluvial plains of Colmar were being torn apart as the US Army struggled to push forward across the Rhine. The roads were clogged with overladen farm carts as thousands of refugees – old people, women and children – stumbled along, seeking what food, shelter and safety they could find.

In this, as in most other campaigns, ordinary journalists were not obliged to take the same risks as their photographer colleagues. They could sit in the safety of a press camp miles behind the action gathering their material at press conferences or from the supply teams. The only way photographers could get their pictures was to go and find the action. It is worth remembering that Lee's Rolleiflex did not have a telephoto lens, auto-wind or built-in light meter. Under pressure, every exposure was an automatic guess. To compensate for having only twelve shots on a roll and to guard against malfunction, Lee alternated her shots on two cameras. This made caption writing a nightmare, but more than once it saved her from failure.

Battles came in all sizes, from the sharp, furious encounters between patrols, to the enormous set-piece assaults with masses of tanks and artillery. There were two common denominators adding to the ferocity: the marrow-chilling cold and the fact that the Germans had their backs to the Rhine. The US Army was fighting alongside the Free French and some of the contingents were Moroccan, French Foreign Legion, Argentinians, Russians, Hungarians and Spaniards. Lee had her own jeep and moved freely among the troops, pushing south from Strasbourg towards Colmar. There was no sunshine thrill of liberation here, just bitter, endless toil and bloodshed as villages were captured, sometimes to be retaken and then captured again. Lee penetrated everywhere. Her previous experience earned her ready acceptance by the tough infantry soldiers whose ways she now understood well. She wrote and photographed 'Through the Alsace Campaign' for *Vogue*'s April 1945 issue.

I'll never see acid-yellow and grey again like where shells burst near snow without seeing also the pale quivering faces of replacements, grey and yellow with apprehension. Their fumbling hands and furtive, short sighted glances at the field they must cross. The snow which shrouds innocent lumps and softens savage craters covers alike the bodies of the enemy and of the other platoon which tried before. The new craters are violent with black circles of clods around, the smell is choking. In the ditch a waxen-faced dead German was frozen in a heroic pose, and the new boys stamped their feet because the others did. They were too numb to feel the cold. Mostly they twisted one foot around the other, shyly. . . . A lieutenant who was holding his cut face leaned against a tree. He left a bloody hand mark and walked on. He started down the ditch and sat on the edge, slowly, with his hands to his belly. He sat there for a while. Soldiers who passed him spoke. He motioned them on. One stayed and then went back to the mill. Two guarded German prisoners came with a litter, but he was dead. They left him covered up by the side of the road. The guard and the prisoners saluted

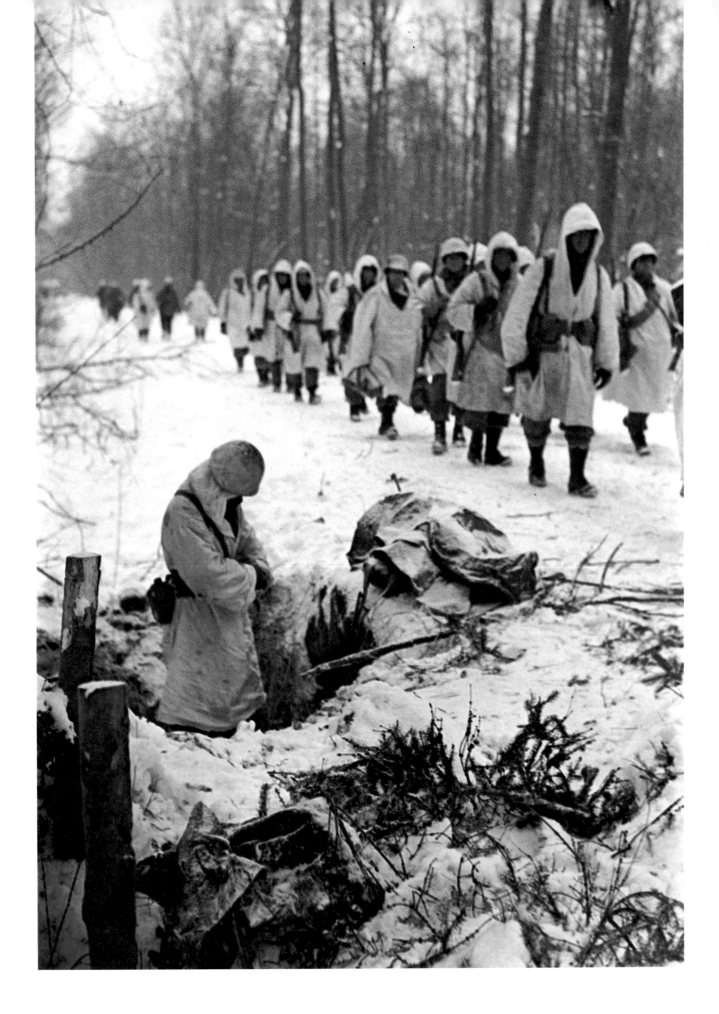

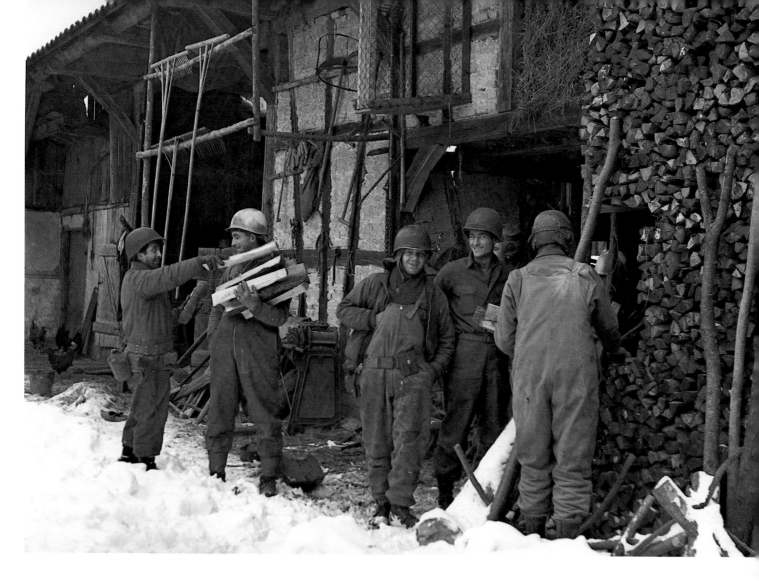

and returned towards the mill. . . . What kind of an atavism are we creating for hordes of people and children who peek out of their cellars at dawn to find the strange men who were eating soup in the barnyard before the 'noise', pale and dead in the snow?

Returning to her base at the Hôtel Scribe, Lee filed her story and took stock of the situation. By now there were so many correspondents in Europe that there was intense competition for the already strained facilities offered by the army. Lee switched her accreditation to the US Air Force who, now that their role in Europe was less spectacular, were offering far better facilities to journalists as an inducement for publicity. Lee now had priority for airfreighting film and despatches, and *carte blanche* to go where she liked. Far from changing to routine reporting about airforce activity, she stuck with the infantry, whose efforts she admired most.

Dave Scherman had just acquired a large 1937 Chevrolet for 120,000 Francs which had been sprayed the regulation olive drab colour and which had a large white American star on its bonnet and LIFE stencilled on its mudguard. He and Lee set off for Torgau, to cover the Russian–American link-up on the banks of the Elbe. This official meeting between the armies was the product of a deal made at Yalta between Stalin, Churchill and Roosevelt to limit the Russian advance into Europe.

United States tank crew and infantry billeting in an Alsace farmyard. 1945. (Lee Miller)

Opposite: Moroccan replacement troops arrive to join the fighting in the Colmar region of Alsace. 1945. (Lee Miller)

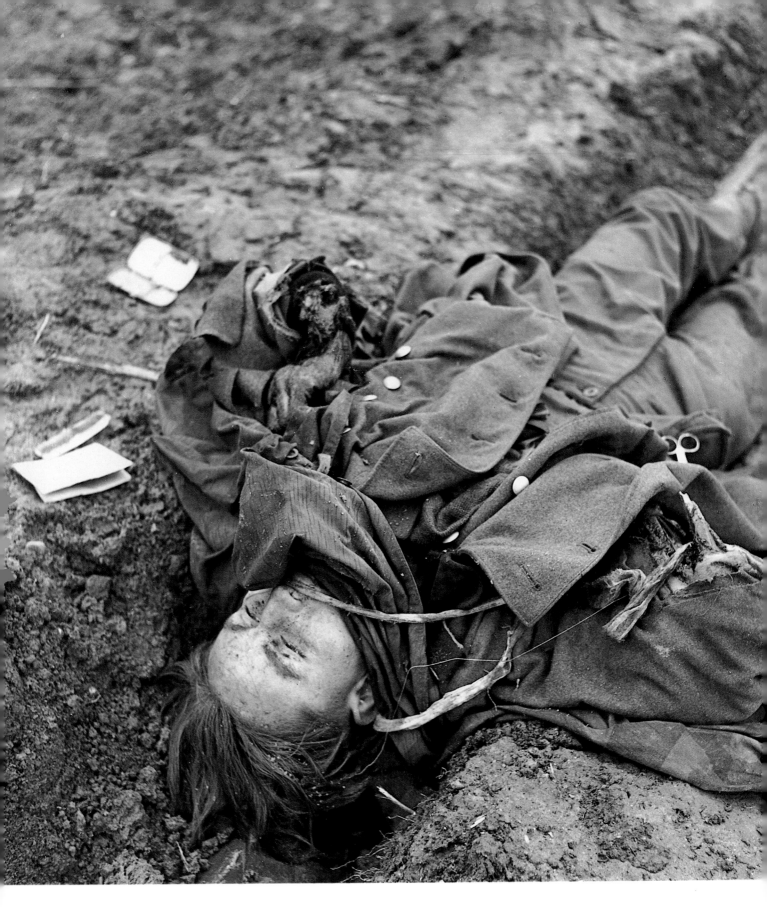

Dead soldier. Lee wrote: 'This is a good German, he is dead. Artery forceps hang from his shattered wrists.' Cologne, 1945. (Lee Miller)

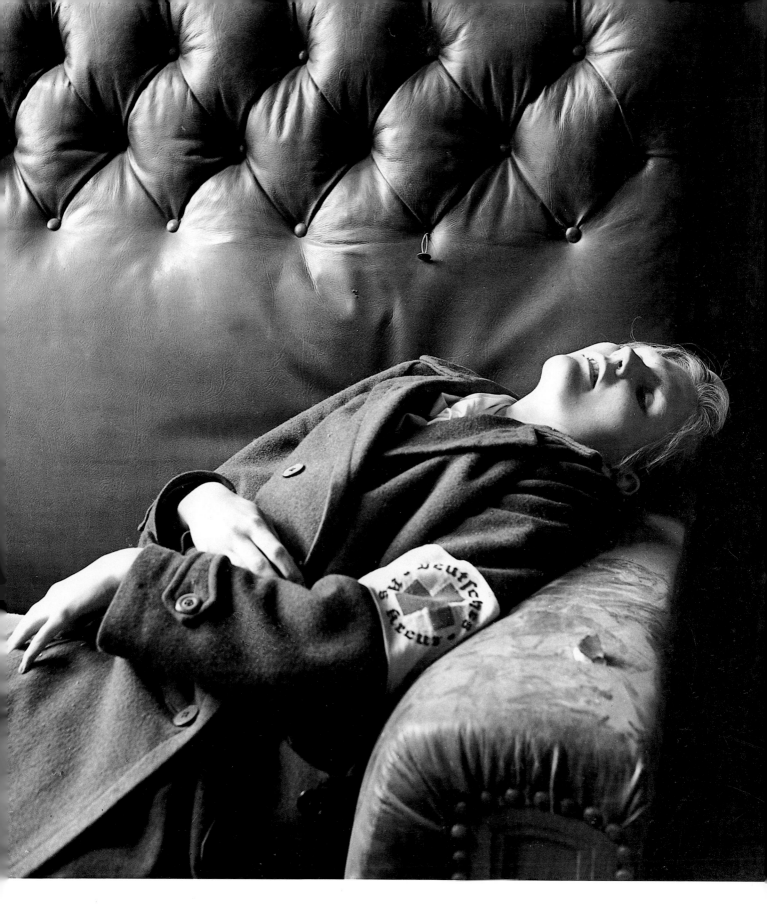

Daughter of the burgomaster of
Leipzig. She and her parents killed
themselves as the Allies took the
town. Lee wrote: '. . . she had
exceptionally pretty teeth.' 1945.
(Lee Miller)

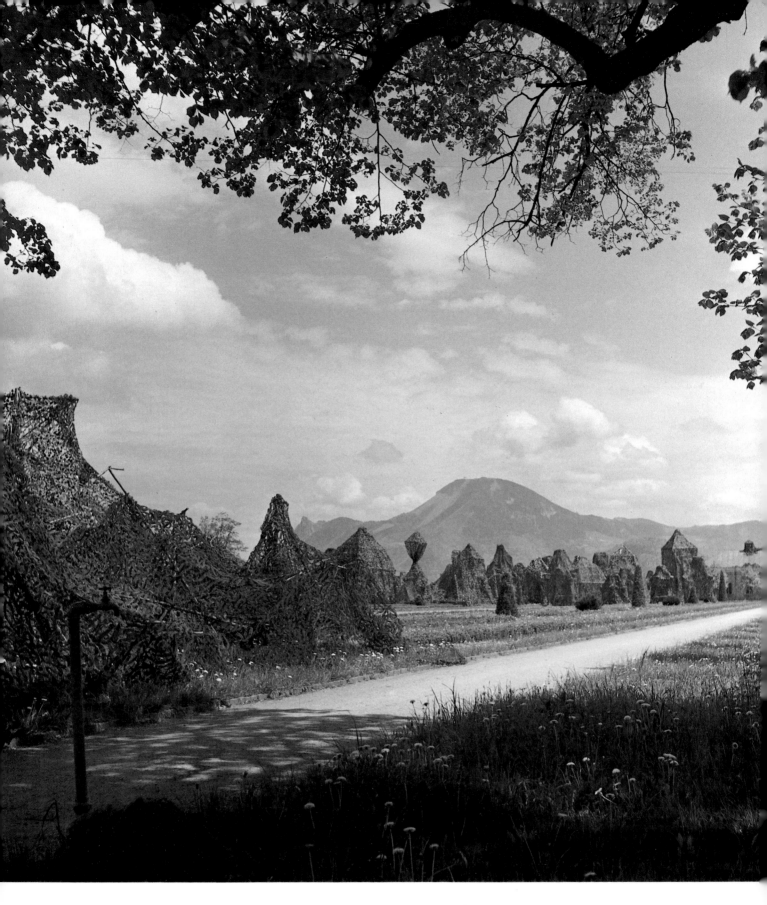

Statues covered by camouflage nets
make a landscape like a painting by
Yves Tanguy. Germany, 1945. (Lee
Miller)

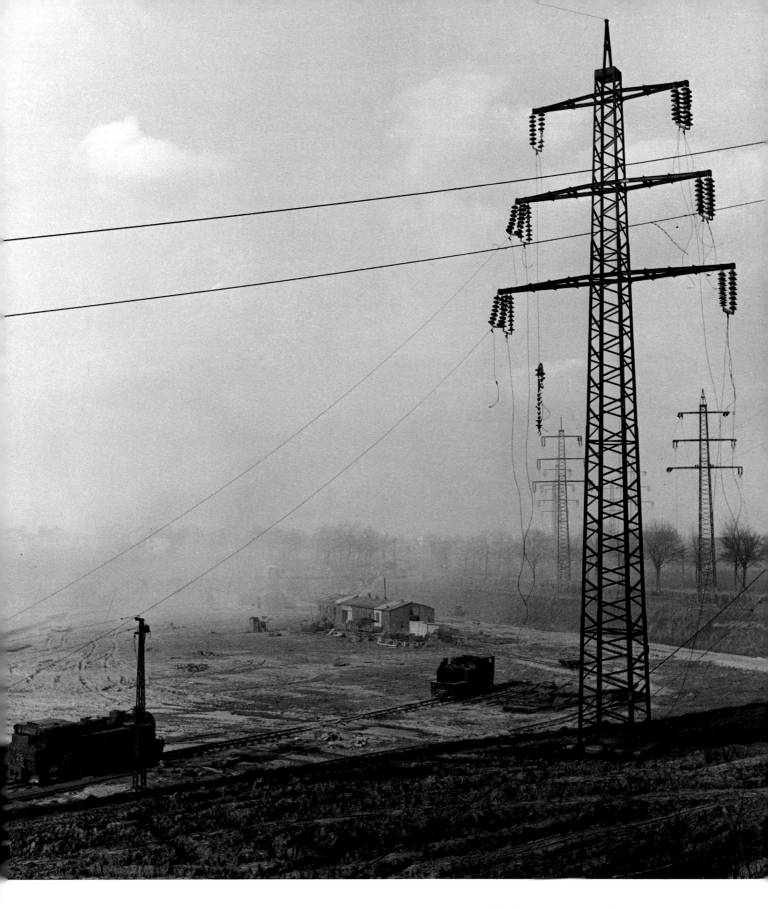

The locomotives and the eerie
stillness of this landscape are
reminiscent of the work of Giorgio de
Chirico. Germany, 1945. (Lee Miller)

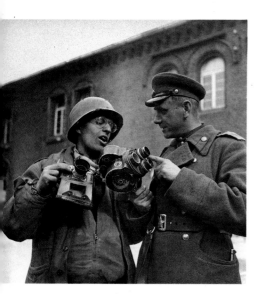

Dave Scherman and a Soviet cameraman. Torgau, 1945. (Lee Miller)

Torgau consequently became the target for a huge convoy of reporters. Dave held back because someone else from *Life* had been assigned the story, but Lee jumped on a heavy weapons jeep with four G.I.s from H company, 273rd infantry regiment of the 69th Division, and went a different way. The jeep tore through small towns, whose inhabitants, thinking the dreaded Russians had arrived, scattered in all directions. Displaced people cheered and armed German soldiers ducked out of sight. The wrecked and abandoned streets of Torgau were choked by two columns of refugees heading in opposite directions. The Poles and Russians were trying to go east to get home while the others were fleeing to the west ahead of the Red Army. At the Russian command post there was the usual flag-waving and handshaking, but providentially Lee got her pictures ahead of the other reporters. Soon after, the vodka started to flow and everyone got drunk in an orgy of bearhugs, whooping, yelling and firing weapons into the air.

The G.I.s were fascinated by the strange lumpy shapes of the Russian female orderlies. The women were disinclined to reveal their secrets to the soldiers, but struck an immediate rapport with Lee because they in turn were fascinated by her shape. They invited her to their quarters and several stripped to reveal amazing brassieres of heavy material with masses of thick straps. When Lee gave a reciprocal demonstration, they were baffled to find that she was bra-less and offered touching sympathy about her comparative lack of endowment. The press corps were still arriving as the vodka began to take a firm hold on the gathering. Lee and Dave, knowing they had got the best out of the story, were making their getaway when Marguerite Higgins of the *New York Herald Tribune* turned up. She complained to Dave: 'How is it that every time I arrive somewhere to cover a story, you and Lee Miller are just leaving?'

Travelling south, Dave and Lee came across a group of G.I.s looting the cellars of a wine merchant. They wanted only the sweet wines, so Lee picked out the Sauternes and some liqueurs. There were several cases of Framboise which Lee 'liberated', and, to save space in the Chevrolet, she decanted the bottles into a jerrycan which had held water. The can remained in the car for the rest of the campaign, and since petrol was more precious than gold, no one was surprised to see her guard it so closely. What did astonish people was the sight of her taking a swig out of it with apparent relish. As the level of Framboise dropped, Lee topped up the jerrycan with whatever liqueur or wine came to hand until the taste was indescribable but the potency unrivalled.[8]

Nuremberg was taken by the forces of General Patton, who declared that Munich was now only 'one piss-call down the road'. Lee and Dave followed hard on his heels to the 6th Army press camp. The public relations officer was ex-*Life* reporter Dick Pollard, who took all Lee and Dave's film and gave it priority shipping back to England. He also advised them that Rainbow Company of 45th Division were that evening going in to liberate Dachau concentration camp.

After a brief firefight with the S.S. guards manning the watch towers, Rainbow Company took the camp. Early next morning Lee and Dave were among the first to enter. Some of their less inured colleagues were immediately reduced to hysterical, vomiting wrecks. Lee's previous experiences had given her a degree of emotional defence against the horrors of war and her main reaction was one of total disbelief. Speechless and numb, she could not accept at first the enormity of the carnage and wanton slaughter. Here, and later at Buchenwald, this reaction was shared by some of the G.I.s. Unprepared for the hideousness of political and racist crimes against civilians, they thought at first that the camp was a grotesque propaganda stunt faked by their own side. Many of the S.S. guards who had survived the firefight had been ripped apart by the prisoners. A few remaining had tried to disguise themselves in cast-off clothing but had been caught because their well-fed appearance always gave them away. If they were lucky enough to be rounded up by the M.P.s, they mostly grovelled abjectly in cells, sobbing for mercy. Many of them were crippled or had been wounded, which had earned them the soft option of running the camp.

The smell, the awful nightmarish cloying stench, is what remains uppermost in the memories of those who took part in the liberation. They recall that it was almost tangible and that they felt they would never be free of it for the rest of their lives. Then they recall the cordwood piles of bodies. Age or sex were no defence, only a vague criterion for the segregation of the cord piles. Men over there, women and children here. The evidence of mass execution and mass starvation could not be concealed because the crematoriums had run out of fuel five days earlier. Huge areas of open ground were covered with the dead and the dying, for whom there could be no comfort as they lay in puddles of excrement and vomit. Every conceivable disease from cholera to typhus was rife and deadly to such drastically undernourished bodies.

A railway siding terminated in the camp, where the prisoners had arrived on a trip that was intended to be strictly one way. Some trains of box cars and cattle trucks were too long to fit into the siding and halted outside the camp. Beside the track were the bodies of those who had died on their last march, yet the civilian population of the town claimed they had not the remotest idea of the camp's purpose.

Lee's sense of outrage fired her to take pictures. 'I IMPLORE YOU TO BELIEVE THIS IS TRUE,' she cabled to Audrey Withers, wanting to confront the world with this atrocity. The prisoners were fascinated by her as she moved among them. Her baggy combat uniform was chosen to divert attention from her sex, but the lipstick and stray wisps of blond hair gave her away. They gazed at her with amazement and adoration. Remembering she had some K ration chocolate in her pocket, she unwisely gave it away. Dave hauled her out from the ensuing mêlée, and after that they stuck close together. In one of the huts they wanted to photograph a bunk, but all the spaces were jammed with the chronically ill. The trusty prisoners hunted through the hut until they found someone who had just died and hauled out the corpse to expose the crude bunk. They stood for a moment with heads bowed, making their devotions, and then invited Dave and Lee to take the picture.

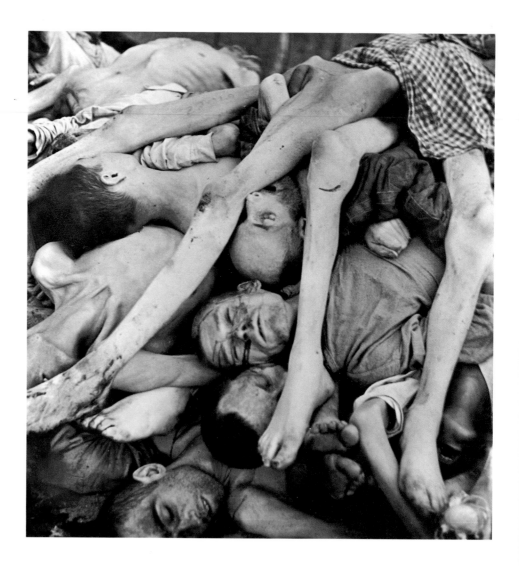

Dachau. 30 April 1945. (Lee Miller)

Opposite: United States medics from Rainbow Company with a dead prisoner at Dachau, 30 April 1945. Some of the troops, unable to comprehend the enormity of the suffering, thought the camp a grim propaganda stunt faked by their own side. (Lee Miller)

The US commanders reacted swiftly to the situation at Dachau. Trucks were sent into Munich and the contents of entire civilian clothing and bedding stores were soon on their way to the camp. All available medical supplies and civilian hospital beds were requisitioned, but food was a different matter. The stomachs of many of the prisoners had shrunk so badly that they could not cope with more than small quantities of gruel; anything more substantial induced violent vomiting and sometimes death.

That night in Munich Lee and Dave wangled a billet in the command post of the 45th Division at Prinzregentenplatz 27. It was in an old-fashioned building on a corner, which showed no outward signs that anybody more elevated than a merchant or retired clergyman lived there, so it seemed an unlikely setting for one of Lee and Dave's biggest scoops. The impression of ordinariness continued inside with furnishings and decor that could have belonged to anyone with a moderate income and no heirlooms. Only the swastika combined with the A.H. monogram on the silver gave it away as Hitler's house. In this banal setting the leader of the Third Reich had lived and conferred with Chamberlain, Franco, Mussolini, Goebbels, Goering, Laval and a host of others.

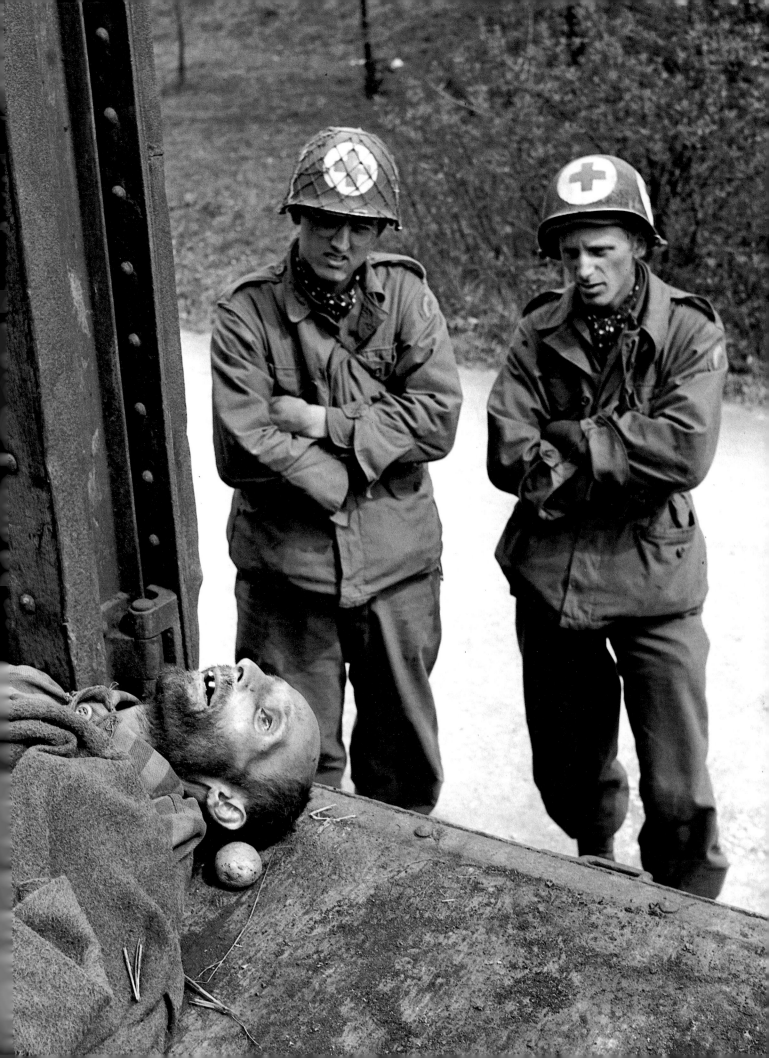

The elaborate telephone switchboard in the aide's adjoining flat was still connected, so Lee and Dave found a German speaking US officer, Lieutenant Colonel Grace, and asked him to call the operator, who was in another, as yet uncaptured, section of the town. Hoping for a quote from the Führer, he demanded a connection with Berchtesgaden. The phone rang and a voice at the other end answered. Then, evidently because the correct password was not forthcoming, the call was instantly cut off and the whole switchboard went dead.

Lee's first thought was to hop into the enormous bathtub and enjoy her first scrub for weeks. Dave took a photograph of her, with her muddy combat boots parked on the bathmat. Later they set up a spoof shot of a G.I. lounging on Hitler's bed, reading *Mein Kampf* while talking on a field telephone. The picture made a full page in *Life* and brought Dave one of the greatest accolades of his career. As souvenirs, Lee carried off autographed volumes of *Mein Kampf*, thank you letters to Frau Winter – Hitler's housekeeper – and endless oddments including a photograph of Hitler which she asked everyone in the command post to sign.

About three blocks away, at Wasserburgerstrasse 12, was the square stucco villa of Hitler's mistress, Eva Braun. The small rooms were furnished in a precise, impersonal way as though everything had been chosen from the same department store. Only the bathroom demonstrated the personality of the occupier; its shelves were crammed with enough medicines for – as Lee put it – 'a ward of hypochondriacs'. She wrote, 'I took a nap on her bed. It was comfortable but macabre to doze on the pillow of a girl and a man who were dead, and be glad they were dead if it were true.'[9]

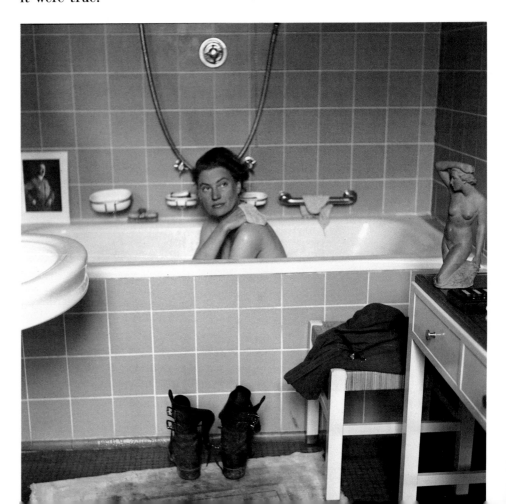

Lee in Hitler's bathtub.
Prinzregentenplatz 27, Munich, 1945.
(Dave Scherman)

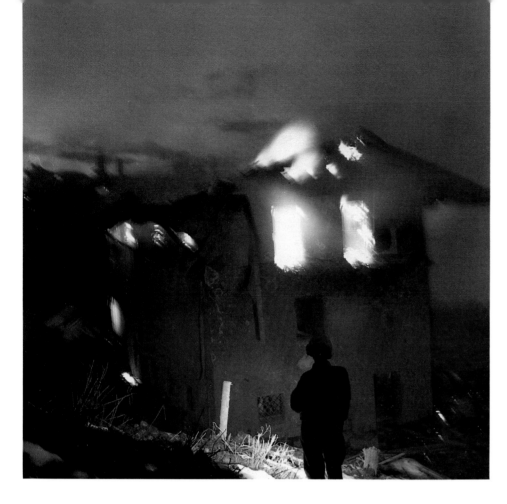

The funeral pyre of the Third Reich. Hitler's house at Berchtesgaden in flames. 1945. (Lee Miller)

Dick Pollard of the 6th Army press camp advised Lee and Dave to hurry to Salzburg as quickly as possible because the 15th Regiment of the 3rd Division, commanded by 'Iron Mike' O'Daniel, was set to attack Hitler's impregnable Alpine fortress at Berchtesgaden. It was a day's drive over difficult terrain, and at one point the Chevrolet slid off the road and had to be hauled back by an army bulldozer. A little further on they encountered a group of G.I.s shooting the windows out of a 1939 Mercedes convertible. Dave persuaded them to stop in return for posing with Lee for a picture for their hometown newspaper. The car's owner was, according to the papers in the glove box, a Hungarian air attaché called Futterer. Dave assumed there would be no official use for the vehicle so he 'liberated' it. Named Ludmilla, it lasted him for many years, ending its days in New York where it was cannibalized for parts.

The impregnable fortress was a pushover for the 3rd Division. After a brief fight the S.S. troops set fire to Hitler's chalet, the 'Eagle's Nest', and fled into the surrounding forest. Dave and Lee arrived on the scene as dusk was gathering and the flames roared from the funeral pyre of the 'Thousand Year Reich'. They climbed up the mountain behind the building and held flashguns for each other. G.I.s swarmed everywhere. 'How many guys you got down there?' roared a voice from the mountainside. 'Four lootin' an' one shootin', sur,' came the reply, scarcely audible above the crashing masonry and roaring flames. The following day large areas of the house and underground bunkers were found to be unscathed, but the looters took care of them and soon not a shred remained of anything movable. The first to go were the huge stocks of wines, champagnes and scotch which Hitler had amassed despite being a health fanatic who claimed to loathe alcohol and tobacco. Inside the mountain miles of tunnels connected living quarters to a library, cinema, kitchen and dining rooms, as well as a store for treasures looted from all over Europe. Lee and Dave took their photographs and then helped themselves to souvenirs. Dave took the complete works of Shakespeare in translation with Hitler's bookplate on the flyleaf, and Lee left with a large ornate silver tray with the A.H. swastika monogram stamped on it. This later became the drinks tray in her London home.

The press headquarters were set up in a schoolhouse in nearby Rosenheim. Lee and Dave were hard at work on their captions and stories when a soldier walked in and said, 'I thought you guys might want to know Germany has just surrendered – the war in Europe is over!' The beat of Lee's Baby Hermes hardly faltered as she glanced up. 'Thanks,' she said. Then the tapping ceased. 'Shit!' she exploded, 'That's blown my first paragraph!'

German boy. The *Scharnhorst*, a giant German battleship, sank at 19.45 hours on 26 December 1943 off North Cape, following a fierce engagement with British and Norwegian destroyers. Out of the ship's complement of 2,000 men, only 36 survived. (Lee Miller)

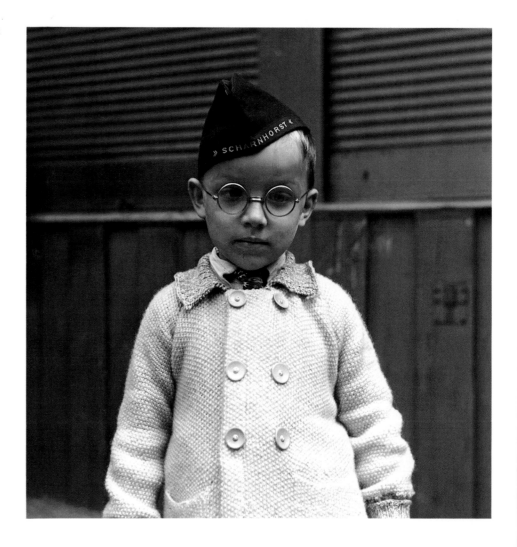

Opposite: Lee, London, 1943. (Dave Scherman)

Chapter Eight

Spinning It Out: Austria
1945

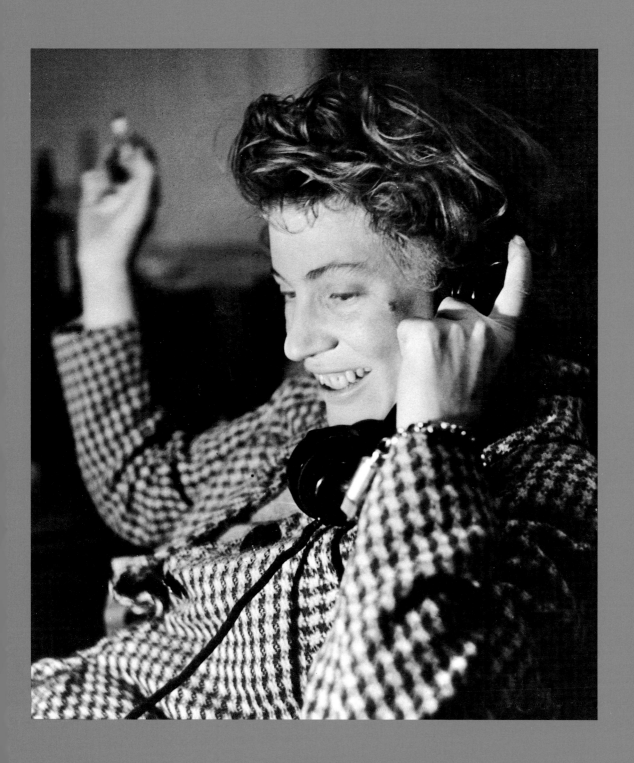

The period following armistice was a devastating anticlimax for Lee and her journalist colleagues. The tension that had vitalized them suddenly evaporated. 'Encased in a wall of hate and disgust', Lee drove across Germany to Denmark, assigned to report on Danish fashion and social life. The photographs she took outside the assignment were beautiful: tranquil landscapes, farms, markets and crowds of people enjoying themselves in the Tivoli Gardens in Copenhagen. It was as though she were deliberately seeking a visual antidote to the previous horrors. Her writing gave a truer indication of her state of mind and Audrey Withers had to slash the eight thousand words and three drafts to the bone to make it coherent.

In London, *Vogue* gave Lee a rapturous welcome. A lunch was held for her, and Harry Yoxall, the managing director, made a speech warmly commending her for her work and her courage: 'Who else has written equally well about G.I.s and Picasso? Who else can get in at the death of St Malo and at the re-birth of the fashion salons? Who else can swing from the Siegfried line one week to the new hipline the next?' He went on to pay a tribute to Audrey Withers, her assistant Grace Young, the art department, and the studio, but he could not resist implying that it had been *Vogue*'s initiative to send Lee to picture the world at war – which was not the case.

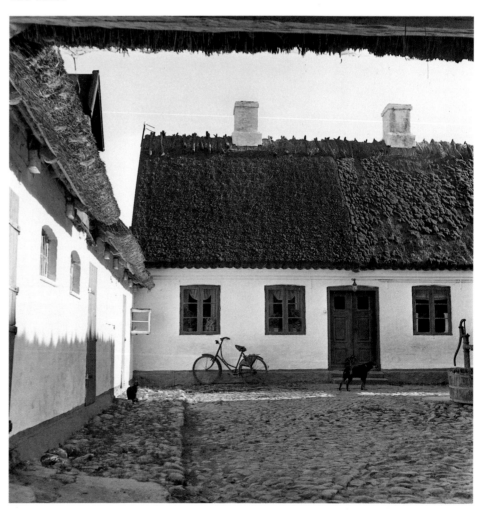

Farmyard in Denmark. 1945. (Lee Miller)

Lee's relations with Roland were strained by the changes she had undergone. They still loved each other but the turmoil of her emotions was beyond the understanding of either of them. At the root was a basic conflict – he wanted to clip her wings and keep her at home, but she could not settle. 'I'm not Cinderella, I can't force my foot into the glass slipper,' she would say, stretching Roland's liberal ideas to the limit by demanding that he should understand motives which she herself found incomprehensible. Volatile tensions simmered, and in mid-August flashpoint was reached. After an acrimonious, passionate, door-slamming row, Lee walked out.

Back in Paris, she succumbed to a particularly cruel bout of mental self-laceration, exacerbated by the backlash of accumulated fatigue. For some time she had been relying heavily on benzedrine to blast herself into activity. Every morning became a crash alert for her body as the drug and strong coffee took effect. At night her jangled nerves would not allow her to sleep without masses of alcohol or heavy sleeping tablets to smash her senses down to a tolerable level. Some mornings the foul, black, winged serpents that flapped slowly round her mind were unconquerable and she would weep alone in bed all day.

Fortunately for her Dave was there – patient, understanding, and, despite his ebullient nature, with similar problems of his own. It was Dave's sense of humour that saved Lee from blowing her brains out. He could turn anything into a joke, and he pulled her round by forcing her to laugh at herself. Slowly the winged serpents were driven back to their caverns, where they resumed their shallow dormancy. She regained some equilibrium and began to move forward again in spite of herself. This letter must have been the product of one of her calmer moments:

Darling Roland,
I haven't forgotten you. Every evening when I could take the time and certainly have the interest to write you I think that to-morrow I'll know the ultimate answer or that my depression will have lifted, or my exaltation ebbed or whatever – so that I'll be able to write you a more coherent impression containing some sort of decision – whether it be that I'm staying or coming home, licked. That moment never comes. You've known that for years already. Either I have had a diarrhoea of words or constipation.

When the invasion occurred – the impact of the decision itself was a tremendous release – all my energy and all my pre-fabricated opinions were unleashed together; I worked well and consistently and I hope convincingly as well as honestly. Now I'm suffering from a sort of verbal impotence – when there was a necessity for stopping being afraid (like you knew how cowardly I was during the blitz) I could and did. This is a new and disillusioning world. Peace with a world of crooks who have no honour, no integrity and no shame is not what anyone fought for.

One Christmas morning I was awakened by the news of an assassination [Admiral Darlan]. Do you remember, I stopped being sick? And the man came by with a coffin and I started laughing? And everything was alright from then on because I knew that we weren't fighting for anything any of us wanted anyway and it didn't matter, we were just stuck with it like always. Then I saw the guys who were grey or bloody or black. The boys who were white with anger or green with fatigue and sometimes shook because they were afraid, I was awfully sorry that the war wasn't for anything at all – and I was very angry.

Really great groups of humans are suffering the same shock symptoms caused by peace that I'm combatting – and I don't in the least mean the boys going back home to find that they've become dependent upon a benevolent maternal army – that they have outgrown their wives or become socially unfit or drunks or misanthropes. Its just an impatience with the sordid dirt which is being slung around now compared with the comparative cleanliness and the real nobility of the men in the lines, or men and women in the lousy little jobs they thought were helping to win the war – and the people who bought bonds so that their disreputable government could continue after the war loan had been paid off – the families who are still short of rations so that a lot of grasping bastards with greedy gloating appetites should have enough schlag on their coffee. A more disorganised, dissolute and dishonest population has never existed in the history books.

The room and my affairs are a hopeless mess and I'm incapable of sorting them out; however they hang over me and depress me all the time. Paul doesn't answer his phone, nor Picasso, nor Dora – the whole town is closed down and everything is shut, not only for August but also for a series of V.J. Days, alternating with Assumption days etc. I'm leaving for this Austrian trip tomorrow morning, Saturday, at dawn with a great deal of dread and boredom. Davie is hanging round waiting for me to get off because he knows that if he doesn't, I'll never leave.

Love Lee

The winged serpents triumphed insofar as Lee did not post this or any other letter to Roland for the next seven months – a silence that came perilously close to destroying his love for her. Her disregard for him stemmed from the fact that at this point she saw him as just another transitory love affair. Undoubtedly she was very fond of him, but she vested no commitment to the future in their relationship. This fact was borne out by her attempts to interest Dave in a scheme for working together in the United States as a photographic team. Dave turned down the idea because he believed that he would be breaking up what he supposed to be her solid, long-term union with Roland.

Salzburg was Lee's first stop. The place was in an uproar with truckloads of French, British, American and Soviet soldiers in town for the music festival. The smart hotels took on the appearance of transit camps for displaced persons as a babble of ten or eleven languages filled the air. Fifty Soviet infantry men, official guests of US General Mark Clark, gawped at the sights and gave a hero's welcome to the conductor Reinhardt Baumgartner. Much of the organization of the festival fell to Barbara Lauwer, a young Czech, more accustomed to daring deeds of spying and sabotage. She managed to assemble a strong group of performers despite having to eliminate those who had played more than music for the Nazis. Baumgartner had been exiled in Switzerland and had to be fetched and identified at the border, and others in hiding needed convincing that the persecution was finished. One of the greatest problems was food supply but the authorities were finally persuaded that music was heavy labour. At the end of the festival you could tell by looking at the faces in the street who had been singing for his supper.[1]

Music broke the nationalistic barriers and for a few hours at a time the demarcation zones between the French, Soviet, American and English

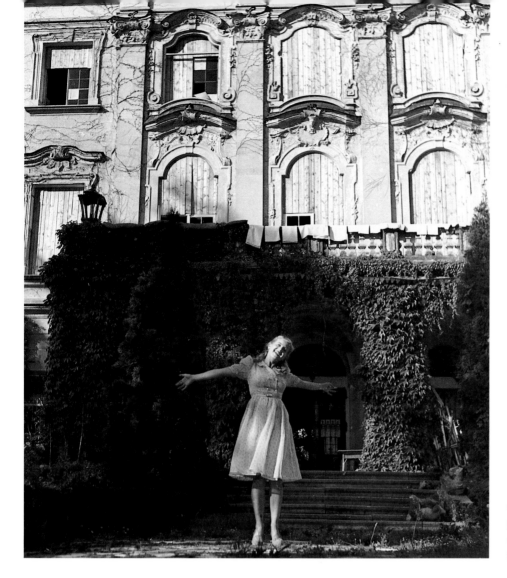

The Viennese singer Rosl Schwaiger in 'the perfect setting for romantic opera' – Leopoldskron Castle. 1945. (Lee Miller)

occupying forces were forgotten. A bemedalled Russian shared a score with an aristocratic Hungarian landowner who had fled the approach of the Red Army a few weeks before. The dozen languages of a dozen peoples were laid aside while they listened to the grand purity of Handel's Messiah or were enraptured by Mozart. Music was everywhere and musical shop-talk became the lingua franca of Salzburg.[2]

It was the opera that Lee fell in love with and, in particular, the opera stars. The performer who stole the festival was Rosl Schwaiger, a local girl from a poor family whose father had managed to send her to the Mozarteum. In her manuscript for *Vogue*, Lee described Schwaiger as 'a dainty little girl who looks as if she were pretending to be grown up, wearing a pink fichu, her hair on top of her head, and stockings instead of socks. I heard her sing Blondchen in *Abduction from the Seraglio*. She had everything – acting ability, personality and a startling soprano voice.'

Schwaiger took Lee to see Max Reinhardt's former residence, Leopoldskron Castle, which overlooked a lake. They thought the bomb-blasted gardens and shuttered windows the perfect setting for romantic opera, and Schwaiger flitted through the rubble singing arias.

Romanian-born Maria Cebotari sang Constanze in *The Abduction* with true bravura despite spending several nights at the bedside of her film-star husband, Gustav Diesel, who had suffered a heart attack.

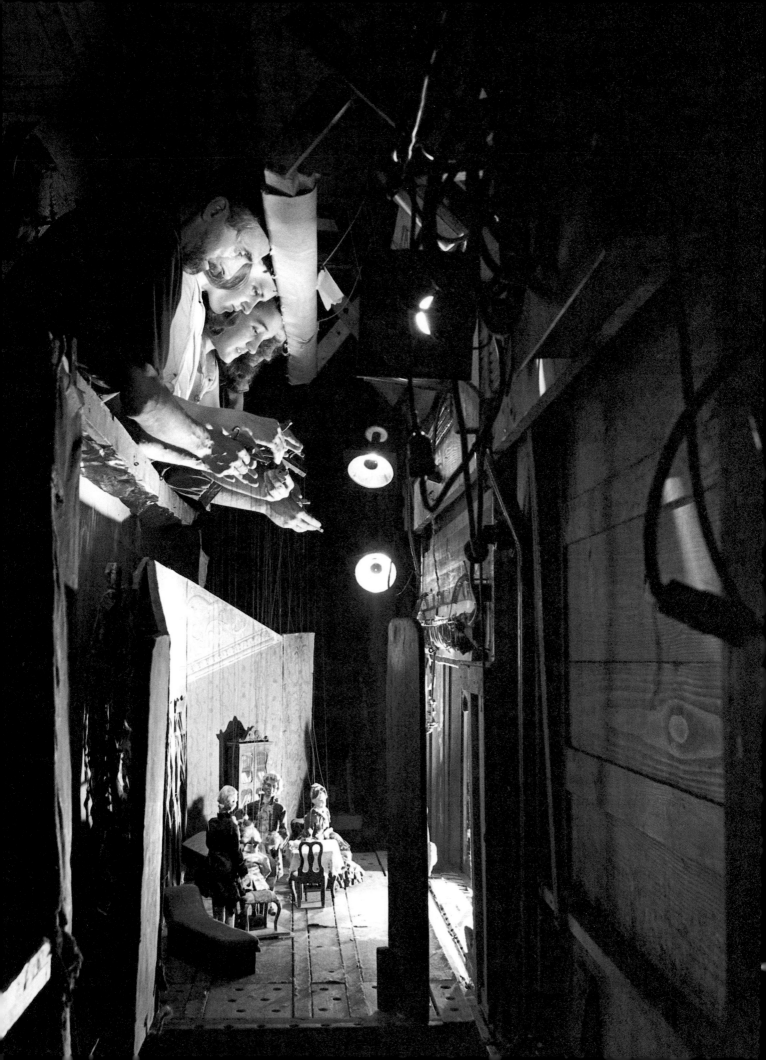

Maria Cebotari suggested visiting the famous White Horse Inn at Saint Wolfgang. She thought nothing of climbing into the back of a canvas topped weapons-carrier to zip thirty miles of sharp turns and sharp braking. She was thrilled with the rare opportunity a civilian has for travelling. I'd always thought opera stars babied their voices and gargled at unsociable intervals but she paid no attention to her flying hair and the whirling dust. She has a warm voice and warm personality.[3]

The marionettes of Hermann Aicher were speaking English for the benefit of the British and American soldiers. Operettas were performed with singers hidden under the floor boards. One show, a Jules Verne spoof, was about an individual who gets invited to travel in a space rocket.

The rocket whooshed across the three foot wide stage with a bang and a shower of sparks, all too redolent of the V1s we were on the receiving end of last year. It lands on a queer planet where all the flowers dance and talk and the inhabitants look like beetles. There are skinny lizard-like creatures crawling around with greenish skulls and protruding ribs, making squawking noises . . . it's a comedy, but I didn't laugh. The rocket is serious and the lizard beasts were like Dachau.[4]

After ten days in Salzburg, Lee left for Vienna. Fearing bandits who were said to operate in remote areas, she enlisted the company of Fred Wackernagle, a reporter for the US Army Informational Services Branch. On the east side of Linz they showed their papers and were issued with a rich pearl-grey card with their names in flowing italics that looked more like an invitation to a *vernissage* at a snob art gallery. Threading through

Opposite: The marionettes of Hermann Aicher. Salzburg, 1945. (Lee Miller)

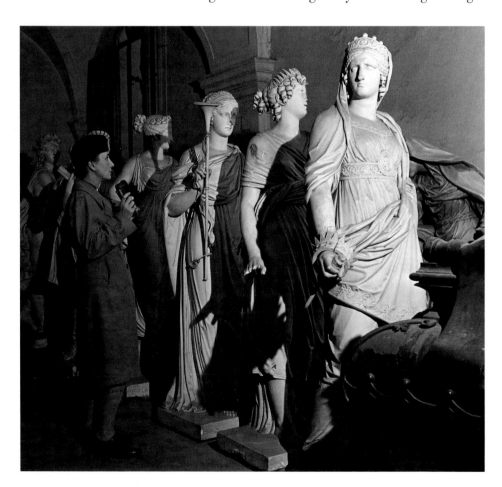

Statues queue in the shelter where they were moved for safe keeping. Vienna, 1945. (Lee Miller)

the byroads, they came to a checkpoint at a little bridge over a small river. Two Russian- and German-speaking American sentries manned one end, and two Soviet guards were stationed at the other. It was the usual routine of wisecracks at the American end: 'Say, lady, are you a driver or a nurse?' or, 'Say, lady, how long do you think that car will hold together?' 'Take my pitcha an pudit ina paper, lady!' and, eyeing up the cases of equipment in the back of Lee's car, 'Isn't it just like a woman to have so much luggage?'

The few road signs necessary for the limited traffic were painted white on infantry badge blue in cabalistic letters – candelabras, bedsteads and an assortment of our letters and numbers upside down or backwards like a witch's looking glass. At main town intersections Russian traffic M.P.s wigwagged indecipherable messages of stop and go with red and yellow flags, then with sleight of hand as complicated as the Great American Knife And Fork Switch Over When Eating they managed a smart salute as the car passed. At each of the climbing hairpin bends approaching Vienna a traffic signalman was doing this trick but I couldn't salute back as pulling my tail loaded car around the bends was two-handed work.[5]

Vienna was divided into five zones of occupation: Soviet, French, American, and English, with the fifth and most fraught being internationally controlled. No chauvinistic trick was overlooked in the rivalry that ensued, but the cleverest ruse was the division of the city into three separate time zones, with the result that Lee always found herself turning up either two hours too early or two hours too late for everything. It was a wonderful opportunity for the bureaucrats and they made the most of it. All permits had to be in quadruplicate – one for each nation – but some passes did not remain valid long enough for them to be completed with a countersignature at the next country's offices.

All the hotels had been taken over by the military, and hostelries of all classes sported two bayonetted guards of some nationality on the doorstep. Light music seemed pervasive – too light and frothy for empty stomachs. Because food was strictly rationed, with fish and meat practically unobtainable, malnutrition and its related diseases were rife throughout the civilian population. The American forces were characteristically well supplied but the other nations were much less fortunate. To ease their lot, some enterprising Russian soldiers rigged up a striped awning to trawl the partly dried-up ornamental pond in the Belvedere Gardens. They soon had a bucket filled with wriggling carp, but the last two fish eluded capture until a soldier drew his revolver and shot them.

Worst of all was the shortage of drugs and other medical supplies. These were available only to the military, and the glossy well-equipped civilian hospitals were crammed with patients who had little hope of survival. Diapers and bandages could be made from the soft brown paper wrapping from aircraft parts, but there was no substitute for penicillin. Lee visited a children's hospital and cabled this to Audrey Withers:

For an hour I watched a baby die. He was dark blue when I first saw him. He was the dark dusty blue of these waltz-filled Vienna nights, the same colour as the striped garb of the Dachau skeletons, the same imaginary blue as Strauss'

Danube. I'd thought all babies looked alike, but that was healthy babies; there are many faces for the dying. This wasn't a two months baby, he was a skinny gladiator. He gasped and fought and struggled for life, and a doctor and a nun and I just stood there and watched. There was nothing to do. In this beautiful children's hospital with its nursery-rhymed walls and screenless windows, with its clean white beds, its brilliant surgical instruments and empty drug cupboards there was nothing to do but watch him die. Baring his sharp toothless gums he clenched his fists against the attack of death. This tiny baby fought for his only possession, life, as if it might be worth something, and as if there weren't a thousand more right here on the doorstep of the hospital waiting for a bed as an arena for their losing battle.

At this point in Lee's notebook her pencil slashed at the paper as her rage boiled over: 'This is a silly, fatuous, stupid town – it's not evil, wicked or tragic. Tragedy is the fate of the undeserving, not the earned justice of the wicked Nazis.'

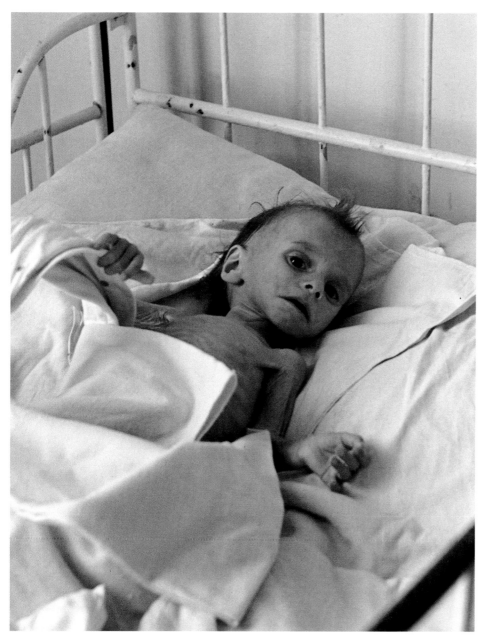

Child dying in Vienna's splendidly equipped children's hospital, which had everything but drugs. 1945. (Lee Miller)

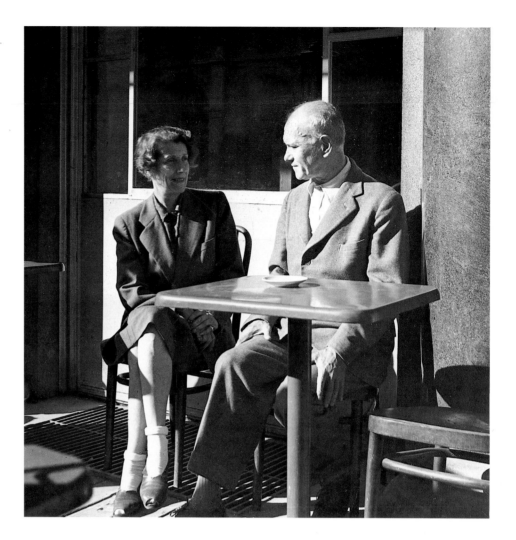

Nijinsky in Vienna with his devoted wife, Romola. She hid him from the Nazis, fearing that he might be a victim of their 'mercy death' campaign because of his mental illness. 1945. (Lee Miller)

Opposite: Opera star Irmgard Seefried singing an aria from *Madame Butterfly* in the burned out Vienna Opera House. 1945. (Lee Miller)

Amid all the despair and depression, and living precariously in the internationally controlled zone, was an amiable, demented old man – Nijinsky. The Nazi policy of so-called mercy deaths for the insane had forced his wife to keep him hidden throughout the war. His confused senses were just getting used to the idea of being able to walk in the street again or sit at a café. Lee described him in the same cable:

He's like a nice speechless backward child and goes out with his nurse to the park to sit and think his own thoughts while his wife Romola bucks the various frustrations of modern Vienna, regulations, queues, evictions, permits, barter and blackmail, all multiplied by four nations' paper work. They had been on their way to America when they got stopped in Hungary who'd been neutral. When Germany moved in they were scheduled for a concentration camp but managed to settle for house arrest. Waiting until they believed the Gestapo were busy elsewhere, they broke away and hid in Sopron until the battle and our airbombing overtook them. Their villa alone in the whole street was left standing. Nijinsky's excitement at the sound of Russian after his fright during the battle made him forget his fear of uniforms. He spoke for the first time and danced around the bivouac fire. The soldiers were shocked that the great Nijinskaya had no shoes, and looted a red leather sofa from under the debris next door and cobbled her a pair of sandals. They aren't quite Perugia, but they carry her on the constant walking and standing errands which comprise modern living here.

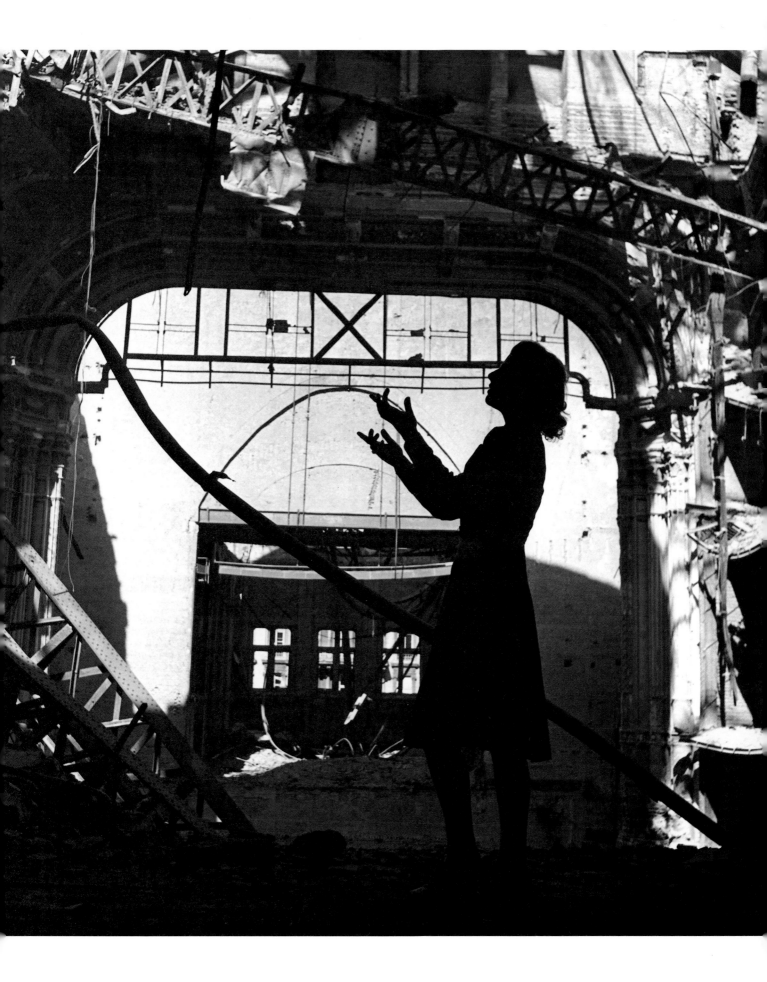

To an extent Lee was killing time in Vienna. She wanted to be where it was hardest to get to. It proved impossible to obtain visas for Moscow despite Audrey Withers' intervention, so next-door Hungary became her objective. The perversity of heading for the Balkans in the middle of winter may have added to the attraction of entering a country that was virtually a closed door for most people. The paperwork for Lee's clearance dragged on for weeks. There was a continuous round of queueing at the different military missions, usually to be told that some additional technicality needed clarifying, which would mean five more visits to different offices over the next three days.

For company on these boring gloomy occasions Lee had a kitten she had rescued from the gutter. Named 'Varum', he went everywhere buttoned into the tunic of her uniform. With the unfailing psychic power of all cats, Varum knew just when to emerge and be an amusing distraction and he invariably worked wonders with stuffy officials – except for one. As he strutted across the desk of a colonel in the Soviet Mission, a door slammed. Having lived through gunfire and bombs, Varum associated unpleasant events with bangs, so he bolted, knocking over the ornate inkstand and flooding the desk top. The Colonel leapt to his feet, roaring like a bull; the door flew open, and an armed sentry burst in. Varum took in the scene at a glance. Clearly the only safe place in the world was Lee's bosom and he made for it at speed – via the desk top. Ink splattered everywhere as he got up speed for his leap towards Lee. Totally disregarding the inky paws and the roaring colonel, she stuffed him into her tunic and fled.

She filled in the days of waiting for the passes by 'goofing off' with the other correspondents or indulging her newfound interest in opera. The opera star Irmgard Seefried took Lee to visit the burned-out remains of the opera house. The whole building was gutted, as the roof above the stage had caught fire first and the proscenium had acted as a giant fireplace. Standing on a plank across a drop into the ruins of the auditorium, Seefried sang an aria from *Madame Butterfly*. The acoustics remained impressive and the crashing of hammers and falling masonry were a dramatic counterpoint.

When the travel permits came through, the boondoggling had to stop. Lee was not entirely sure if she was pleased or sorry to be on her way again. On 25 October, against all advice, she set out in the Chevrolet with Varum and two passengers to drive cross-country to the Hungarian border.

Lee being massaged by a Romanian dancing bear. She called it, 'The only effective treatment for fibrositis'. 1946. (Harry Brauner)

Chapter Nine

The Last Waltz: Eastern Europe 1945–1946

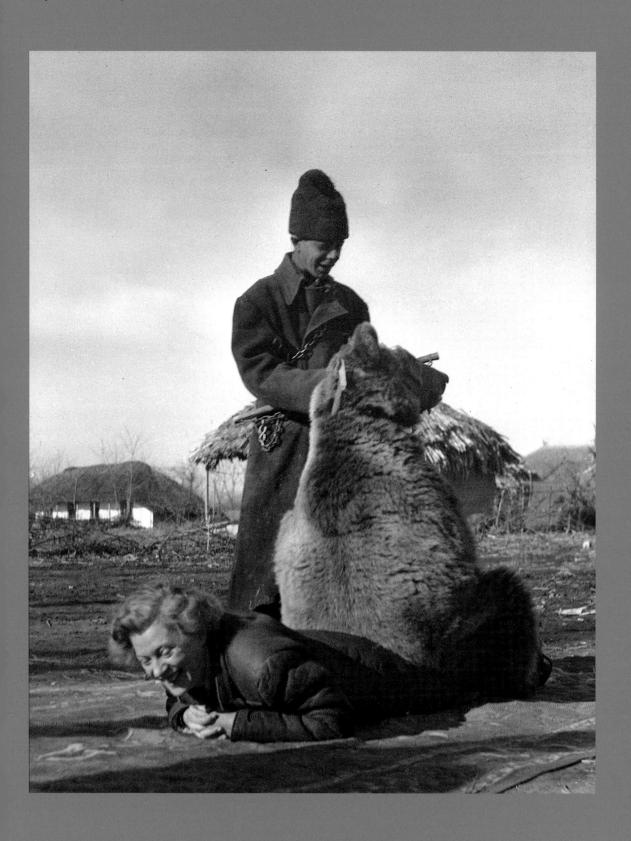

Lee's sense of achievement and elation at finishing her long and difficult journey to Budapest is evident in a letter she wrote to a friend she had left behind in Vienna. The person has never been identified but that fact is not important. This may be yet another letter Lee did not post. Perhaps she never intended to do so, and this was her way of recording her adventures and organizing her thoughts.

Thurs Eve, Oct 25 '45

Dear Ralph,

You all should really have made a pool or laid some side bets on whether I'd reach destination or not – what were the odds anyway? It was a long deserted road and the guards told me I was the only one to go thru that day.

The adventures were good cinema and included a chase by armed Russian guards who closed in on my car from both sides. One of them swerved around in front blocking me off. With the greatest of innocence I had driven through a check-point. An extremely gruff ruffian hauled my two passengers out and they were tommy-gun-waved into one of the cars. He got in beside me and growled at me about *schnell* and other directions. His large revolver dug in my ribs quite uncomfortably, and Varum decided to be playful, causing me to reach round and grab him several times, which annoyed my guard even further. Naturally I was driving as slowly as conceivable – it was an extremely bad stretch of road, so when he insisted on my going faster I hit a bump, braked and smashed his nose against the windshield, which toned him down for the next ten kilometers. After going to several different buildings in Bruck we finally alit at a main Kommandatur and were received by a full colonel, a major and other assorted characters. Everyone was extremely courteous but puzzled by the combination of an American driver, a Hungarian major with jaundice and an Austrian radio artist who was travelling for the Red Cross.

An extremely handsome, charming Lt Colonel arrived to take charge of the situation. He spoke better English than us, had a great sense of humour and all his wits about him. After a cross examination of why I, an accredited war correspondent, should be assigned as driver, instead of secretary or colleague, we discussed movies and new books. He will probably try to get orders for Vienna immediately as he was so interested in the film situation in Austria. My papers were in order, except the fine letter from Major Betz was written on such bad quality paper that no one could really believe it carried the authority of the American Government. We settled for the paper shortage being caused by so many triplicates, and departed.

At the Hungarian frontier there was some inspection of the actor's Hungarian passports. Already it was late and dark. The Danube had been like a mirage for hours before Budapest rose like a jewel-studded icon across the water. I was tired of driving, three in the front. The strain had been terrific all day, and the Bristol hotel was frightening – empty, gloomy and smelling of damp plaster and rat turds. My companions insisted on finding a better place for me so we promised to return and barged off. Varum, who had enchanted and softened hearts all day was still full of energy and charm. I didn't miss him until we went into the Astoria. He'd last been seen on my seat as we got into the car from the Bristol and I slewed there like a fire-engine, hoping to see a little pair of green eyes in the headlights. He was lying on the pavement, quite dead – all fluffed out and arched like when he was pretending to be a warrior. I couldn't even cry, for five minutes, but when I did, my tears were the accumulation of weeks of frustration bursting on the doorstep of my objective as well as the loss of my pet. The Astoria took me into a bare sheet-less room and your alarm clock awoke me to a new day; I'd put my red scarf (ex-Nazi flag) on the pillow so that at least it'd be my own dirt, and

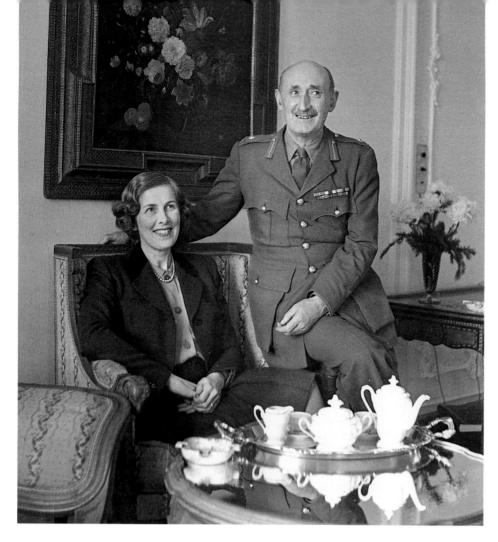

Major General O. K. Edgecombe, OBE, MC, and his wife. Edgecombe was Commanding General of the British Military Mission to Hungary. Budapest, 1945. (Lee Miller)

the color came off on my nose and eyes from crying. In spite of that some M.P.s invited me to their mess which is wonderful. Having been given and eaten scrambled eggs, I then ate three fried ones. The coffee was good, the butter was real and the toast was not slightly charred warm bread. The conversation was heartening. The sergeant in charge of passes said they'd been expecting me for weeks, where'd I been? Colonel Hegge said I couldn't live at the Astoria, but must move to the convent which is where I am now listening to the tramcars grind by.

Had a drink at the Park Club after dinner, before returning to write you this FYI. Walking along the street with a British girl correspondent dressed in civilian clothes, I felt like a lesbian. I had my little Walther in my hand in my pocket and felt very odd being protecting strength to someone.

The main Colonel of the U.S. mission was there at the bar, and in banter with us gave a sinister foundation of his real policy. He said that correspondents interfered with his business and the work of the mission – they caused too much trouble and only came down on a binge camera hunting. Senators were even worse and spend sometimes five thousand dollars in a day – but at least did not get into bar room fights like the journalists. He didn't think anyone ever filed a story, and that they were taking advantage of their position as correspondents to junket around. Now he was happy because he had handed over all question of passes to the Russians and they could deal with keeping everyone out as they liked – and damn well did. At the same time he admitted that the Russian general was fed up with seeing 36 names on the list of people accepted to come here, when only a very small percentage were sufficiently interested to turn up after all the work to clear them. In fact, where had I been for all these weeks . . . . . ? Well I'm glad I'm here, but my delay does look as if it was only my own fault for not grabbing that old bull by the balls several weeks earlier, and getting a move on myself. Also I miss you.

Love Lee

The Hungarian fascist troops and their German allies had been cut off from the rear and had holed up in Budapest in a desperate stand against the Russians. They were driven back to the ancient Turkish fortress of Buda and conducted the last defence of the seven week siege from the cellars and tunnels hewn beneath the fortress. The airless and dirty bunkers were already crammed with refugees who had fled there at the beginning of the fighting, expecting it to last only a few days. The bridges across the Danube linking Buda and Pest were all smashed, and the temporary ones that replaced them were frequently swept away by ice floes.

An unpublished part of Lee's manuscript for *Vogue* reads:

The wall enclosed Var section housed the great names and families of Hungary in graceful houses in narrow streets. Artillery fire and tactical bombing has crushed and battered the palace and the homes, it scarred the coronation church and blasted the little confiserie, Ruszwurm, where for the last quarter of a century the hundred-year-old spun-sugar reliefs of bouquets and weddings defied the heat of slander and the fog of corruption as the wives of ministers and palace officials, of traitors and the few men of good faith, battled over teacups and invitation-lists to dispose of democracy and geography along with the careers of their men-folk.

The Sisters of Mercy Catholic Convent where Lee was billeted was on the Stefania Ut. It had become the unofficial press camp for US journalists, with John Phillips of *Life* and Simon Bourgin of *Stars and Stripes* already in residence. Lee decided she needed an interpreter and an assistant and the right place to start looking seemed to be the studio of the distinguished Budapest photographer, Bela Halmi. She found that the maestro had been gaoled on a convoluted charge that was never fully explained, but in his absence the studio was being run by his son Robert, who was quietly playing a game of chess when Lee burst in. Chespy, as Lee dubbed him, had escaped from a German prison camp in Czechoslovakia and had barely survived the siege of Budapest when the building he was hiding in was bombed. He spoke fluent Ukranian, Russian, Hungarian and English, and had the guile and disposition that enabled him to travel with comparative freedom. These latter qualities were to prove most useful at a time when people with cameras around their necks were generally unwelcome.

Many years later Halmi recalled:

Lee's story was 'Women's Fashions After The Siege'. The Russian battle with the Germans had left half the city in ruins. The story was bullshit: I found the girls I knew, and any rag on them became fashion. The girls were so pretty that fashions didn't matter. I was with Lee round the clock. I was not attracted to her. She was way too masculine for a young Hungarian. She wore those baggy army slacks most of the time and she drank too much. She was an excellent photographer and she knew what she was doing. She was also absolutely fearless. She probably

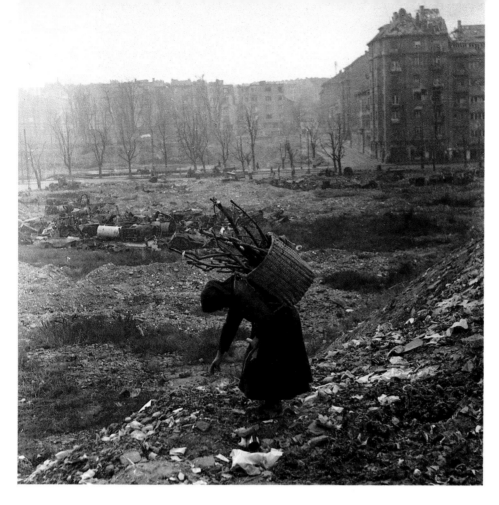

'Field of Blood'. Budapest, 1945.
(Lee Miller)

would have been raped a hundred times if the Russians hadn't thought she was a boy. And she had a marvellous sense of humour. It was one of her best features. We got to be good friends and I took her home every night when she got loaded. It wasn't easy-going at the convent: Lee had given the nuns lipstick and silk stockings, and Margit Schlachta, the Mother Superior, strongly objected. She said, 'You don't do that in a convent.' I said that we didn't know. There were hysterics when one of the nuns came into Lee's room one morning and found me astride her, rubbing her back, as she lay in bed. I was trying to revive her, and I did this every morning. She had discovered she could get out of her hangover this way, and she preferred it. Schlachta told us, 'We don't do that either' – in Hungarian of course. I told her, 'I'm sorry, I didn't know, I never lived in a convent.'

After Lee had been at the convent for nearly a month, she rescued some Hungarian refugees from being run in by the Russians. She installed the refugees in her room, and moved in with Bourgin and Phillips. Mother Superior was outraged: 'We have survived the Milos, we have lived through the Nazis and the Communists, but you people are the limit!' she exclaimed. The inevitable happened when another correspondent was caught entertaining a whore in his room: they were evicted *en masse*.

Social life in Budapest revolved round the Park Club. This glamorous haven had been one of the world's most exclusive clubs, the treasured domain of the Hungarian aristocracy who, by this time, had been dispossessed of practically everything except their titles. They now relied on invitations from the present incumbents, the allied officers of the control commission, for access to this bastion of their former privilege. Thanks to the incredible rate of inflation which rendered the Hungarian

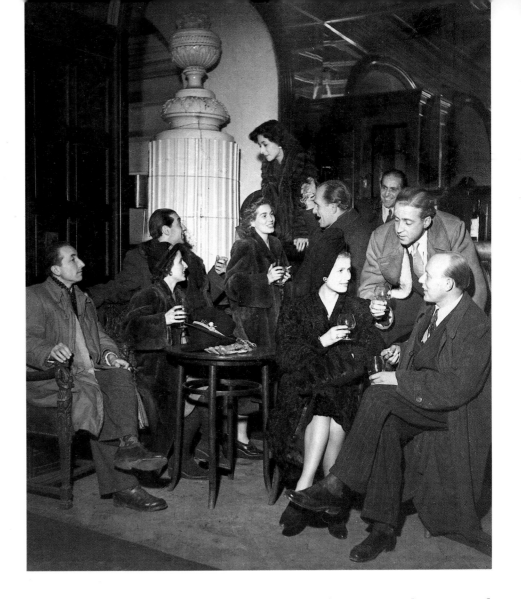

Hungarian aristocrats clinging to the last vestiges of gracious living at the Park Club, Budapest. 1945. (Lee Miller)

pengo practically worthless, the hundred or so Americans, who were paid in dollars, found to their surprise that they were now the elite of the new aristocracy. It was natural that the Americans who appreciated luxury and the aristocrats who remembered it fondly should get on so well. The British, who had the misfortune to be paid in pengos, and the Russians, who hardly got paid at all, did not fare so well.

Invitations to the Park Club were avidly pursued by Hungarian intellectuals and displaced *bons viveurs*. The attraction was not only the chance of a good feed and entertainment by the 'Two Georges', a band who were the envy of all other bands in Budapest because they had the latest sheet music flown in from the United States. It was also, given the willing complicity of the waiters, the opportunity to sell the last gold cigarette case, or finally dispose of the diamond earrings, in return for those coveted dollars.

The regular Friday night gala party was the most sought-after occasion because it was the last chance to pick up an invitation for a weekend's shooting. The sport had become a business enterprise, since the game was sold to restaurants all over the city. Only the best shots were invited, as it did not pay to average more than two cartridges per kill. The shooting took place on vast estates by the people who had only recently been dispossessed of them. It was not unusual for a count or baron to meet the new landowners who only a few months ago had been his former servants. Conscious that a reversal of fortunes always remained a possibility, the new owners would bow low to their former masters and say, 'I beg pardon for trespassing on your property – please forgive me – I dream of the day you return.' It was good insurance against the next change of power.

In the countryside food production ground to a halt as peasants refused to part with their produce for worthless currency, and most people in the towns resorted to barter. A shopping trip necessitated carrying a huge laden basket both ways. A kilo of salt, a stolen uniform, some empty bottles, loot from the homes of people who had been interned, were all items that could be swapped for food. It was the lower classes of urban people who suffered the most. Rural peasants fell back on self sufficiency. Craftsmen who had a skill to barter fared the best.

The aristocrats' only resources, apart from their few salvaged heirlooms, were their wits and natural resilience. Centuries of precarious tenure of wealth had ensured that they were made of stern stuff. John Phillips described them as the sort of people whose 'childhood nannies had made them run barefoot through nettles, and spanked them if they cried. Now they sought regular employment, and their wives did likewise. The latter became barmaids or cab drivers and walked to work in their mink coats, until these were sold.'[1]

Lee, however, was unimpressed by the men, listing 'drug running, abandoning pregnant girlfriends, blackmarketeering, stealing the penicillin supplies of the country, sleeping with their own or other people's wives knowing themselves to be infected with V.D., and accusing rivals of political alliances so they'll be slung in clink' as quite ordinary social behaviour. Of the women she wrote:

The women were brought up in a tough school. They learned courage and endurance and a long term sense of values. Some set of laws makes all women property-less, so girls knew from the first time they cried for a toy that they'd have to fight for everything they'd ever own – for husband, property and power. They were bullied by English nannies who gave the hot water bottles to the boys, they broke their bones out hunting, or bore children or mourned without a whimper, and they were devoted wives and looked beautiful.

Now it's paying off. What's left of the men all seem to sit in banks and offices despairing of the use of working. They struggle in ministerial political intrigues or continue their jobs as directors of foundering industries for a yearly salary which does not cover the electric light bill for a month. The women who are practical and logical knew that nothing would be done unless they did it with their own two hands so they rolled up their sleeves and took off their rings which they sell, one by one, and started doing it. Countess Pal Almassy, who was famous for her horses and internationally known as an equestrian, makes her living as a teamster on the reconstruction work of the Margit Bridge. Now after six months she owns two teams and employs a driver. In the glacial dawn she harnesses and feeds the horses and goes to the Danube to haul building blocks and debris.

Many of the 'expressos' and café restaurants are staffed by the former elegants of the town. In the beginning there was probably a snob value to the management in having baronesses and countesses wait on table or wash dishes,

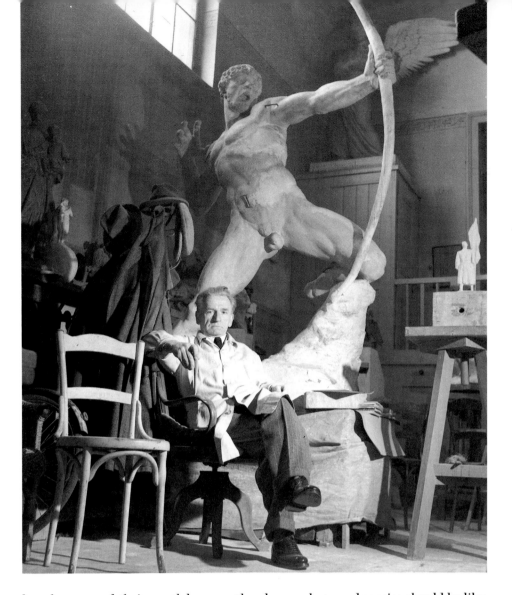

Sigismund Strobl, whose sculptures were much in demand by the Allies for war memorials. Budapest, 1945. (Lee Miller)

but they proved their worth because they knew what good service should be like and weren't ashamed to give it. In the winter these jobs are especially clung to – warmth, a meal a day and gossip with client friends. The waitresses' and nurse-maids' trades union register of Buda Pest reads like the Almanach of Gotha and these women, from practical experience with employers, now realise that maybe those horrible revolutionists, the 'Unions', had an idea.

Baroness Elisabeth Ullman 'bicycle-delivers' muffins her aunt made and Princess Gabrielle Esterhazy is now in the furniture delivery business, having used her covered wagon for food hauling during the siege.

The fortune of Count and Countess Joseph Teleki was wiped out after the last war in the bank failures and inflations of 1920. He became a director in a cheese factory and eventually retired in fairly frugal comfort though fragile health. Now they are broke again. They walk kilometers to the cheese factory and stagger back with a load to peddle door to door in the city, and no one, least of all themselves, find it pathetic that a deaf old rheumatic man and a thin delicate woman should have to start at the bottom again.[2]

Famous artists and scientists were far from immune from these misfortunes. Lee visited Albert Szent-Györgyi, the scientist who had won the Nobel Prize for his work on Vitamin C, and found him dissipating more of his energy in keeping himself and his staff fed and housed than in running his research experiments. He had been obliged to operate a black-market enterprise to fund his laboratory. The sculptor Sigismund Strobl

164

was in a better position because of the recent demand for war memorials by the Allies, particularly the Soviets, who were fond of commissioning lofty columns topped by victorious figures.

Seeking some adventures outside the city, Lee and Chespy made a trip to Mezőkövesd, a small town in the north-east famous for the richly decorated and embroidered dress of the peasants. October and November were particularly colourful months of the year. With the harvest safely gathered in, days getting shorter and time on their hands, young couples' thoughts turned to marriage, so courting and weddings were rife. Unmarried girls seeking husbands paraded the street in fours and sixes regularly in the evenings or all day on Sundays and holidays. A girl successful in her promenading soon found herself encased in a formidable arrangement of cascading waterfalls of white fringing, tied at the waist with coloured ribbons. Wedding feasts lasted several days and were attended by ambulatory gypsy bands who brought their romantic, sensuous music, poetry and customs.

Lee moved freely and photographed all over the village, aided by Chespy. She wrote:

I had just been talking to the most wondrous old 'dame' (for once I use the word correctly) who wore a head-dress of large pink pompoms and the black dress of mourning. She was sitting on the stove showing me how she did the freehand drawings of flowers for all the local women to embroider during their winter hibernation, except that now there's no more thread – when I got arrested.

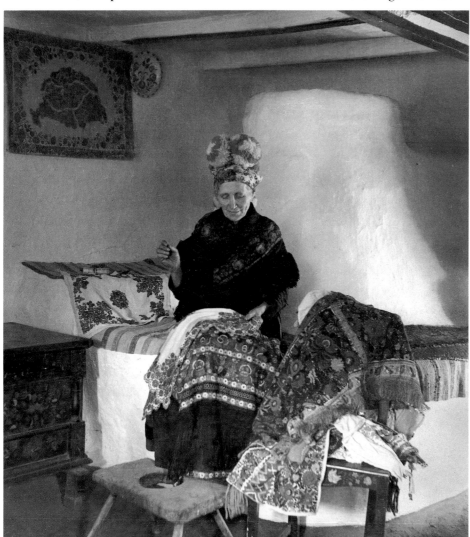

The 'wondrous old dame' Lee was photographing in Mezőkövesd when she was arrested. 1946. (Lee Miller)

The dusty little Russian soldier with the banjo-gun was in a hurry. He kept yelling DAH VYE!, DAH VYE! It means 'come on', but it is also Russian Army slang for 'hand over your watch or gun or whatever'. It's very frightening at first, to hear Russian soldiers talking to each other. They yell at the top of their lungs in a tone of voice like the preliminaries to an axe murder. The first time I heard a polite friendly conversation done in this manner I looked instinctively for cover and a place to duck when the shooting began. That conversation turned out to be about a happy outing the night before, and an invitation to the theatre.

I was taken to Miskolc, the provincial capital, and for the next few days I lingered round the *Kommandatur*. I sat in austere rooms under a photo of Stalin, to be interviewed, scrutinised and asked to wait by officers of various rank, amiability and branch of the service. Everybody was very polite and patient and I was given delicious cigarettes with long paper self-holders. I was under guard but not in jail, and was billeted in a good hotel at rates based on pre-war pengos. I taught the officer in charge of me that game with the paper napkin on a glass when you burn cigarette holes until finally the coin drops into the glass, and we solved all the fox and geese problems that can be done with coins as there were no matches. We made pictures of imaginary monsters by each drawing a head and passing it on hidden for the next to make the body. Hungarian playing cards baffled me as they have bells and other symbols that I am unfamiliar with, besides which the cards are circular.

I couldn't think what I had done wrong. Was it enough for Siberia? Would my cameras be seized? Would I be exiled from Hungary?

As soon as Lee was arrested, Chespy hurried back to Budapest. The situation was entirely familiar to him and he knew exactly what to do. In his studio he quickly faked a pass. It had to look important, so he made the cover of red card, with a photograph of Lee and lots of slightly smudged official looking rubber stamps. The wording proclaimed that Lee had permission to travel everywhere and take photographs of children.

The guards in Miskolc were extremely impressed and, never having seen a splendid red pass of such importance before, they released Lee immediately. By now they were all on such amicable terms that they probably felt embarrassed at keeping her under arrest. Lee continued her manuscript:

A few days later I went back to the scene of my crime and detention and called politely on my captors, who were delighted to see me, gave me a party and took me to the theatre. We danced in the café and made thousands of toasts to our presidents, prime ministers, our heroes and our absent friends. We described our countries, criticised our enemies and felt awful the next day.[3]

Before dawn a few days later Lee and John Phillips assembled in the icy anteroom next to the condemned cell of László Bardossy, the fascist ex-Prime Minister of Hungary who was about to be hanged as a war criminal. The power went dead in the prison and they waited interminably by the light of a broken-chimneyed smoky oil lamp. An unpublished part of Lee's manuscript reads:

When the gendarme beckoned us out we could hear the pressure and the murmur of the several hundred people with permission to witness the hanging waiting to get into the yard from the far side. They thought the delay meant that they were being barred from the performance. In the yard it was almost light – as light as it would probably ever get in that weather and between those walls. The whole set-up was being changed. Instead of the big beam-like vertical stake, attendants were stacking sandbags against the brick wall. They had changed their minds and were going to give him the dignity of a firing squad. The crowd surged in and clambered on windowsills – moved great big stones and shifted a wagon round to form a grandstand. There was a long wait.

Some officials with papers and dossiers came to the table under my window. Then, accompanied by a priest and some gendarmes and a noise of the silent crowd shifting, a cocky little man jaunted in from a dark archway. He wore the same plus-fours tweed suit, ankle high shoes with white socks turned over the edges as when he'd been arrested. He held his beaky grey face high and his gestures were taut. He listened to the words of the judge and as he walked in front of the sandbags he waved his hand refusing the blindfold. The four gendarmes who had volunteered for the execution stood in line awaiting the order to fire. They were less than two yards from him. Bardossy's voice orated in a high pitched rasp, 'God save Hungary from all these bandits.' I think he started to say something else but a ragged tattoo of shots drowned it. The impact threw him back against the sandbags and he pitched to his left in a pirouette, falling on the ground with his ankles neatly crossed.

He was dead before the sound of the guns at two meters could have reached him. The priest, who had been standing very close by, knelt and prayed for ten minutes. He had a bad cold and kept reaching up his lace edged sleeve for a very tatty handkerchief. The prison doctors listened to the bared silent chest. The little gold cross on a chain lay over one of the three bullet holes. The fourth bullet had hit him on the chin which was covered with a handkerchief. At my usual hangout, the Café Floris, everyone was talking about the hanging. 'Wasn't it disgraceful, hanging, a common criminal's end for a distinguished brilliant Prime Minister?' I globbed a large drink and remarked, 'It's alright, he'd been shot after all'. 'No, he'd been hanged!' and they went on with their stories. Next edition he'd been shot and writhed in agony for forty minutes. No absolution had been given, and the press forbidden to take pictures. And so the embroiderers added and added. Finally, he'd be a great hero, and one day I'd be walking down a reverently named 'Bardossy Street' to the execution of the present democratic leaders. I gave up and left Hungary to its world of fable.[4]

László Bardossy, fascist ex-Prime Minister of Hungary, facing the firing squad. Budapest, 1946. (Lee Miller)

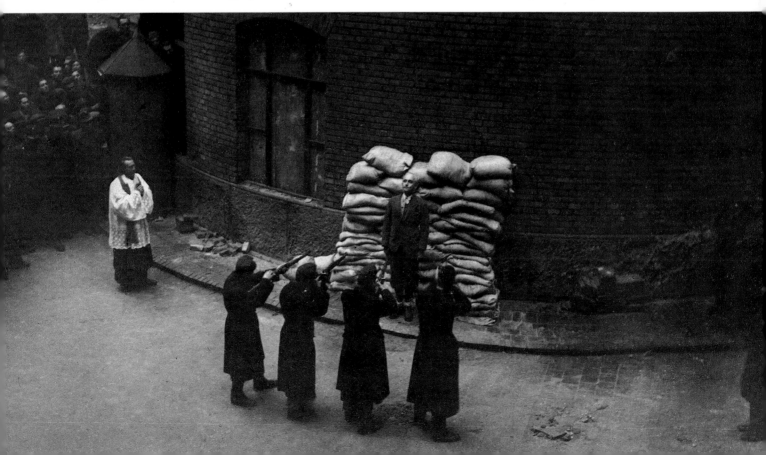

Christmas and New Year passed in Budapest, in a series of wild drunken parties at the Park Club with the correspondents and their aristocratic acolytes. John Phillips, an expert at making a screeching whistle through his fingers, recalled that on New Year's Eve he whistled through Lee's fingers, something that he had never done before. Beneath the frivolity there were always the tragedies; Lee and her colleagues found themselves inextricably involved in trying to help by getting hold of penicillin, donating blood for a sick child, fixing passes for refugees or trying to get people out of goal. The war was no longer full of heroic gains and reversals centering on bombed refugees or the suffering of soldiers. It was now the universal massive misery of countless pathetic civilians, and even the most inured could not fail to be drawn into an attempt to alleviate such suffering.

Neither Phillips nor Lee seemed to have the remotest idea of what they were actually trying to achieve in their wanderings around the Balkans. 'It's my damned itchy feet,' Lee wrote to Dave, 'they just won't let me stop moving.' Lee's 'excuse' for further travel was of course her work for *Vogue*, but Harry Yoxall was getting more than a little uneasy as the bills for Lee's expenses kept thudding in and the flow of usable material slowed to a trickle. The reality was that Lee was on the run from herself.

Romania was her next bolt-hole. At the end of January she took a fond farewell of Chespy and, with Phillips in Jemima the Chevrolet, and Phillips' driver Giles T. Schultz accompanying them in a decrepit jeep, headed across the wide southeastern plains of Hungary. In places the land was so flat and utterly featureless that the curvature of the earth made the horizon circumscribe a perfect circle around them. The cars crawled like insects on a meridian carelessly scrawled across a flat disc that hung in space. On the Romanian border the country changed gradually to become more rolling and then came the sharp, wooded undulations of the northern foothills of the Transylvanian Alps. In her article for *Vogue*, Lee wrote:

Through eyelids tightly squeezed against the brilliance, I peered at a snowy expanse of white plains and lovely mountains topped by blue skies. It was Roumania, and a late blizzard had made it anonymous. Transylvania, this province, had slightly ambiguous nationality anyway: every war puts it on the other side of the Hungarian frontier. Now it is Roumania again, like it had been when I was there in 1938.

I was rhapsodic about Roumania. The people were Latins, the language was understandable, or at least readable, if you knew French or Italian and subtracted the final 'iuls' from the words. In case you couldn't read, every shop had gay, primitive paintings by the door, of pork chops, sausages, hats, gloves, hammers, saws and ploughs, whatever was stocked inside. The peasants wove their own textiles in traditional local patterns and stitched their sheepskin coats with bouquets, and the date of acquisition. In the market towns you could tell from which village any peasant came by the designs embroidered on his jacket, or the colour and weave of a scarf. They had swirling music, with patterns as bright as their costumes, and customs which were even more fanciful.

There were no road signs in the glaring wilderness. The Hungarian place names had been taken down and the Roumanian ones had not yet been put up. I might have been in Russia, or Michigan, or Patagonia instead of making slow progress through Transylvania. The roads were devilish – deep snow drifts alternated

'The prying eyes of Sibiu'. Romania, 1946. (Lee Miller)

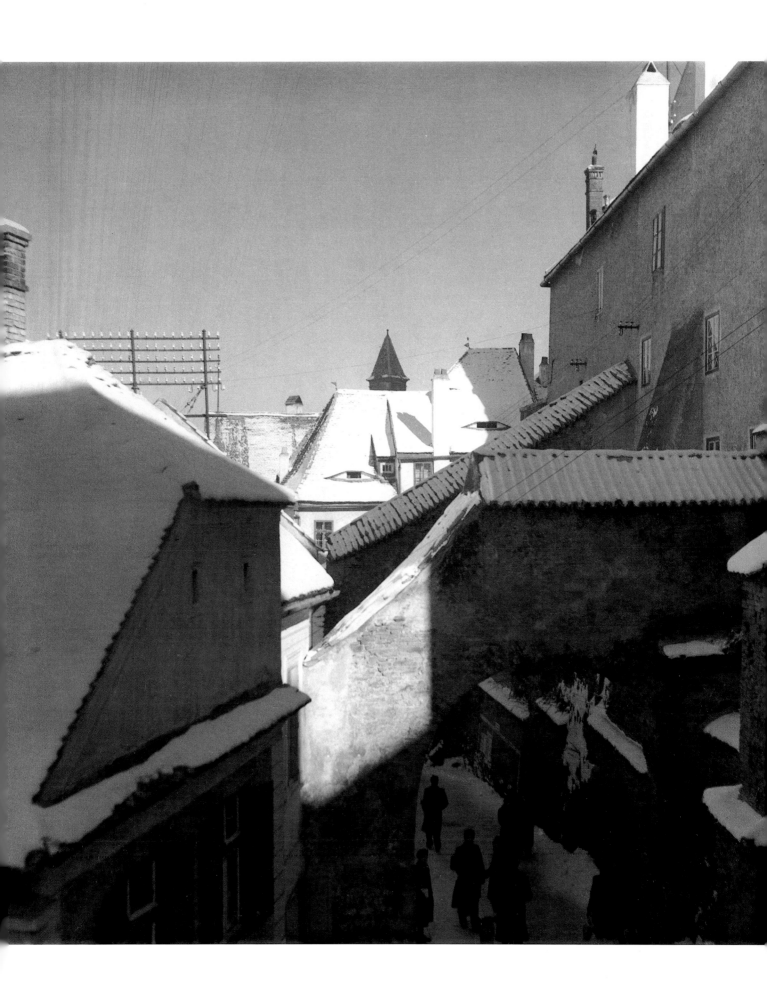

with icy curves where the sharp gale swept the road. By nightfall we still hadn't reached Sibiu, where we'd find a hotel. I remembered Sibiu as a mysterious-looking town. There are staircases in the streets, arcades under buildings, and the slanting roofs had little windows let into them, the shape of peering, prying, calculating eyes. I was thinking of the evil eyes of Sibiu when I went into a long whipping skid down a steep curve ending up in the wrong direction in a down-sloping snow bank.

John Phillips recalls Lee saying coolly, 'I am terribly sorry about this, John,' as the Chevrolet ploughed over the edge of the road, smashing through small saplings until it came to rest at a crazy angle. There was little they could do to budge it. A detachment of Russian soldiers almost succeeded in towing the car back onto the road with their truck, but gave up when their own vehicle nearly plunged over the edge. The jeep was scarcely mobile, but they piled all the most valuable things into it and set off to find help. By the time they returned, the rear window had been smashed and everything stolen. Clothes, rations, maps, petrol had vanished, but, worse still, so had all four wheels. Leaving a couple of Russian soldiers to guard the remains, Lee and her band retreated to Sibiu.

Lee's article continues:

This was a complete disaster. I finally slept on the two sleeping tablets I'd carried in my pocket since the war began, thrashing myself with bright ideas I'd been too tired and shocked by the rude punch of the steering wheel in my middle to create at the time. There were a dozen methods to have either prevented or remedied the accident, any one of which would have been sufficient. I shouldn't have been talked out of putting on the chains. We had been warned not to travel after dark, and we should have camped in blanket rolls in the local constabulary. I shouldn't have been thinking of the evil eyes of Sibiu, but of my driving. I should have unloaded jerry cans of gas and the luggage to lighten the car. I should have dug down to the soil and sprinkled the ice with dirt. I should have taken all my luggage in the jeep. I should have stayed with the car while the jeep fetched a guard. Not one of these endless possibilities came to me when the need arose – they only came in time to give me a sleepless night.[5]

The next morning among the dilapidated taxis of Sibiu they found an antiquated Chevrolet. They hired it for $1.50 an hour and unscrewed its wheels. Later that day, after plenty of risks and some strenuous efforts, the car was temporarily fitted with the borrowed wheels and driven to a garage where Lee formally abandoned it, lying in state jacked up on blocks. A fact she overlooked in her article is that the car actually belonged to Dave Scherman, who was none too pleased with the proceeds of his $1500 motor car, remitted many months later by Dr Eugene Popp of the American Military Mission. Dr Popp's genuine and diligent efforts netted only $250.

The first person Lee looked for in Bucharest was Harry Brauner. The last time she had seen him was in London just before the war, when he had brought a troup of Calusari peasant dancers to perform at the Folklore Festival at the Albert Hall. They had been a tremendous success, though the floors of their little Kensington hotel and of 21 Downshire Hill were nearly pulverized by their smashing footwork at rehearsals.

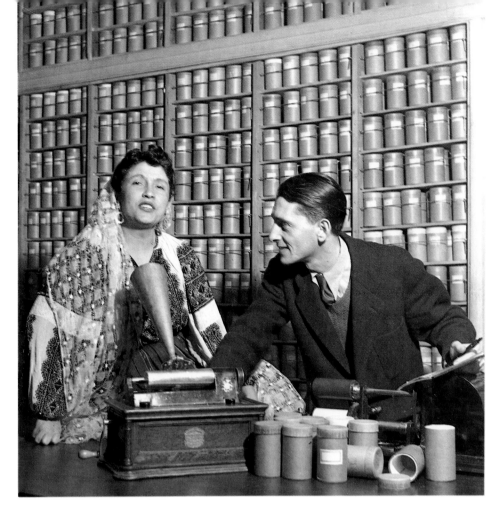

Harry Brauner recording a song by Maritza, the Romanian folk-singer. The drums contain folk-music recordings collected by Brauner at Bucharest University. 1946. (Lee Miller)

Harry was located at Bucharest University, where he had recently returned to the chair of Musical History after some near-fatal years condemned to a labour battalion. His immense library of cylinder recordings of gypsy and folk music miraculously remained intact.

Among her many imaginary conditions like 'starch poisoning', Lee had one genuine ailment – fibrositis, a muscular complaint aggravated by her frequent spells of hard living and sleeping on the ground in a blanket roll. She was sure that the only possibility of relief for her aching bones lay in being massaged by a Carpathian dancing bear. With Harry she set off to look for gypsy bear-owners, but government settlement orders and fascist persecution of non-Aryans had rendered both performing bears and gypsies nearly extinct. First they hunted through the gypsy quarters and the shanty towns of Bucharest looking for the old Bear Hotels. Lee described the occasion:

A Bear Hotel is really a café-courtyard where the animals sleep, their masters curled up alongside them to keep each other warm. Café hotels who cater to this clientele don't usually have any other guests.

We had no success until Harry Brauner activated his grapevine information service through the villages. Sixty kilometers away, a notary public, the only telephone subscriber in the place, said his village was a center of bear training. We hired the same ancient taxi with the amiable driver who had helped us search the outskirts, and rumbled forth into a mysteriously foggy country on frighteningly bumpy roads, squashed through snow and ruts to find a typical peasant community: thatched plaster houses, one-story high with dilapidated gardens. The mountains of sunflower stalks looked like the gypsy tents I'd known before the war. It seemed wrong for them to be living in houses.

There was only one bear left. One was all I wanted. . . . My bear was asleep. She was chained to a stake amid a litter of cornstalks. Two plumes of vapor snorted out of her nostrils at every breath in the frosty air. Sleepy and sulky, she snapped a few times at her keeper. There'd been no business all winter so she'd reverted to hibernation, and was cross at being put to work again.

They muzzled and led her to the open space in front of the owners' house where she continued growling and snarling until the music started. The shrill fifes and the thumping tambours urged her on her feet and she stamped around on her back legs in time to the different tunes played, both in solo numbers and partnered by her master.

Dozens of snotty-nosed brats pressed around, hooting, and nearly all the neighbours arrived to find out what was happening. I hadn't countenanced having such a big audience for my magical treatment, but that was not going to stop me.

I was invited to lie face down on a gaudy carpet they smoothed onto the frozen earth. Well, I'd asked for it and there it was! I showed Harry how to operate my Rolleiflex and had a lot of misgivings as I calculated kilos into nearly three hundred pounds. I caught sight of the beast's long paw-nails, and decided to keep on my coat, a local affair of reversed sheepskin, thick and tough. I was terribly cold anyway.

The bear knew her business. She walked up and down my back on all fours as gently as if on eggs. Each big paw felt its way until it found an area which wouldn't squash in, and the weight was transfered from foot to foot with very little change of pressure. As the music started again, she raised up on her hind legs and shuffled up and down my back. It was crushing and exhilarating. All my muscles clenched and relaxed to keep from being flattened. Then she was led off, to return, facing the other direction. She sat her great, furry, warm bottom down on the nape of my neck and, with gentle shuffles, went from my neck to my knees and back again. At first I kept my fists doubled-up underneath my collar bones so that I could trust her not to give an unexpected thump. The gulp of air I snatched as she moved each inch was enough, like swimming the crawl in a lake of lead.

I felt marvelous afterwards, racing circulation, flexible and energetic. I discovered I could move my neck and shoulders in patterns I'd forgotten. Here is the answer to 'Oh, my aching back'.

The owner was delighted. His virtue in not having risked his bearskin by travelling without movement orders from the gendarmerie had been rewarded. The money we gave him, the equivalent of a dollar and a half, was all we had left with us at the end of a couple of months peregrinations. At first he would accept nothing at all. He begged only that we should try to get the ban on bears lifted so they could wander around the country lawfully. It was tough explaining that it was a hygienic measure, and the gypsies were held to be typhus carriers, but we said we'd do what we could, although we disapproved and doubted any favourable results until after the epidemic months of early spring were passed.[6]

North of Bucharest, with its back against the south-facing slopes of the Carpathian Mountains, is the former summer capital of Romania – Sinaia. Its resort-like atmosphere of casinos, skiing and grand hotels seemed highly appropriate for the collection of several mismatched royal palaces. In the biggest and most fanciful, Lee was received by His Majesty King Michael and his mother Queen Helen, although they themselves lived in a cosy villa nearby. Lee wrote:

The formal, over-retouched portraits of a severe lady choked in beads I'd seen of Her Majesty in all the cafés and ministerial offices, flanked by starry-eyed

Queen Helen the Queen Mother in her palace at Sinaia, Romania. 1946. (Lee Miller)

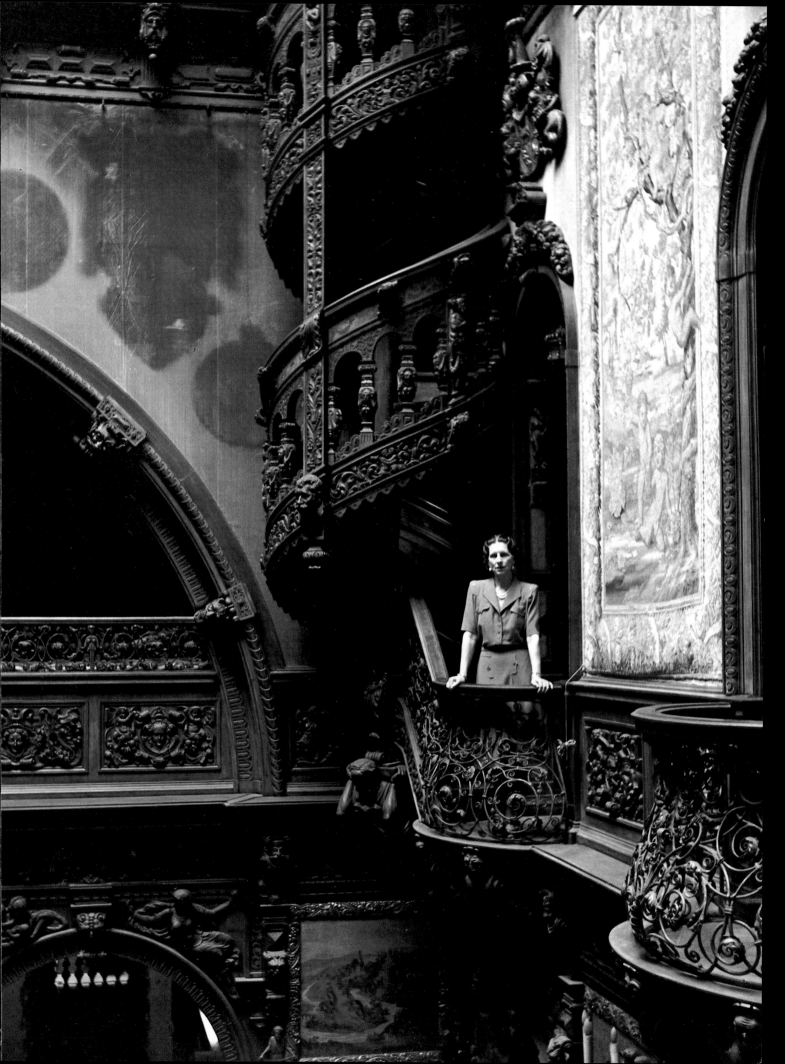

pictures of Michael at the age of 15, were poor preparation for meeting a graceful, beautiful woman with a sense of humour and a great deal of charm. She was dressed in green and even I recognised that the ostrich egg pearl earrings were real in spite of the fact that they, like her manners, were worn in the simplest possible way.[7]

Lee got on well with King Michael. He was strangely shy, she found, but she soon got him talking about his two passions in life – fast cars and photographs. He used a Leica and did all his own processing and printing, with impressive results.

Not far from the palace and the resort, as a grim counterpoint, lay a vast US cemetery. Eight hundred graves had already been dug and filled, mainly with airmen who had lost their lives in the disastrous Ploieşti raids. The men from the War Graves Commission were still digging and the final death toll was expected to be over a thousand.

In a sense it was here that Lee dug a grave for part of herself. Her journey had come full circle as she crossed the trail she had laid with Roland Penrose and Harry Brauner eight years before. Physically and emotionally she was spent and there was no further place that she could summon the enthusiasm to visit. Try as she might to write the Romanian piece, the words would not flow. Assailed by rising panic and despair, she found she could neither stop nor go on. Through her self-alienation from Man Ray, Aziz and Roland she had forced herself into a position where she could not go back without a crushing loss of pride. She was broke, and therefore likely to have to become dependent again. Worse still, she had to recognize that since Berchtesgaden there had been none of the excitement that had provided that vital catalyst for her talent which could have assured her of continuing a productive and rewarding career. The factor that allowed her to master herself and channel her abilities had vanished. Lee's winged serpents had triumphed again. They had driven her into a corner from which there was no uncompromised escape.

The latest in a long line of unanswered letters from Roland Penrose was likely to be the last. He had despaired of continuously sending letters chasing after her and never getting so much as a flicker of response. The only way he could get any news of Lee was to keep pestering Audrey Withers. When he and Lee had pledged never to allow their love for each other to impinge on their individual freedom, this wall of silence was not what he had had in mind. By now he had been snubbed too long and found he was drawn towards a permanent relationship with another woman. He firmly stated that unless this last letter received a reply, he would assume that Lee was not returning.

It is doubtful that Lee would ever have responded to this threat but for a cablegram from Dave Scherman. Kathleen McColgan, seeking to warn Lee of her rival's presence in Downshire Hill, managed to telephone Dave in New York. Tracking Lee down through John Phillips, Dave cabled from New York: 'GO HOME'. More than a week elapsed before the reply came: 'OK'. If a telegram could convey a tone of voice, then this one would have exuded total resentment.

The cemetery at Sinaia where 1,000 US airmen who died during the Ploieşti raids are buried. 1946. (Lee Miller)

174

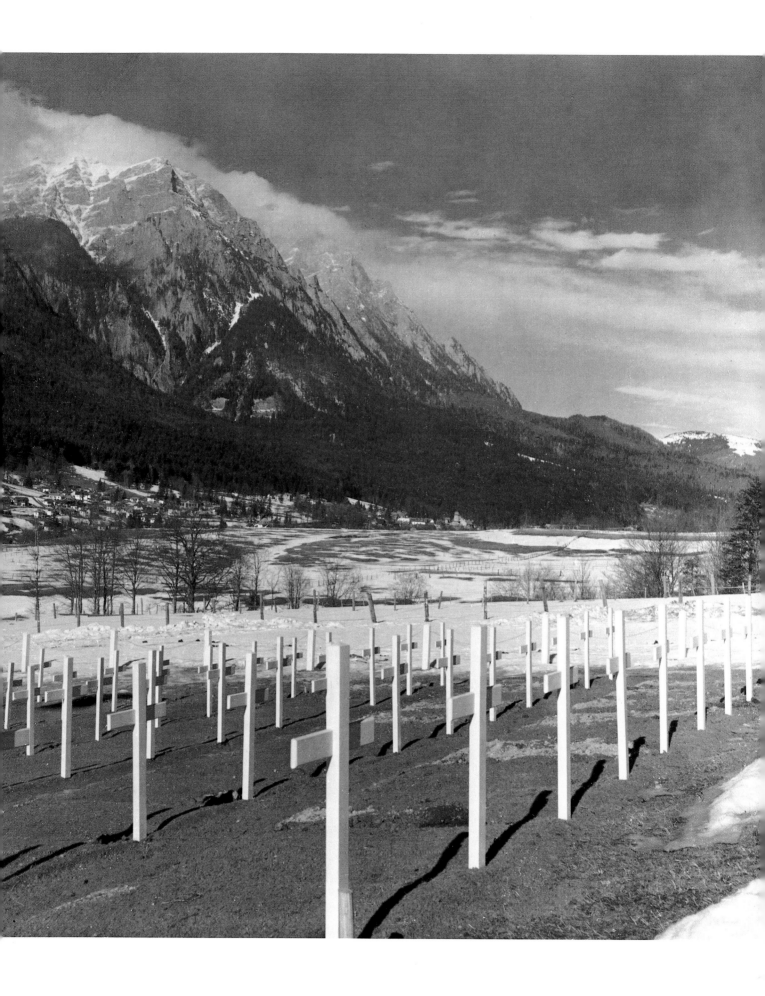

Lee returned to Paris, travelling mainly by rail. People who knew or had heard of the fabulous beauty of Lee Miller were staggered by the red-eyed haggard apparition that confronted them. She had contracted a disease which blistered her lips and made her gums bleed almost continuously. Her complexion was pasty and her blond hair lank. Whenever she tried to do anything intricate her hands shook with exhaustion. She stayed only long enough to collect a few things from the Hôtel Scribe before travelling on to London.

Lee and Roland were quickly reconciled. The rival departed amicably and Lee set about trying to recover both her health and her life. Late one evening, Roland was indulging Lee with one of her greatest passions: massaging her feet. Lee murmured, 'Darling, that's wonderful, it gives me such calm. If only someone had massaged Hitler's feet like that there would have been no massacres.' 'Whoever would have done that?' Roland asked incredulously. 'Mary Magdalen,' replied Lee.

Back in London on his way to France, Dave helped her through the usual agonies at the start of writing the Romanian story. Before she could finish, he had to leave to take up his job in Paris. Timmie O'Brien took over the invigilation, dispensing whisky and comfort in equal quantities. The article was acclaimed, and *Vogue* ran it in the May 1946 issue as a big spread using ten photographs, two of them full-page. It was the swansong of Lee's days of high adventure.

Homeless girls in Bucharest. 1945.
(Lee Miller)

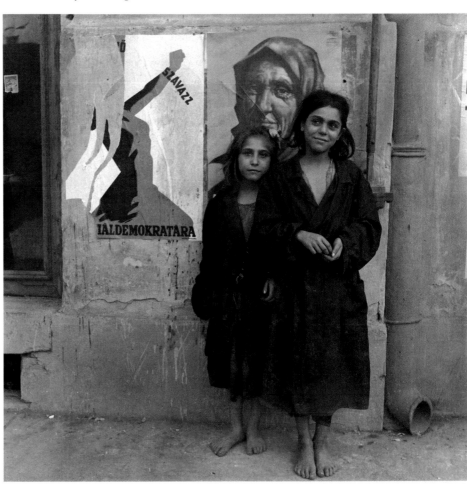

Opposite: Lee on a fashion assignment in Switzerland, March 1947.
(Photographer unknown)

Chapter Ten

Winged Serpents: Married Life in Hampstead and Sussex 1946–1956

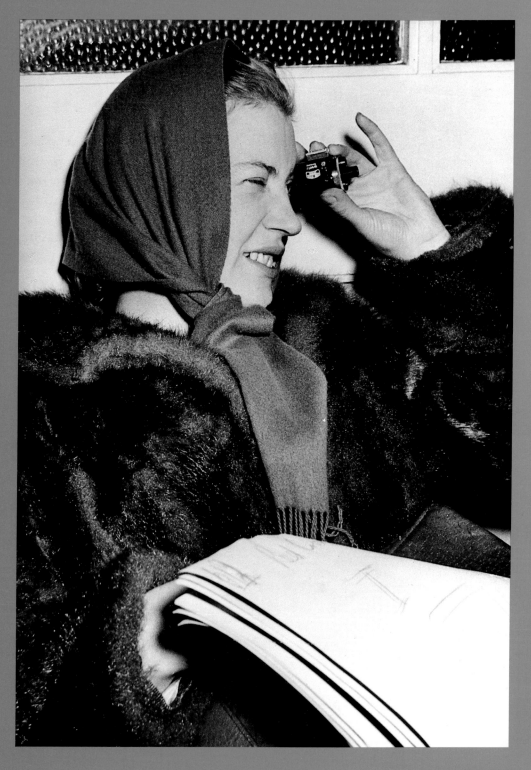

In the summer of 1946, the new scheduled air services gave Lee the welcome opportunity of visiting her parents in the United States. Roland was keen to make the trip, so in July they flew across the Atlantic.

Their first priority was a journey by train up the Hudson River to Poughkeepsie for a visit to the family home. It was nearly twelve full years since Lee had left as the bride of Aziz. Now she was returning, still as Mrs Eloui but with a different partner. The rarity of Lee's letters home left them guessing about her new lover. Theodore Miller had housed some of Roland's collection of paintings for the duration of the war, including a few of his own works, so the prospect of meeting the originator of these outlandish pictures added to their curiosity. Not for a minute did this natural inquisitiveness get in the way of the effusive welcome Lee's parents gave Roland. It was quite evident to them that he adored Lee, and she him, and that she seemed carefree and happy, but a touch of reserve lingered in the air.

The local paper sent round a photographer and a reporter who quizzed Lee about her exploits. The photographer posed the family group and was just about to click the shutter when Lee flew into a rage at a chance remark by her brother John, and stormed off. The family best-behaviour routine was shattered by this sudden return to the tantrums of childhood. Eventually Lee was coaxed back for the sake of the photographer, but the incident had served to blood Roland into the family.

In New York, *Vogue* was planning a celebration in Lee's honour and as part of their hospitality booked accommodation at the Sheraton Hotel. To Lee and Roland's dismay, they found that single guests were rigorously separated by being given rooms on different floors. The womens' floor was guarded by a beefy chatelaine stationed at the door from the lifts. All night this grumpy creature remained in the corridor, glowering from behind a small desk to discourage nocturnal wanderings among the guests. This was definitely contrary to Lee and Roland's scheme of things, but alas no other hotel room could be found.

Enquiries to their friends about a spare room were all met with polite refusals. Even Julien Levy, who was known to be leaving town for a while, could not help, but he did invite them round for a drink. That evening he phoned them at the Sheraton. 'I noticed that you only asked for beer,' he said gravely, 'and that you stubbed your cigarette in the ashtray. If you had asked for scotch I could not have considered this, but you are obviously more restrained than you used to be, so you can use my apartment while I am away.' They moved over the next day. His pleasant apartment was crammed with Surrealist paintings and they felt completely at home.

The *Vogue* party for Lee was both lavish and friendly, and it naturally spawned a succession of other parties. Among the new friends Lee and Roland made was Alfred Barr, whose work in creating the Museum of Modern Art made a tremendous impact on Roland, giving vital encouragement to his early ideas for founding the Institute of Contemporary Arts.

Isamu Noguchi, the Japanese sculptor, in his studio. New York, 1946. (Lee Miller)

178

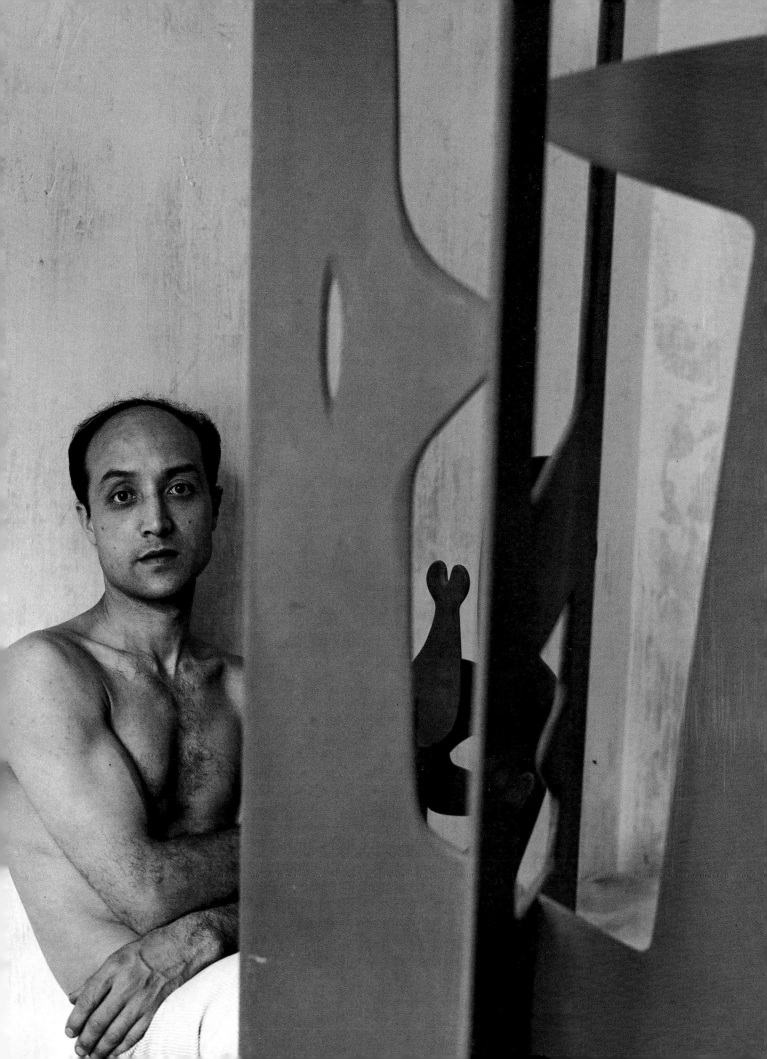

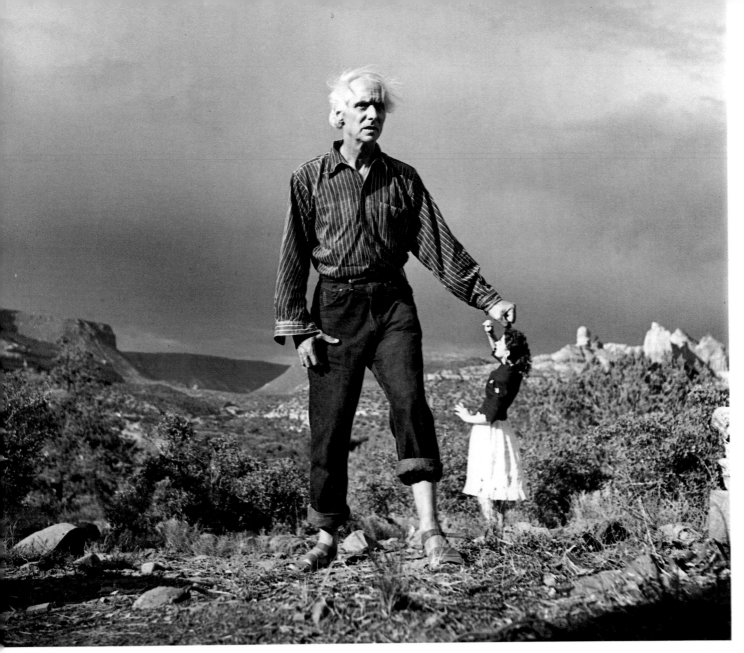

Max Ernst and Dorothea Tanning.
Arizona, 1946. (Lee Miller)

Max Ernst, who was now living with the painter Dorothea Tanning, had settled in Sedona, Arizona, where he was building a studio. Lee and Roland flew to Phoenix to visit them and found themselves entering a landscape composed of chunky profiles and dramatic colours so redolent of Max's paintings that it seemed he had designed it himself. Every afternoon the sky would darken and lightning forks stab at the mesas to the accompaniment of rolling echoes of thunder in the canyons. Against this background Lee's photograph of a diminutive Dorothea railing at the giant, dominant figure of Max had prophetic overtones for the fate of Lee's own creativity.

In the inhospitable environment of the mesas, the indigenous Hopi Indians live in a harmonious and frugal style. With Max and Dorothea as guides, Lee and Roland visited their village and perched on top of the flat-roofed houses to watch the Hopi rain dance. The stamping, swaying file of Katchina dancers emerged from the underground kiva, their bodies and loincloths painted all over with bold geometric patterns. The dance leaders held their arms outstretched and clutched live writhing rattlesnakes in their hands. From inside their masks came a hypnotic humming chant, so compelling that it instantly made everyone tense their shoulders as the little hairs prickled on the backs of their necks.

The dance continued all afternoon and looked set to last for several hours more when Max, knowing what to expect, insisted that they should leave. The efficacy of the ceremony was proved when, a moment after they had departed, the skies opened and the other visitors found their cars stuck fast in the mud.

In Los Angeles a welcome awaited Lee that was the most cherished of all. The fortunes of Mafy and Erik had suffered outrageous reversals since they left Lee in Cairo in 1939. Erik had endured a long period out of work and Mafy's health had been severely damaged by a tropical disease. Their luck had begun to change in 1941 when Erik got a job with the Lockheed Aircraft Corporation as a photographer. By now he had built a distinguished reputation with his aircraft shots which combined the best of the dramatic and the aesthetic. Of all the people in Lee's life it was Erik and Mafy for whom she had the deepest and most enduring affection although, characteristically, she saw them infrequently and almost never wrote to them.

Los Angeles was full of old friends and new. In the old part of Hollywood off Vine Street, Man Ray had his studio in a courtyard where

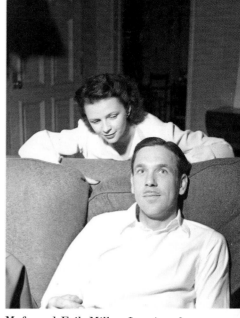

Mafy and Erik Miller. Los Angeles, 1946. (Lee Miller)

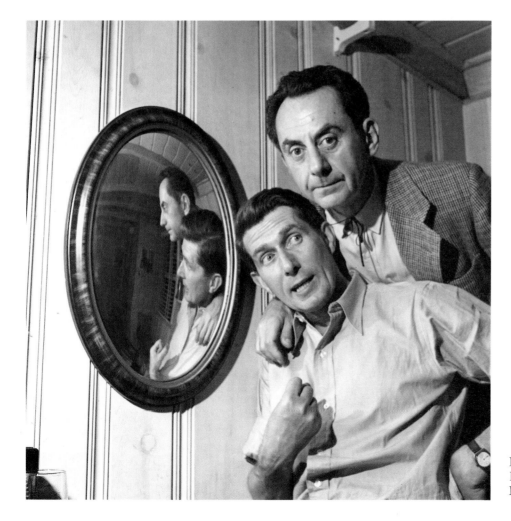

Man Ray and Roland Penrose in Man Ray's studio. Los Angeles, 1946. (Lee Miller)

181

palm trees and flowers grew in profusion. The atmosphere of this quiet oasis, only a few paces away from the bustle of Hollywood, had strong similarities with the Paris he had fled after the German occupation in 1940. Man Ray's attention was now concentrated on his painting to the virtual exclusion of photography. His success was increased by the unexpected discovery that he was an excellent and provocative lecturer.

A few weeks before Lee and Roland's arrival Man Ray had married Juliette Browner, a dark-eyed, slender girl. It had been a double ceremony, shared with Max Ernst and Dorothea Tanning, and the two couples were each other's witnesses.

The following three weeks were a social whirl. Based at Erik and Mafy's house, Lee and Roland were continuously moving around and meeting people. Lee enhanced one of Roland's greatest talents: his gift for friendship. Her gregariousness countered his English reserve and unlocked doors for both of them. They visited such Hollywood celebrities as Gregory Peck and his wife Greta, the poet and Surrealist collector Walter Arensburg, Stravinsky, and the film producer Albert Lewin and sound engineer Dick Van Hessen who arranged several tours of film studios for them. Lee was too much of a professional to waste this access. She took pictures for *Vogue* everywhere she went but none of them was ever published.

Lee could easily have stayed in the United States. Photo-journalism was as yet unthreatened by television and she had excellent prospects for a career with *Vogue, Life,* or *Picture Post,* all of which were in their heyday. But on balance she felt too Europeanized to settle in America and, besides, life with Roland was an attractive option. He looked set to do some frontier trashing of his own in the art world and Lee found that enticing.

It was not until January 1947 that Lee undertook her next assignment for *Vogue.* It was a fashion and celebrities story set in Saint Moritz where high-society people were flocking to the ski slopes for the first time since the war. Princesses, playboys and fashion designers mixed together on the slopes. Lee had travelled there by rail with *Vogue* writer Peggy Riley and though she was delighted to be working again, an unexpected complication arose which she describes in one of the few letters she actually posted to Roland.

Darling,
This is a hell of a romantic way to tell you that I'll shortly be knitting little clothes for a little man – but it seems to be true. I feel rather peculiar about it both physically and emotionally. Physically it's heavy and lethargic-making – the morning sickness is probably nothing to do with it as I've always had it anyway – but emotionally I'm very pleased. So far no resentment or anguish or mind changing or panic – only a mild astonishment that I'm so happy about it. I've had to tell Peggy, as otherwise she couldn't understand my insistence on returning so immediately to London when the job isn't really thru – leaving her in the lurch on her first story. She's madly pleased about it and cherishes me like mad – worries that the prenatal influences of three-legged tripods will be bad. We're so preoccupied with that damned instrument and losing it always so we're both fearful that junior will be born with three legs.

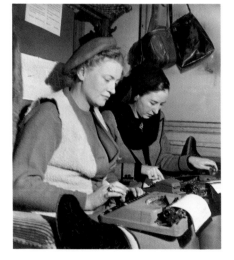

Lee with Peggy Riley (now Rosamond Russell) on a fashion assignment in Switzerland. It was on this trip that Lee discovered she was pregnant. January 1947. (Photographer unknown)

Let me know how you feel about being a parent – sure you want it? and why? There is only one thing – MY WORK ROOM IS NOT GOING TO BE A NURSERY. How about your studio? HA HA.

Darling I love you – will telephone London to-night or to-morrow.

Love Lee

The pregnancy was far from easy and its early complications were not helped by a move in March across the street to a larger house, 36 Downshire Hill. It was the famous 1947 winter, one of the coldest ever. Wind whistled up through the cracks in the uncarpeted floor. Coal was still rationed and the only fuel to be had were meagre supplies from log and peat vendors in the street. Roland resorted to burning old canvas stretchers, frames and the wooden bases from his sculptures.

As Lee's confinement drew closer, her principles began to take a more conventional shift. During the war years few of Aziz's letters had got through, and after the war those that arrived were invariably pleading for answers to previous letters. This was not without some justification, because in his enormous generosity he had passed over to Lee a controlling interest in his two most important businesses. Without her to sign papers or give him power of attorney he was powerless to resist a boardroom coup to oust him. He lost a fortune, and so of course did Lee.

Despite his ruin, Aziz bore no malice towards Lee and at the earliest opportunity he travelled to London, arriving in June 1947. That month 36 Downshire Hill was an unusual household even by Surrealist standards. Valentine had arrived and in the evening would sit down to supper round a card table at the foot of Lee's bed with Roland and Aziz, who held everyone enchanted with tales as fantastic as those in *The Arabian Nights*.

Aziz could not have been more affectionate or generous to Lee. He had unfailingly given her everything he could during their marriage, and now the moment had come for his last gift: Lee's official freedom. He stood before her as she lay in bed and using his prerogative under Moslem law he recited steadily: 'I divorce thee, I divorce thee, I divorce thee,' thus terminating thirteen years of what must have been one of the world's strangest marriages.

A few days later, on 3 May, Lee and Roland were married at Hampstead Registry Office. *Vogue* studio boss Sylvia Redding and the painter John Lake were the witnesses and the only people present at the brief ceremony. At Downshire Hill there waited a beautifully calligraphed envelope, decorated with blue watercolour and addressed to Mrs Lee Penrose. It was from her husband of one hour and contained simply three playing cards from a spelling game – I, O, and U–, the Ace of Diamonds, a foil heart and a corner torn from a page saying 'and love Roland'.

Being pregnant was a wonderful excuse for Lee to indulge her hypochondria and compound it with fancies of a characteristically original nature. She insisted, for example, on having pets. The first passion was an axolotl – a revolting aquatic salamander that resembles a drowned penis. Then it had to be hedgehogs, and not just one single animal. Lee despatched Roland into the country with the threat that unless he returned with a complete family of the creatures their child

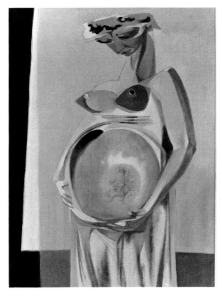

First View, by Roland Penrose, 1947. Roland was fascinated by Lee's changing shape and made many studies of her, culminating in this oil painting where the foetus appears as a green lizard.

would undoubtedly be born covered in prickles. A friendly gamekeeper obliged and Roland came back with the menagerie in a basket. Although Lee was delighted at first, she soon perceived that the hedgehogs were suffering, so Roland had to go out on to Hampstead Heath and turn them loose.

The influence of the hedgehogs must have been benign because on 9 September 1947 Lee was successfully delivered of a healthy son by Caesarean section at the London Clinic. Named Anthony William Roland, he was at first known to all as Butch, on account of his pugilistic features, but later Lee insisted on his being called Tony. 'I don't want him growing into a thug,' she explained. Lee, the arch child-hater, had become a mother. A few days after the birth, Paul Eluard, who was staying at Downshire Hill, seized a large piece of plywood and drew on it two bird-like figures – one large, elegant and protective, the other immature and stubbly, like a chick. He wrote underneath:

> *La beauté de Lee aujourd'hui.*
> *Anthony,*
> *c'est du soleil sur ton lit*
>   Paul Eluard

(The beauty of Lee today. Anthony, it is sunlight on your bed).

The first few weeks of motherhood greatly appealed to Lee as she dominated stage-centre from her nursing-home bed. She wrote this account for the April 1948 issue of *Vogue*:

For me a white bed is a symbol of security. A long row of high, white beds, presided over by a starched white nurse, is my heaven. But different people have different images of safety when they are hurt or frightened. Some want to crawl away, alone. Some want mother. Some are alarmed by the unfamiliar and dream of being at home, comforted by well-known objects, noises and routines.

I wanted my white island of safety, but I didn't want it surrounded by a sea of austerity. A few months before, the matron of the nursing home had sent me a printed list. It was headed in banner type, 'PLEASE BRING RATION BOOK WITH YOU' and ended 'Please have all baby's clothes, ESPECIALLY NAPKINS, marked in full'. In between there was no glamour whatever. No hint of dreams tied up in satin ribbon, or how tiny everything seemed or how soft. Just, 4 woollen coats, 4 night gowns, safety pins, carrying shawl, bonnet, crepe bandages, 2 brassieres, etc. Half the items had been crossed out to adjust the list to minimum coupons. There wasn't a word about how trimmings could be switched from blue to pink (just in case), or about a fluffy elephant, or a film for the camera or a bottle of gin for the visitor, or a book, because a fortnight is a long time to be socially dependent on one member of the family, and a stranger at that.

The article continues with tips for make-up, clothes, permanent waves and 'keeping your elbows well greased unless you want to be able to use them as a nail file after a fortnight's rubbing on the sheet'. In conclusion Lee offered this advice:

When a friend says, 'Darling, you have lots of flowers, and you seem to have everything, what can I bring you?' – discard all shyness and dive into this list, coming to the surface with not more than one thing at a time:

Tomato Catsup, Worcester-type Sauce, Horseradish Sauce, and real Mayonnaise (they'll do wonders to a hospital menu).

Smoked trout, pâté de foie gras, red or black caviare, a tin of Nescafé, evaporated milk, tins and tins of grapefruit juice or tomato juice, lump sugar, lemons, a pepper mill, home made biscuits, a freshly washed green salad matched with a bottle of French dressing, a standing order for ice-cream from Selfridges with a jar of chocolate sauce, a constant supply of ice-cubes in a large-jawed thermos jug, a girl from Elizabeth Arden's to do your face, a subscription to a nappy laundry service.

And now is your big chance! Say boldly to the owner, 'How about lending me your Picasso or that Sutherland to put on the wall for a fortnight?' The friend can hardly refuse, your room will become a palace and the nurses will treat you with great attention as a patient liable to become violently demented if not handled with caution.

Finally, unless you want all your visitors to tear off to the nearest pub at opening hours, don't forget the bottle of gin.

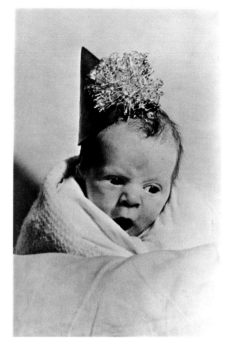

'First Baby, First Christmas'. Tony, photographed by Lee for *Vogue*'s 1947 Christmas issue. The hat would not stay on and had to be photographed separately and pasted to the print.

Once back at Downshire Hill, away from the haven of the London Clinic with its hordes of nurses at her beck and call, Lee's maternal instincts soon began to fray. Fortunately Annie Clements was still there, and she took over Tony and doted on him. This left Lee free to start working again, and her first major assignment was to cover the Venice Biennale. The article, printed in *Vogue*'s August 1948 number, was straight from Lee's heart, a mixture of witty gossip and sharp observations:

Guttuso, a 'young prize' winner, is a vast untidy and charming Roman whose themes are woodchoppers, laundresses and landscapes with birds. He blends abstraction with social realism; his colours glow with countryside richness . . . a further young sculptor's prize was given to Viani, a talented Venetian whose sensuous anatomic abstractions in marble take off from their pedestals like soap bubbles. He's a serious young man – and looks like René Clair.

The warmest comments are reserved for Henry Moore:

He left for London before the announcement that he had been awarded the prize of half a million lire as the best foreign sculptor, but he'd had a week in Florence and a few days in Venice arranging his work. He prowled around, stocky, un-Latin, serious and simple. He talked with Italian-speaking artists and critics, sculpting his inarticulate verbal intentions with his hands like an Italian, and being interpreted by his fans. He liked the sun, Americanos (a vermouth and soda drink) and a bronze statuary group at the right edge of St Mark's.

In the summer of 1948 Theodore and Florence made their first visit to England. Florence, who had always been exemplary in her honesty, was so moved by Lee's tales of postwar rationing that she smuggled a large number of silk stockings through the customs by folding them between the leaves of books.

At Downshire Hill the grandson was the focus of much of their attention and as if on cue took his first steps, toddling from Theodore to Florence's arms, much to Lee's delight. Roland took them on guided tours far afield and found that they were interested in everything and therefore easy to please. Needless to say, the most successful tours were those that included bridges and other engineering works for Theodore to admire. Towards the end of their stay Theodore took Roland aside and with a perfectly straight face said in a grave tone, 'Roland, Florence and I have considered everything very carefully, and we want you to know that this is all not half as bad as we expected it to be.'

Roland had always aspired to be a farmer. Originally he hoped to be a poet–farmer in Ireland, but his deep involvement with the London art scene made this impossible. Instead, he started to look for a farm in south-east England. Proximity to the cross-Channel ferries was important as air travel was still expensive and unreliable. Also, since he knew he was never going to bury himself completely in rustic surroundings, London had to remain accessible. Many different properties were offered for consideration, but none seemed suitable until some friends of Harry Yoxall mentioned Farley Farm, situated in a hamlet with the sympathetic name of Muddles Green. Roland and Lee visited the property on a bleak February day and fell in love with it, buying it at auction a few days later.

The 120 acres of grassland rolled away to the south and west of a large isolated house, whose bleak appearance gave little hint of a potential that Roland immediately recognized. New windows to the south to let the sun stream in, a larger kitchen, and the creation of a huge garden were the first items. The masses of wall space would give ample opportunity to hang the rapidly increasing collection of paintings. What no one could have foreseen was Lee and Roland's discovery on the next visit. Bright sunlight disclosed an unbroken panorama of the South Downs ten miles to the south, presided over by the giant chalk drawing of the Long Man of Wilmington, a presence that augured well. Further observation over the years was to bear out the importance which at first they were able only intuitively to attribute to him. When viewed from the house at midday on Midsummer's Day, the sun stands directly over the Long Man's head, and at night on Midwinter's Night an even greater giant in the mighty constellation of Orion occupies the same position. Thus they felt assured that they were protected by the right guardians.

Roland was wise enough to concede that he knew nothing about farming and that his dreams of verdant acres and fecund cattle needed expert help in their realization. He had the immense good fortune to engage Peter Braden as his farm manager and he retained most of the farm's existing workforce. The dream of a garden needed similar help before the cold, hard Wealden clay would provide a seductive retreat and the house could be ringed with newly planted trees. Grandpa White, a rustic sage, and Fred Baker were engaged for this task and over the years wrought a transformation. As housekeeper and cook came Paula Paul, an earthy Irishwoman of unparalleled kindliness who introduced her daughter Patsy Murray to look after Tony following the retirement of Annie Clements.

At one blow the staff had grown to Victorian proportions, but Lee's innate sociability caused her to run the household as a family. This was not an echo of the trendy left-wing views of the time; it was simply Lee's natural friendliness which overrode impediments of class and status. Her friendship was never patronizing; it was direct – drunk or sober, in fair mood or foul.

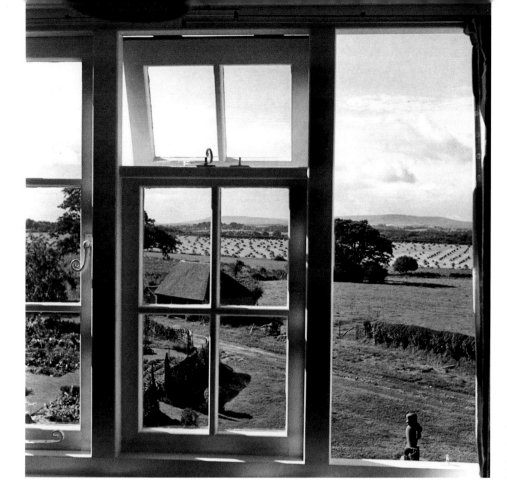

View from Farley Farm, looking towards the South Downs. *Mother and Child*, by Henry Moore, is on the lawn (*bottom right*). 1952. (Lee Miller)

Lee immediately took an interest in the garden, although she limited herself to a strictly supervisory role. She secretly devoured several tomes on gardening. This new knowledge, coupled with her scientific attitude, soon turned her into a formidable expert, capable of taking on the doyennes of the Chiddingly Horticultural Society on their own ground.

Lee's 'self sufficiency' jag was less successful. First, she decided that the family had to make butter from their own milk, so the latest design of churn was bought. It was carefully filled up with masses of cream and milk and the handle expectantly turned. Several hours and many exhausted crankers later the mixture showed no sign of turning to butter. 'God dammit!' cursed Lee, 'I'll take it back to the shop.' No one had the chance to savour the idea of Lee lugging a contraption full of rancid cream back to Harrods because at that precise moment the entire contents suddenly became butter. Despite the triumph, the experiment was never repeated.

The next attempt was much messier. Under the aegis of the Women's Institute, selected pigs were sent for slaughter and the carcasses cut up and cured for pork and bacon. The scene in the back kitchen was unimaginable. The abattoir, at Lee's request, had sent back all the entrails, as she had great plans for their use. The job was started in the morning and seemed endless. Fortification was needed, by way of several shots of whisky, and it was not long before the pails of offal began to get kicked over. By the afternoon Lee had had enough and retired for a snooze, allowing Patsy and Paula to finish the task. The pigs had their revenge; there was something wrong with the formulation of the brine and nearly all the meat went putrid.

The first few years of Lee's marriage to Roland were, by her own testimony, among the happiest of her life. She had both security and freedom, and she also had the excitement of battling on the frontiers of modern art at Roland's side as the newly formed Institute of Contemporary Arts swept forward. An early success was the exhibition 'Forty Years of Modern Art', then, in 1949, 'Forty Thousand Years of Modern Art', illustrating the influence of so-called primitive art on contemporaries like Picasso, Henry Moore, Miró, Hepworth and many others. For this show Lee wrote a perceptive and erudite article for *Vogue*'s January 1949 issue which gave 'quite enough reasons for lingering at the show until you have "museum feet" and the filing departments of your subconscious are crammed and disorientated.'

Then came a trip to Sicily aboard a BOAC flying boat with three models, an assistant, a fashion director and a mountain of equipment. *Vogue* had made arrangements with the airline to provide free transport in return for a favourable mention in the fashion feature. Naturally none of the niggling delays and frustrations of the trip showed through in the finished article's stunning ten-page layout. It is only the contact sheets that provide evidence of the problems creeping up on Lee. The file runs to more than a thousand shots and it was quite clearly very hard going – not because of the girls or the dresses, but because Lee was having trouble in maintaining her interest.

In London Lee's established reputation gave her a firm lead in her field but it was a routine that she found crushing. 'I get so depressed,' she wailed to her close friend and doctor, Carl H. Goldman, who replied sternly: 'There is nothing wrong with you, and we cannot keep the world permanently at war just to provide you with excitement.'

The assignments ebbed and flowed. The only relief in an endless succession of dresses were items like 'London Spotlight' or 'New Writers of Fiction' which brought contact with old friends and new from art, literature and drama. The interiors of Downshire Hill appeared as backgrounds with increasing frequency as Lee put less and less effort into her work. The results were always technically excellent – the problems were not in the camera, but immediately behind it. Fortunately for everyone concerned, Timmie O'Brien was still willing to take it upon herself to make sure Lee delivered.

One article that Lee did not need to be nagged to write appeared in the November 1951 issue of *Vogue* for Picasso's seventieth birthday, an occasion marked by an exhibition at the Institute of Contemporary Arts. Picasso had stayed with Lee and Roland when he visited England for the Sheffield Peace Congress, leaving shortly before the show opened.

If Picasso is ever going to be a Grand Old Man he'd better start now as he will need considerable practice. He's just reached seventy and he has yet to acquire any of the characteristic aura of a G.O.M. Grand Old Men should live in retirement: brittle, fragile, unapproachable. Their youth of struggle, revolt, insecurity and wild oats should be unimaginable, and if they work at all they should be well-mannered enough to continue in the style for which they were revered. Picasso is unlikely to make the grade.

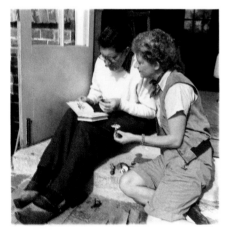

Roland Penrose with Timmie O'Brien at Farley Farm. Timmie and Roland, both avid mushroom hunters, speculate on the likelihood of getting poisoned. Summer 1953. (Lee Miller)

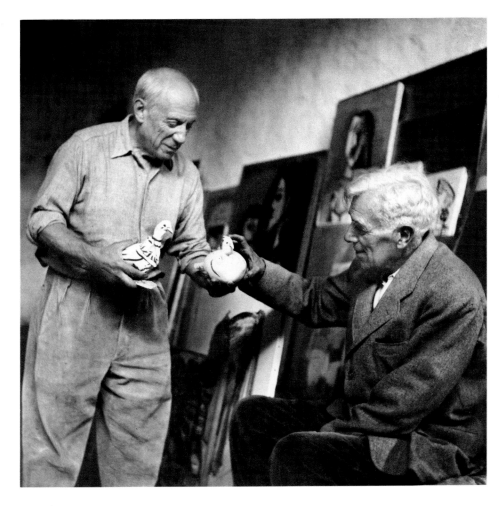

Picasso offers Braque a gift of ceramic doves – a gesture of peace and affection. Braque had visited Picasso at his studio in Vallauris after a separation of many years. 1954. (Lee Miller)

The piece goes on to refer to the trip Lee, Roland and Tony had made to Picasso's house at Vallauris near Saint Tropez the previous year when Roland selected the works for the ICA exhibition. By a wonderful coincidence, Paul Eluard was there, and they extended their trip for a few days to attend his wedding to Dominique Laure. At the ceremony in the town hall Picasso and Françoise Gilot were witnesses and Lee took the photographs. Afterwards Picasso invited the party, joined by Tony and Marcel, Picasso's chauffeur, to lunch in the courtyard of an old inn in the town.

With her special talent for blending the erudite and the commonplace, Lee goes on to give us this personal portrait of the artist and his way of life.

Picasso doesn't collect – he just never throws anything away. Each thing has some aspect of beauty or meaning to him that he does not want to lose. Even my own used flash-bulbs, which had caught his fancy, are still in the corner by the stairs where I left them in Liberation week, six years ago. When a studio or apartment gets too crowded, even for him, he locks it up and starts anew elsewhere. His house in Vallauris must already be filling up – I wonder if in five years' time I'll find some of the things he collected on his recent English trip. Besides Kwells [travel sickness pills] and postcards of Brighton Pavilion, they included a peaked school cap for himself and his son, a Bournvita plastic mug of a sleepy man wearing a nightcap lid, a photograph of Roland's great-aunt Priscilla Hannah at the Bath Peace Congress in 1875, and a toy red London bus.

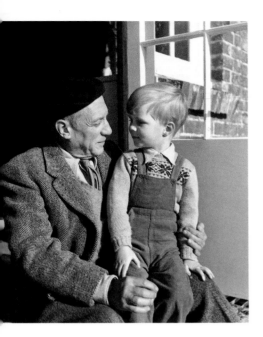

Picasso and Tony Penrose at Farley Farm, September 1950. Picasso was in England attending the Peace Conference in Sheffield. He visited Farley Farm twice, showing a particular interest in the bull, and claiming that he too wanted to establish himself as a Sussex farmer. (Lee Miller)

During his visit to England, Picasso stayed twice at Farley Farm.

At our farm in Sussex, Picasso found the world was very English; the landscape of Downs with Constable clouds, the prudish Long Man of Wilmington, left-handed driving, red and white Ayrshires, open log fires, whiskey and soda nightcap, hot water bottles, cooked breakfast and tea. A tinned plum pudding, holly wreathed and flaming was indeed English, *very* English and quite unimaginable.

Our three-year-old son Tony was in ecstasy. Picasso and he became great friends, telling secrets, finding treasures of spider webs and seed pods, rough-housing, and looking at pictures. In Tony's early vocabulary the word picture and Picasso were synonymous, I suppose because Roland and I refer to the same painting as 'picture' and 'Picasso' interchangeably and the words started the same. Later he realised that Picasso was a man, who, like Daddy and himself, made pictures. 'Pictures' include Craxton, Max Ernst, Klee, Braque. Although I don't know which generic term he uses for them, naturalistic or whimsy illustrations and photographs are *not* 'pictures'.

Picasso and he agreed on this instantly, and illustrated books, particularly *Farmer's Weekly*, became tools to clarify misunderstandings in their mysterious mutual language. I've only recently realised that Picasso probably speaks a great deal more English than he admits. Only that, not magic, would account for the perfect accord and the whispered conversations.

You can't have a rough-house in secret. Picasso and Tony pummelled each other amid squeals and roars. Each meeting, here and in France, added to the repertoire: giggling ambushes from behind sofas, bellowing bulls, the *olé olé* of approval. The crescendo of violence rose through ear-twisting and kicking to biting. Picasso bit back sharply – 'the biter bitten' and in the astonished silence which followed said, '*Pensez! C'est le premier Anglais que j'ai jamais mordu!*'

I can't imagine why Picasso took on this ordeal of 'sparring partner' unless to keep in training for Claude, his own small son. Claude is a strenuous customer who is only quiet while his father shaves. In Picasso's special children's performance, he lathers everything from Adam's apple to the crown of his head, leaving a horrifying blank. Then with his fingernails ploughing through the soap to the brown skin underneath, he draws a clown's face. He continues, covering with the brush, gouging with his finger through a hundred subtle expressions until the audience falls backwards into the bath tub.

Tony is still within Picasso's ambience. He tells perfectly true 'tall' stories about what he and Picasso did in St. Tropez – about deep-sea divers, processions with gunfire, and a flower vase Picasso gave as a wedding present to Paul Eluard – 'taller than himself and covered with ladies with no clothes who looked very happy.' He wears a beret and St. Tropez sandals just like his hero, and his current excuse for all odd behaviour is: 'That's the way they do it in France – just like Picasso.' He dunks his bread and insists on eating his ice cream with his dish in his hand and his back to the table – 'Just like Picasso' – who had done exactly that otherwise he would have missed the sights of the port and the procession of pretty girls.

Good going for a G.O.M. Happy Birthday, Picasso!

Farley Farm soon took on the air of a perpetual arts congress. Both Lee and Roland loved entertaining. For them the company of friends brought the satisfaction and stimulation that nothing else could provide. Art was vital and had to be lived and shared, otherwise it became academic, sterile and as good as dead. They both enjoyed creating the kind of atmosphere in which new ideas and projects could be spawned, and the eclectic assemblies of weekend guests were an agreeable extension of this idea.

There were *habitués*, such as Timmie O'Brien and her husband, Terry, and Tommy Lawson of the ICA and her husband, Alastair. The American artist Bill Copley visited at the time of a dance in the village hall, and, deciding he was the 'Green Man' of local folklore, garlanded himself in ivy and passionately wooed the local lasses. William Turnbull availed himself of the welding equipment in the Golden Cross Garage to complete his wind vane sculpture for the top of the pigeon-house. Audrey Withers, now married to the photographer Victor Kennett, arrived with a basket containing a pair of tumbler pigeons destined to occupy this unique residence. 'Oh, don't let Mummy see them,' pleaded Tony, 'she will put them straight in the deep freeze.' The arrival of eccentrics at Newhaven became so commonplace that when Jean Dubuffet disembarked from a cross-Channel ferry unable to speak a word of English, a taxi driver brought him straight to Farleys.

The goings-on were observed with interest by the locals, who found that with only slight exaggeration they could regale each other with tales of nude dancing on the lawn, plenty of laughter interspersed with violent quarrels, incomprehensible pictures adorning the walls and weird statues sprouting in the garden, people in foreign clothes who chattered in foreign tongues. Man Ray was one of the few visitors to be taken seriously, because he appeared on BBC TV's *Monitor* series with Huw Weldon.

Lee was aware of the unusual qualities of her *ménage*. She loved her role as hostess, particularly with Patsy and Paula to help her, because tormenting her accomplices was always a special component of her creativity. Man Ray once remarked that regardless of what Lee was doing, she could make more work for other people than anyone else he knew. The sight of others sitting around idle was unbearable to her; she insisted that they be involved in some task under her direction and with enormous ingenuity invented schemes to keep everyone occupied. With a perceptive candour that could be mistaken for offbeat humour, she wrote about her scheme, 'Working Guests', in *Vogue*'s July 1953 number:

There are columns of print by experts advising guests and hostesses on how to behave toward each other with tolerance. They contain hints and reminders – they abound in fabulous invitors and invitees. Although there are planning charts and menus to make the single-handed hostess carefree and leisured, the conspiracy to simulate the good old days of silent service for relaxed guests more often produces instructions for rehearsed team-work on the part of the husband and wife to make it seem like a bevy of pixies flits around doing the background chores. There was one article, so orthodox in its 'gracious living' that it told how to evade offers of aid on household projects.

That isn't the way I want it or do it, and I've devoted four years of research and practice to getting all my friends to do all the work. There is scarcely a thing, in or out of sight, from the wood-pile to the attic water tank, from the chair coverings to the brined pork and the contents of the deep freeze, without the signature of a working guest.

Since most of the visitors sleep all morning, and I'm siesta-minded after lunch, it takes dove-tailed planning to keep industry on its feet. The visitors' book is flanked by a photo album of grim significance: in it are no 'happy hols' snaps of leisured groups wearing sun glasses and sniffing Pimm's Cup. It could easily be taken for a set of stills from a Soviet workers' propaganda film. Everyone busy doing a job: Joy through Work.

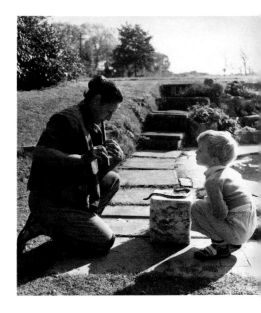

Valentine Penrose charming both a grass snake and Tony. Farley Farm, *c.* 1952. (Lee Miller)

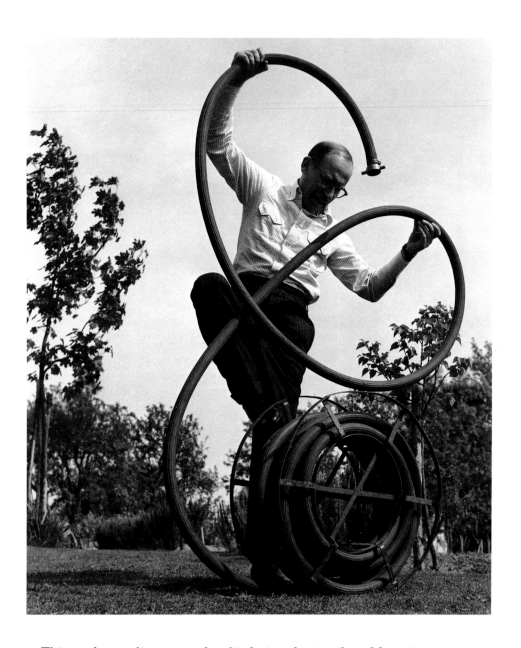

Saul Steinberg, the New York cartoonist. Farley Farm, 1959. (Lee Miller)

This catalogue of 'merry workers' is designed to instil confidence in newcomers and manual morons who can herein see some butter-fingered acquaintance doing highly skilled work, to show the variety of scope of the projects, and to suggest social ostracism of drones and sit-down strikers.

Lee goes on to outline ingenious ways of ensnaring helpers to paint, upholster, garden, sew curtains or build an ornamental pond. The story, which was only partly exaggerated, was firmly authenticated for the readers by shots of the guests hard at work. Alfred Barr, director of the Museum of Modern Art in New York, was pictured feeding the pigs. Saul Steinberg wrestling with the garden hose turns himself into one of his own cartoons, and Henry Moore hugs his sculpture. Renato Guttuso dons a chef's hat for a cooking spree and fashion editor Ernestine Carter injects an antique chair with a hypodermic filled with woodworm poison. Madge Garland (Lady Ashton), a professor at the Royal College of Art, demurely powders dried marjoram, while Vera Lindsay (Lady Barry) clamps a knife

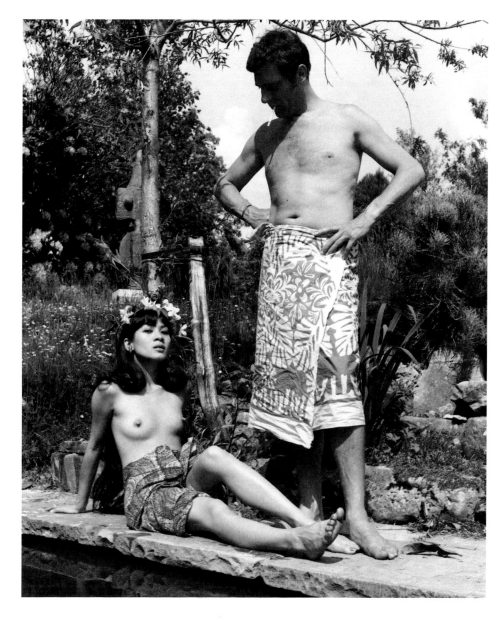

Philippe and Yen Hiquily at Farley Farm, *c.* 1962. Hiquily is a well known Parisian sculptor. Yen is Chinese from Tahiti, and cooked many fish dishes with Lee. (Lee Miller)

between her teeth for an assault on the vegetable patch, cradling a stricken, captured pumpkin in her hands. The last picture in the article is appropriately of Lee herself, fast asleep on the sofa.

'Working Guests' was the last article Lee wrote for *Vogue* and the penultimate one of her life. The process of writing had become so traumatic that the turmoil it caused threatened to engulf Roland. He wrote secretly to Audrey Withers – 'I implore you, please do not ask Lee to write again. The suffering it causes her and those around her is unbearable.' Audrey had long been aware of the difficulties involved in using Lee's work. It was so distinctive that it actually required accommodating in the magazine rather than simply including. There were also the problems of deadlines, but most difficult of all was finding Lee an assignment that interested her enough to do it. In the face of all the new talent available to Audrey, it must have stretched her loyalties to use Lee for as long as she did. In the event, it was Lee herself who decided to quit writing for the simple reason that she could not think of anything further that she felt compelled to say. Cooking was emerging as her new metier and it had the understandable attraction that it was far more sociable and less solitary an occupation than the combined flagellation of herself and her typewriter keyboard.

In spite of the copious *bonhomie* of Farleys, Lee was happiest in London. The house at Downshire Hill had been sold, and during the week Lee and Roland now lived in a small flat in Kensington. Its size was no drawback as, when not at school, Tony was happily established at Farleys with Patsy. The flat was looked after by Elsa Fletcher, a quiet, genial woman who soon became unswervingly devoted to Lee, and Lee to her. The flat was Lee's refuge, and Elsa her confidante and a vital source of sympathy and understanding.

By 1955 Lee was in the grip of a vicious downward spiral that nearly killed her. Following the birth of Tony, she had suddenly found herself unable to get any pleasure from sex. She was also rapidly losing her looks. Her face no longer had its fineness – wrinkles and folds were proliferating and her eyes were becoming puffy. Her hair was getting thinner and lifeless. The fat was piling on, making her body look coarse and bulky. To make matters worse, the woman who had once been described as a 'snappy dresser' was fast becoming a slob. She would turn up at smart dinner parties in scruffy or unsuitable clothes – calf-high stockings under a knee-length skirt, or an ill-fitting suit jacket worn over slacks. But of all the vicissitudes of age, it was the deterioration of her face that wounded Lee the most, and drove her to a painful face-lift and ill-fitting wigs.

Roland, on the other hand, was on the springboard of his career. The ICA was making a contribution that was changing the whole ethos of contemporary art in Britain. Success followed success and recognition was coming from all quarters. On top of that was the irony that age had improved his looks.

To add to the other strains of this period, Lee's chosen method of giving up smoking created extra problems. She had been accustomed to around fifty cigarettes a day. It was a miracle that she never burned houses to the ground with her technique of keeping several cigarettes on the go simultaneously, smouldering in ashtrays or perched on the edges of furniture. In the middle of a cigarette one night at the restaurant Chez Anna near the Trocadero, she announced she was going to stop smoking forthwith. For the next year or more life was absolute hell for her and those around her as she rode out the withdrawal symptoms.

It is hardly surprising that Lee became difficult and quarrelsome and that those closest to her in the firing line became the target for venomous vituperation. A vicious feud began between her and Tony. Neither missed an opportunity to snipe at the other with the knowledge that they both knew exactly where to hit to inflict the most damage. Attacks and counterattacks were sparked off over trivia, and the opponents pressed home on their targets with relentless ingenuity. The obvious result was that Tony transferred all his affections to Patsy. Enormous quantities of whisky exacerbated all of Lee's problems and tightened the spiral. Lee drank because she felt unloved, and she was unloved because she drank.

Roland found this crisis incomprehensible, mainly because Lee took care not to allow anyone the opportunity to completely understand her. She wallowed in her own misery, revelling in this prolonged bout of self-laceration, and wreaking a hateful vengeance on anyone within reach.

In 1954 the publisher Victor Gollancz commissioned Roland to write *Picasso, His Life and Work*. This was another blow to Lee – 'Christ, how can you write?' she said, 'You can't even spell to save your life!' But the hurt was deep as she recognized that her own talent was becoming so swiftly eclipsed. Roland's acceptance of the post as Director of Fine Arts for the British Council in Paris served only to plunge her into further fits of depression. The long stays in Paris were spent in the luxury of borrowed apartments and their social life was an incessant round of *vernissages* and parties. Ten years previously this would have delighted Lee, but now she hated it. For the first time in her life she felt she had become an appendage to someone else and no longer controlled her own destiny. Centre-stage, even here in Paris, now belonged to Roland.

At the eye of this private hurricane was the fact that Roland had fallen in love with an acrobat from the flying trapeze, Diane Deriaz. Diane had been a close friend of Paul Eluard, who had written of her:

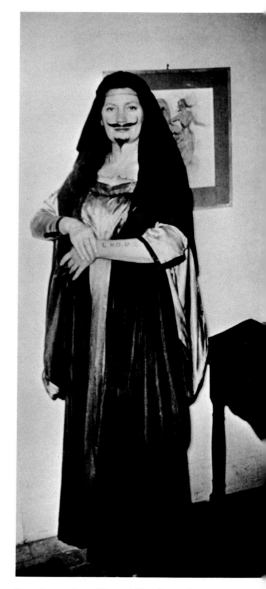

>   *

> *Je suis amoureux d'une voyageuse,*
> *Elle a son soleil*
> *Je n'ai pas le mien*

>   *

> I am in love with a traveller,
> She has her sun
> I don't have mine

Diane's beautiful face, with her piercing blue eyes and mass of golden curls, was solar in appearance and radiated energy. At first Lee had encouraged this affair, feeling confident that it was just another of Roland's passing amours. Then, suddenly, she saw Diane as a threat. Benign permissive tolerance was reversed and Lee became bitterly and openly hostile. The quarrels were devastating and swirled around her and Roland like a maelstrom. In between outbursts Lee would make an effort to 'tough it out' but her own self-confidence was too badly shattered to be able to shrug this one off.

Her hatred was far too consuming to allow her to grasp that it was Diane who was protecting her. Despite Roland's repeated entreaties, Diane steadfastly refused to marry him, but Lee could never believe this and saw her only as a deadly rival. For Lee, Roland's sexual peccadilloes mattered little, and following the loss of her own sexuality she actively encouraged him to have other women. The pain came from being forced to share his love. She felt isolated from everyone around her. Valentine, Patsy, Diane, and many other talented, adoring women formed an admiring circle around Roland. Lee was the outsider who was always

Lee dressed as Marcel Duchamp's *Mona Lisa* at one of Ninette Lyon's parties in Paris. Duchamp himself was at the party, and approved. c. 1954. (Photographer unknown)

195

drunk, untidy and in the wrong. Tony was becoming increasingly distant. Casual remarks like, 'Please ask Patsy to meet me from the school train because if Mummy comes I am not sure if I will recognize her,' left deep invisible wounds. Later, in his teenage years, their relationship was to degenerate into open hostilities at every opportunity.

An element of cohesiveness returned to Lee and Roland's relationship around 1956 when she started to help him with his book. Many research trips were needed to discuss the book with Picasso and also to visit the place of his origin, Malaga. Lee took photographs of the old city, the Moorish Citadel, and the Art School of San Telmo, which were initially used as an *aide-memoire* by Roland. None of these photographs appeared in the book, as nearly all the illustration space is given to postage-stamp-sized reproductions of key paintings. Instead, many of them formed part of the exhibition at the ICA in 1956 titled 'Picasso Himself' and held to commemorate the artist's seventy-fifth birthday. The catalogue for the exhibition was incorporated in a book published by Lund Humphries called *Portrait of Picasso*. The preface was by Alfred Barr, the text by Roland, and the book contained several additional photographs by Lee, appearing beside others by Man Ray, Robert Capa and Gjon Mili.

To some extent the social life in Paris was a palliative for Lee's misery and in between rows she was a hostess without equal. She assembled the guest list for her parties with an almost culinary skill. The result was a name-dropper's paradise: Max Ernst and Dorothea Tanning, Man Ray and Juliette, John Houston, Marcel Duchamp, Jacques Prévert, Lynn Chadwick, Dominique Eluard, Michel Leiris, Philippe Hiquily. But Lee became very close to only one person, Ninette Lyon, a painter who had become a famous writer of cookery books. Ninette and her husband Peter were also great party-givers and their initial friendship with Lee arose from being able to swap recipes and ideas for entertaining.

Even at the grandest party, Lee's tension was very near the surface. The slightest provocation would cause her to throw a scene and embarrass everyone, fully realizing she was alienating herself from the people whose affection she craved. Ninette once discovered the letters NA written boldly on the mirror of Lee's dressing table. Inquiring what the letters stood for she was told: 'It means Never Answer – and it is to remind me that I am expected to carry on without protest.'

By now the winged serpents were rampant and had saturated Lee's consciousness. But, with her horror of mental illness, she denied herself professional help and understanding. All forms of physical illness fascinated her, but she was repelled and frightened by the merest suggestion that she might be suffering from psychological problems. The winged serpents held her in a relentless grip. In the nadir of her depression, she confessed to Ninette that the only reason preventing her from drowning herself in the Seine was that she knew Roland and Tony would be so happy without her.

It was food that saved her life.

Lee in the kitchen at Farley Farm, *c.* 1970. Tile by Picasso. (Christina Ockrent)

Chapter Eleven

Food, Friends and Faraway Places
1956–1977

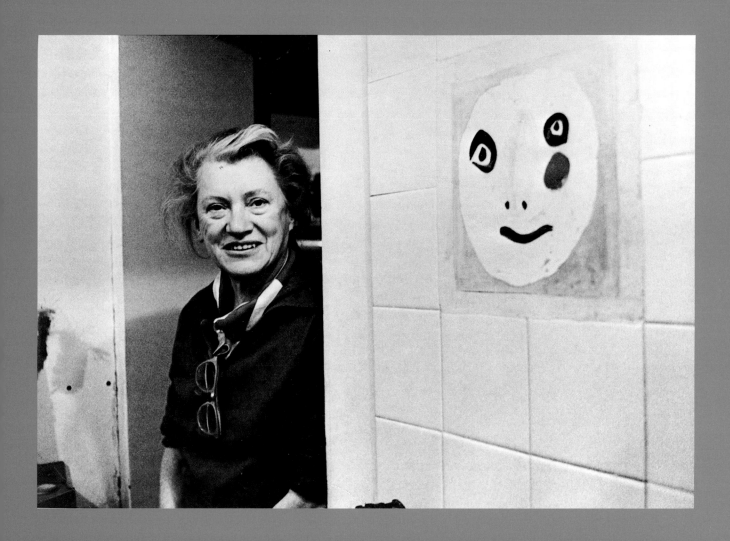

Fortunately for everyone's sanity in these gloomy times, Lee was able to gain some solace from cooking.

Cooking is an art requiring many diverse skills, not the least being the technique of presentation. To justify this and other aspects of their art, cooks need an audience, and Lee's own family were often less than sympathetic to her efforts. Roland would express his desire for English food, and Tony, on reaching an age when he could be involved in farm work, craved plain fare. Valentine on her long visits would grumble about most things, as was her wont. It was Patsy who was most encouraging to Lee. She was a vegetarian so her demands presented an interesting challenge. Lee would spend hours scouring the shops of whatever part of the world she happened to be in for vegetarian delicacies, and return home laden with small tins of exotic vegetable pâtés.

Lee's culinary style, like everything else she did, could hardly be called derivative. She took her Cordon Bleu course in London and passed with flying colours, and she ploughed through *Mrs Beeton's Book of Household Management* and *Larousse Gastronomique* from front to back, but all this was mere foundation. She devoured cookbooks the way some people get through novels and accumulated a collection of well over two thousand volumes. Added to this was a similar sized library of magazines and countless box files with cross-referenced recipes of her own creation. Out of all these ingredients Lee formed her own distinctive style, the hallmark of which was bizarre originality. 'Muddles Green Green Chicken'[1] was actually green, but mercifully 'Goldfish' was made from a cunningly cooked and garnished three-kilo cod, and 'Persian Carpet' was not to be sat on, being made of oranges and candied violets.

Cooking appealed directly to Lee's curiosity about exotic things; there was scarcely a country in the world whose national dish she did not prepare, and if she could find a native from a far-off land who would show her how to cook some ethnic dish, that was bliss indeed. Patsy's friend Stan Peters came from Poland and used to spend hours with Lee making *bigos* and other traditional Polish fare. Renato Guttuso was the expert on pasta dishes, the O'Briens, newly returned from Tenerife, knew about Spanish rice dishes, and Wells Coates found a co-indulger in his unbridled passion for Chinese food. James Beard came to stay and with him Lee took two days to prepare a fish. It was not only the fish that was important, it was the hundreds of other things they were chatting about while they were cooking.

Lee also found that her culinary art could be used as a weapon. One day Cyril Connolly, who delighted in being rude to his hostess, was expounding his views on the decadence of American culture. 'They have the moral strength of a marshmallow and will drown themselves in a sea of that revolting beverage Coca-Cola,' was his contention. Lee said nothing, but disappeared to the kitchen. That evening the dessert was particularly delicious and Lee's eyes gleamed with triumph as Cyril congratulated her. It was made from marshmallows and Coca-Cola.

It was more to Lee's liking to indulge her friends. She kept a notebook of their likes and dislikes: 'Bernard hates mushrooms — Jim can't eat

Left to right: Roland Penrose, Sonia Orwell and John Hayward in the amusement arcade on Brighton Pier, August 1955. Sonia, the widow of George Orwell, worked with Cyril Connolly on the magazine *Horizon*. Hayward was an eminent writer and scholar. They both visited Farley Farm frequently. (Lee Miller)

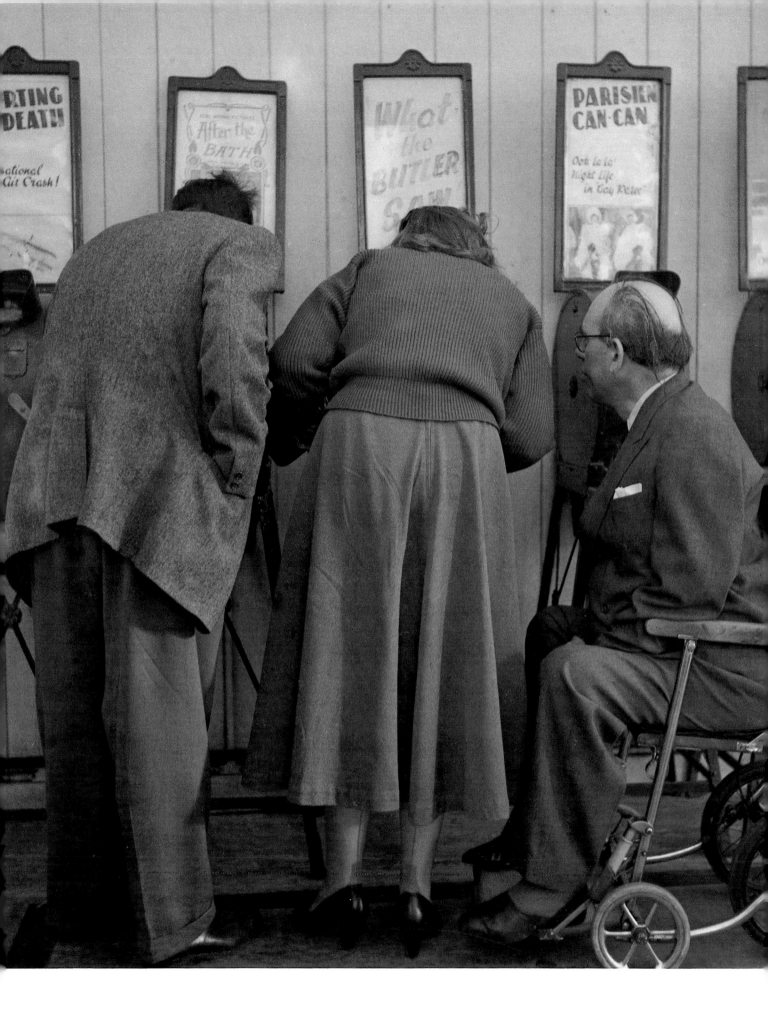

cucumber – Peggy loves guacamole' – and so on for many pages. If she could find someone with a particular passion she could favour, there was nothing she liked better. Terry O'Brien was a stalwart in this sense, with his insatiable hunger for sweet things. Wonderful rich creamy fools would appear, made from gooseberries, raspberries or blackcurrants, or in the winter chocolate and biscuit layercake with whipped cream topping.

If there was a catering trade fair on or an 'Ideal Home Exhibition', Lee would feel compelled to go and she would inevitably return with all the latest kitchen gadgets. Even if doing the job by hand was actually far quicker, the various contraptions would have to be used because they satisfied Lee's penchant for technology. Conversation in the kitchen soon became impossible above the roar and whine of machines that sliced, shredded, mixed, ground, and frequently broke down.

Most of Lee's major *oeuvres* were rehearsed in London with Elsa and fellow gourmet Bettina McNulty. The performance was reserved for Farleys, because the enormous kitchen offered plenty of scope, and there was Patsy, reinforced by Fred Baker's wife, Joan, to battle with the mountains of washing up. The vegetable garden, backed up by the freezer and the delights of the village shop, provided nearly all the other needs. Best of all, each successive weekend brought in a stream of guests who were, almost without exception, far more appreciative of Lee's efforts than her own household were.

No culinary topic was too oblique or obscure to explore – a chance remark by Peter Lyon one long weekend led to the feverish research necessary for the production of Confederate Soup. Books on the American Civil War were consulted, knowledgeable friends were phoned, and the whole scheme plotted more carefully than the Battle of Gettysburg. It took two days to cook and the guests pronounced it delicious – but was it worth the effort? For Lee the answer had to be yes – how else could she satisfy so many passions at one stroke?

Lee's cuisine was not the art of a woman harnessed to a casserole. Preparations for supper often started early in the morning and did not preclude the elaborate preparations for lunch that also had to be fitted in. After lunch Lee would have a sleep while Patsy wrestled with the pots and pans, then cooking proceeded at a relentless pace until the creation was ready for dinner. Hitches or interesting side tracks could easily delay proceedings for hours, so that everyone was thoroughly stewed from Roland's generous drinks by the time they sat down at the table. This kind of evening nearly always went well as Lee loved both pleasing and surprising her guests. By contrast, nothing was so chaotic as the occasions when Lee obliged Roland by cooking some traditional English set-piece like a roast leg of lamb. Because she had no creative interest in the dish, it would languish in the oven until it was ruined while she enjoyed herself drinking with the guests.

Over the ensuing years Lee often threatened to write a cookbook – an idea that struck terror into the household. She wanted to make a compilation of her favourite stolen recipes and to this end filled her handbag with various ingenious cutting devices so that while seated in a

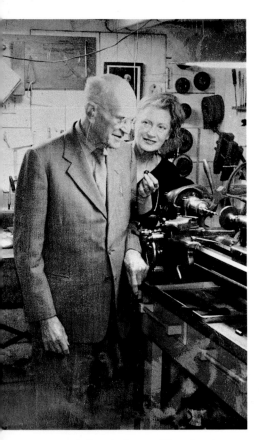

Lee with her father in Theodore's workshop in Forbus Street, Poughkeepsie, New York, *c.* 1958. From a Polaroid print. (Photographer unknown)

doctor's waiting room she could eviscerate magazines. She kept this project going for many years, cramming cardboard boxes with her booty. Quiet weekends were also spent foraging in magazines bought for the purpose. 'It's my work,' she would say in counter to Roland's protests as the tide of shredded paper engulfed the sitting room at Farleys. Valentine echoed the general contempt – 'What is this you call work – this business of tearing up a lot of magazines and going to sleep on them?' But Lee was not to be deflected, and soon Roland felt that the only way to have a living room that could actually be lived in was to have a special study built for Lee on the south side of the house. It turned out to be one of the most pleasant rooms. Lined with white painted bookcases against the blue walls, it was lit by a large south-west-facing window and french windows that looked out to the Long Man. Two thousand cookbooks filled the shelves and the cupboards kept the magazines out of sight, if not under control.

Lee's interest in cooking dated from her days of travelling in the Egyptian desert, but it was not until the early 1960s that it reached its peak. It not only counteracted her depression but also gave her a new set of friends who were not involved in the art world – an area that was now dominated by Roland. Faced with the heat of the kitchen, the winged serpents began to retreat to their caverns, glowering and undertaking occasional rearguard actions. What finally overwhelmed them was not the cooking, but a new jag that Lee had never considered before – music.

How she ever became interested in classical music is a mystery to all who knew her. Her musical ability was such that she was described as being 'unable to carry a tune in a bucket', but by dint of sheer study she suddenly became an aficionado of classical music with very definite tastes. Schumann and Brahms were her favourite composers. Mozart was valued, but Wagner absolutely out – he was unforgivably a German. About this time there was a regular broadcast on BBC radio by Anthony Hopkins on the subject of music appreciation. Nothing would induce Lee to miss this programme. Of course the next development was to tape-record the talk and soon countless spools of tape were added to the piles of torn-up magazines. Concerts were her supreme delight, and Lee became a regular at the Wigmore Hall and the Festival Hall. She also visited the Glyndebourne Opera House, where it is traditional to take a picnic dinner to eat during the interval in the elegant, romantic gardens. In this instance, Lee's passion for music meshed with her passion for food.

By 1960 the British Council job in Paris was over. Roland's Picasso book was successfully published. He had become a trustee of the Tate Gallery and undertook the organization of what was to be the most important exhibition of Picasso's work ever to be held in Britain. More than 250 works were borrowed from all over the world, including several from the Hermitage Museum in Leningrad which gave everyone the jitters by not arriving until the night before the opening.

With shrewd diplomacy Roland managed to turn the opening night of 5 July into a fund-raising gala for the Institute of Contemporary Arts, a sparkling occasion with a host of famous names including HRH the Duke of Edinburgh. Marquees were erected on the lawn of the Tate to accommodate the guests and, as well as helping with the selection for the menu, Lee rashly undertook to write a short piece for the gala brochure. With Roland close to being overwhelmed by the final stages of the exhibition and gala, Lee's dilatory approach went unnoticed. Two days before the event the deadline was suddenly upon her and no amount of pleading could get an extension.

'How shall I start?' she wailed to Roland. 'Well – try imagining Picasso is going to be there at the opening,' he said, and rushed out of the flat. Lee spread newspaper on the kitchen table and spent hours arranging her Baby Hermes, dictionary, typing paper, carbons and whisky bottle in many different orders. The day disappeared. When Roland came home late that night there were not more than a dozen words on the page. He went gloomily to bed, leaving Lee hunched over the typewriter.

The next morning the kitchen floor was covered in tightly screwed up balls of paper. Beside the empty whisky bottle was a second bottle with only a drop remaining. The margins and every other available space of the newspaper were entirely filled with doodles. There was no sign of Lee, but plenty of snores were coming from under a pile of blankets on the living room sofa. Clipped together on top of the typewriter lay three immaculately typed sheets, signed, with some assertion, LEE MILLER. Later in the day when she got up she insisted Roland telephone the printer and change the byline to LEE MILLER PENROSE as a conciliatory gesture.

'Picasso Himself'
If Picasso were here tonight, to greet you and shake your hand, you would experience in his touch what the 18th century Dr Mesmer called 'animal magnetism.' His flashing black eyes have fascinated everyone who has even only seen Picasso but those who meet him feel thrown into an exciting new equilibrium by the personality of this small, warm, friendly man whose name means modern painting.

Wherever he is, he lives an unbelievably simple life in the midst of an unbelievable chaos of possessions. They are all treasures, motley, matched, chic, shabby, beloved or forgotten. Masterpieces lie next to junk which in his hands will become other masterpieces. Old iron, shards and bones await their moment of glory.

At *La Californie*, his villa in Cannes, there is a large mirrored sideboard heaped with false noses, beards and hair, costume jackets from everywhere; the harem, the bullring, the circus (no bullet-proof vests or straight-jackets) – and dozens and dozens of hats. Picasso's own pleasure in dressing up and seeing his friends as clowns or choristers is innocent but the game itself like 'Truth and Consequences' can be an unforgettable revelation as well as an ice-breaking gambit.

The crown makes the king and the laurel crowns the poet, so perhaps the 'hat-trying' in which all comedians and most men indulge is the fulfilment of a wish – a form of fortune telling. If the cap fits, wear it. One becomes tinker, tailor, soldier, sailor. The ears and the eyes, like the ego and the id, become protean and the expression can change from malevolent to angelic all because of a 'titfer'.

The *chateau* of Vauvenargues, vast and impregnable, the most recent of Picasso's abodes, is less austere than its architecture and situation suggest. Strawberries and nightingales surround it like an early Renaissance tapestry, and its chatelaine, Jacqueline, and Picasso have brought with them a climate of love and tenderness.

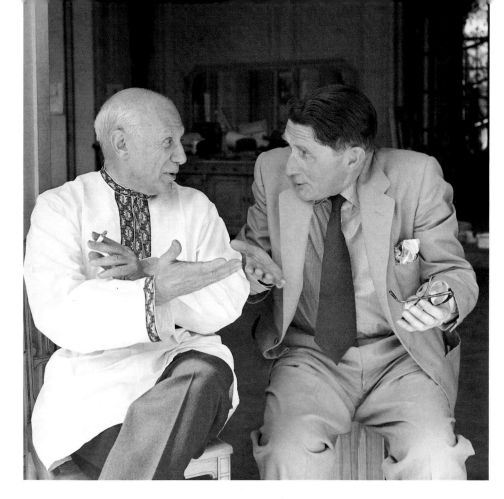

Picasso and Roland Penrose in
animated French conversation at
Villa la Californie, Cannes. 1955.
(Lee Miller)

In spite of the inviting spaciousness, including some dungeons, the noble proportions of the halls prevent Vauvenargues from becoming a dumping ground of unopened crates and mysterious bumpy parcels like *La Californie* whose *passé* banal luxury invites a snub. The dignity of the *chateau* is enhanced by a row of Picasso's sculptures placed at the bottom of the entrance steps (the delivery van unloaded them and left them in chorus formation) which have become household deities and friends, permanently ready to greet or to wave farewell.

Picasso's life is now contained in the south by his work, by love and the Provençal sun. Rarely does he travel further than to a bull-fight in Nîmes or a friend in Nice and although his last visit to Paris five years ago could have easily coincided with a great show of his work in the Louvre, he made no effort to go. Wonderfully he's too busy making new things to pay homage to the old; he's never been his own aficionado. However, if I could use a wish, I'd have him here tonight. I think he'd like it.

Lee Miller Penrose 1960

Picking a fresh path round the giant-sized footsteps left by a work as definitive as *Picasso, His Life and Work* must have been a daunting task in itself, but Lee acquitted herself well, giving us a personal and original vision. Those who knew her circumstances intimately could pick out the neat touches of barbed irony.

Lee's mother had died of cancer 11 September 1954. In the sixties Theodore began a pattern of regular biannual visits to England. Lee, with the help of Tommy Lawson, took him in a wheelchair on a trip to Venice and Rome. It was a great strain on all concerned, but Theodore's appreciation of the civil engineering wonders from all ages was boundless.

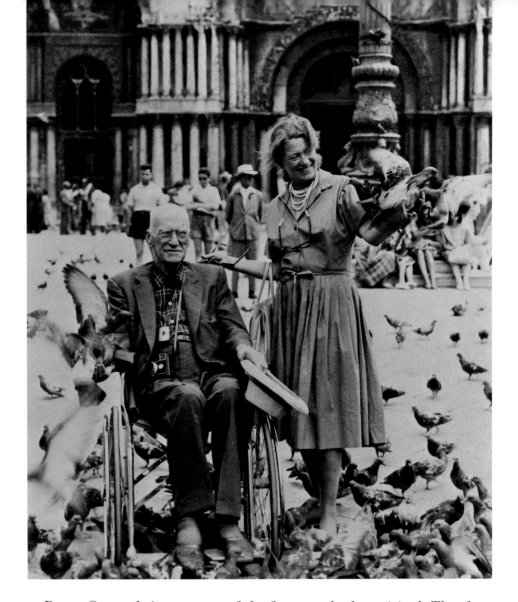

Theodore Miller and Lee in Venice.
1960s. (Photographer unknown)

Peggy Guggenheim was one of the first people they visited. Theodore was politely reserved about her magnificent modern art collection, but he and Peggy got on like old pals and for the rest of their stay, instead of trundling the wheelchair, they cruised gracefully in her gondola.

During his long stays at Farleys, Theodore became something of a landmark in his chair in the corner of the kitchen. Patsy and her daughter Georgina doted on him and he adored them, calling Georgina his 'adopted granddaughter', and insisting that she sign a pledge not to smoke until she was twenty-one years old. Theodore loved the farm and one of his favourite spots was Tony's workshop. He would hang around for hours just quietly watching, never giving advice unless asked, but always generous with his encouragement. Every evening he would retire early and write in his diary, on the flyleaf of which he had inscribed, 'Don't look for scandal – it was not recorded.' In truth his laborious, shaky handwriting encompassed nothing more offensive than the barometric pressure, temperature and the state of the sky.

In addition to Lee's cooking and music, a new jag was emerging. Redolent of previous passions for cards and crosswords, competitions now became the rage. It was not getting the prize, but rather the act of winning that gave Lee satisfaction. She turned it into a sociable pastime by pressing other people to help with the clues. Alastair Lawson – an ace at anagrams and jingles – was Lee's greatest supporter. For multiple choice questions, Lee would work out the permutations mathematically and then submit as many entries as she possibly could, using the names of all her friends and family. Occasionally this system misfired and a coveted prize went to some vague acquaintance, but on the whole the results were remarkably successful. Enough gleaming kitchen gadgets were soon piled up around Farleys and the flat to start a shop.

Cooking competitions were a natural progression. When the Norwegian Food Centre offered lavish prizes to the makers of the best open sandwiches Lee's imagination was fired beyond belief. Days were spent in the library researching the customs of Norway and the origins of its national dishes. Then followed months of trials to perfect Lee's entries. At every possible meal open sandwiches appeared in their different guises. Roland would dream of roast beef and Tony of baked beans as they faced delicately prepared intricate arrangements of pickles, raw fish and salami on flimsy pieces of brown bread. An American visitor was heard to say in measured tones of disbelief: 'I just travelled half-way round the world to the home of one of England's leading gourmets, and I get to eat a sandwich?' For months afterwards pathetic little dehydrated sandwiches could be found, their corners curled up in despair, under the furniture where they had been hidden by less outspoken guests.

The Norwegians took a different view. At the judging in London at the Norwegian Food Centre, Lee submitted three entries in a pool of several hundred, all of which were identified only by a number. The verdict of the jury was unanimous – Lee scooped First, Second, and Third Prize. She generously refused the second and third but accepted the first with alacrity. It was a fortnight's holiday for two in Norway, care of the Norwegian tourist board. 'What would you like to see on your visit to Norway?' the officials enquired. 'I want to visit a fish cannery, cook in a professional kitchen, meet plenty of Norwegians and visit the art galleries,' replied Lee, alight with excitement.

Roland was disinclined to accompany her, so she wasted no time in inviting Bettina McNulty. Lee had met Bettina, a fellow American, at a lunch party at Madame Prunier's restaurant in 1961, and they had swiftly formed an intense and enduring friendship. Bettina, her husband Henry and their baby Claudia became regular visitors to Farleys. Bettina's interests in food, music and travel exactly complemented Lee's.

The fish cannery at Stavanger was the first stop in Norway. Here Lee astonished her hosts with her knowledge of process engineering and physics as well as her overwhelming enthusiasm for seeing everything. It was the depth of winter, and Lee and Bettina travelled by rail in clean and well-appointed trains. In Oslo the Vigeland Art Museum was closed but the Tourist Board laid on a special tour for their two guests. A recent heavy snowstorm enhanced Gustav Vigeland's troubling and complex sculptures.

The climax of the trip came at the ski resort of Geilo on the way back to Oslo. In the kitchen of the biggest hotel, Lee was the guest of the chef, free

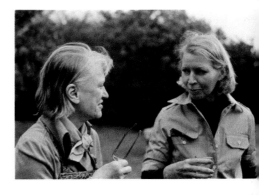

Lee with Bettina McNulty. Farley Farm, 1974. (Photographer unknown)

to do as she pleased in his vast expanse of stainless steel ranges with their array of gadgets and food. A mere culinary exercise was of no interest to her – she elected to work on equal terms with her host and asked to be allowed to produce a dish for the hotel's lunchtime smörgåsbord. She chose to make a traditional Norwegian dish called 'Jansson's Temptation', a succulent combination of anchovies au gratin, onions, potatoes and cream. It was well chosen, because it was not too elaborate but needed careful and skilful preparation. The one-hour baking time gave Lee plenty of opportunity to see how the other chefs were getting on and to watch her host's performance. She enjoyed herself so much in the kitchen that she could not be dislodged. She sent word to Bettina to ask her to watch over 'Jansson's Temptation' as it lay resplendent on the smörgåsbord table, and to report on how it compared with the other dishes offered to the hotel's patrons. All was well, 'Jansson's Temptation' was gone in a flash and, content with this achievement, Lee spent the rest of the day in the kitchen.

Lee made a further trip with Bettina in 1963 that was close to her heart for an entirely different reason. Thanks to Tommy Lawson, the ICA was running a series of trips for art lovers. Lee had been on a Russian excursion in 1961 – one of the first and the most memorable – and on this occasion Egypt was the destination. The tour took in Abu Simnel and Aswan, returning down the Nile on the river boat *Gliding Swan*. Lee hardly appeared on deck, but spent the whole time in the saloon chatting to friends. Bettina, by contrast, was enthralled by the exotic surroundings and took masses of photographs, only to discover later that there had been no film in the camera. 'Never mind,' consoled Lee, 'it is the intention that counts and you have had the fun of *taking* the pictures.'

It was not really the sightseeing that drew Lee to Egypt, though she was undeniably fascinated by the unequal way that change had altered some places beyond recognition, yet passed others by. Living quietly in modest surroundings in Alexandria was Aziz. Old age had not been kind to him. The socialist government had stripped him of everything he owned. Blighted by the infirmities of his years, he now lived on a meagre pension, but was devotedly cared for by Elda, whom he had married in the fifties. After the tour, Lee stayed on in Egypt for a week to be with him. She could not be induced to talk much about it afterwards, but it was evident that, though she was greatly saddened by his plight, there was still a strong bond of warmth and affection between them.

Roland's work 'for the furtherance of contemporary art' in Britain earned him a knighthood in 1966. He deliberated long and hard before accepting – it was not the usual form for a Surrealist to have this sort of recognition and he was never quite reconciled to the ostentatiousness of his new title. The deciding factor for him was that he felt, rightly as it happened, that it would give him more clout when it came to using his influence to further the ICA.

After the investiture Sir Roland and Lady Penrose celebrated with tea at the Ritz. For a joke Bettina phoned the reception so that Lee would hear herself paged as Lady Penrose. She was delighted. The teasing was

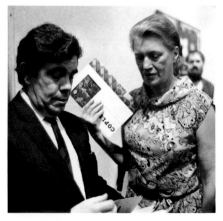

Bill Copley and Lee at the opening of Copley's exhibition in Amsterdam. 1966. (Marc Riboud)

endless: 'Sir Roland, who was that Lady you were with last night?' chortled Bill Copley. 'Lady Lee', as she immediately became known, was not the least bit interested in assuming the airs and graces so common in others of this station. In many ways there could scarcely have been anyone less concerned with filling the conventions of the role, but she did enjoy the dash her title cut in the American press. It was the final enhancement needed to gain her widespread recognition as a cook, and articles about her appeared in newspapers and magazines around the world.

American *Vogue* and *Studio International* ran full-length features about her, but the greatest compliment was from Bettina in her new capacity as contributing editor to *House and Garden*. The article ran to nine pages with three double spreads of photographs by Ernst Beadle whose skill heightened the already abundant sensuousness of the food. The Farley interiors, with only a modest amount of set-dressing and plenty of flowers picked and arranged by Roland, look colourful, welcoming, and informal – which is just how they were. Lee was justifiably proud, and *House and Garden*'s circulation department may have noticed a blip on their graph where she bought dozens of copies to mail to her friends.

The mellowing of age had drawn Lee and Roland closer together. Roland's work gave him more and more opportunity to travel and Lee joined him on some of the trips. Of the many places ostensibly visited for high-minded cultural reasons, Lee particularly enjoyed Czechoslovakia and Japan. Her great delight was to slip away and eat at both famous and obscure restaurants. Whenever possible after the meal she would barge into the kitchen to exchange recipes with the chef, and nothing pleased her more than to return home with yet another pile of cookbooks and lots of strange things in tins.

Through all these travels she took hardly any photographs. The Rolleiflexes gathered dust in the cupboard and the subject of photography raised hardly a flicker of interest. No one could induce her to resume taking pictures. She would firmly brush aside all suggestions of even family snaps by saying, 'You just can't be an amateur once you have been a professional.' Secretly she had purchased a Honeywell Pentax which, with its built-in light-meter and compact size, must have appealed to her love of technology. But she seldom used it. Many assignments were planned and offered to her but the only one of importance that she accepted was to photograph the Catalan artist Antoni Tàpies at work in his studio. The photographs have every bit of the perception and style of the early days and compellingly evoke the atmosphere of Tàpies's surroundings.

Lee's attitude to her previous work baffled everyone. People would come from the great museums requesting loans for exhibitions or books. If they wanted a photograph by Hoyningen-Huene, Steichen or Man Ray she would oblige by rummaging through battered cardboard boxes that contained beautiful original prints. She would declare, her pride tinged with regret, 'I am now the last person left alive who was there at the time,' and launch off into wonderful tales of her life and times.

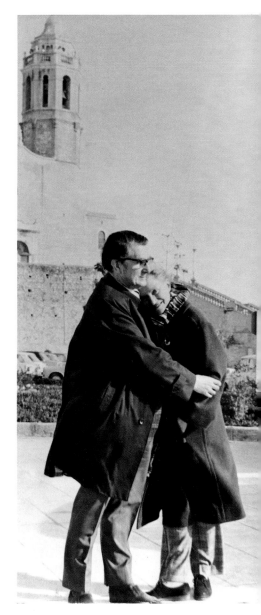

Roland and Lee. Sitges, near Barcelona, 1972. (Photographer unknown)

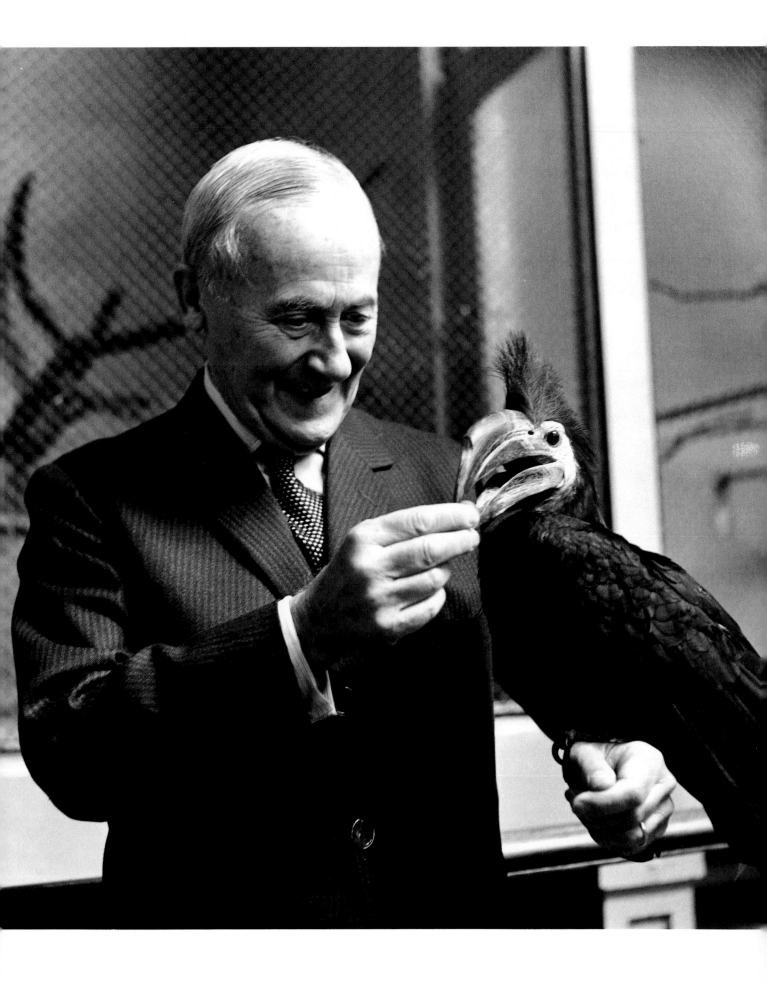

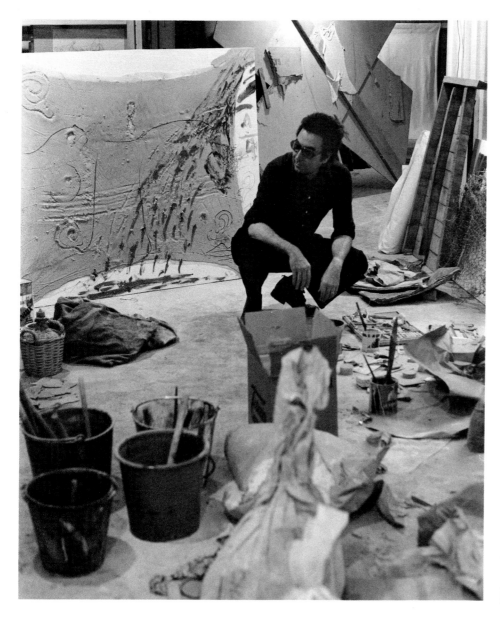

Antoni Tàpies in his studio.
Barcelona, 1973. (Lee Miller)

Her attitude to her own work was quite different. All requests for access to it were politely and firmly deflected. To the most persistent of questioners she would say that everything had been destroyed in the war, always adding that it was of no interest anyway and best forgotten. Her disparagement of her own achievements was so intense that everyone was convinced that she had done little or no work of significance. 'Oh, I did take a few pictures – but that was a long time ago,' she would say. Although she would never admit it, most of her old negatives lay totally neglected in odd corners of Farleys, with more in the vaults of *Vogue* magazine in London. For her a whole part of her life was now a closed chapter. She had absolutely no interest in her own past except where it touched her old friends like Man Ray.

Parallel to Lee's *rapprochement* with Roland, things began to improve with Tony. He had escaped from school and home early and after some years in engineering found he missed the cows and the land too much, so

Opposite: Joan Miró at London Zoo, *c.* 1964. (Lee Miller)

began to study farming. Absence from home for long periods while he worked on other people's farms helped heal the breaches. Gradually he and Lee became more tolerant of each other. Whenever he brought friends home, Lee was as welcoming and hospitable to them as she was to her own guests.

Despite her refusal to take photographs, she had trusted Tony at an early age with her beautiful Zeiss Contax, all its lenses and plenty of film. Barring a few hints on caring for it – 'If you drop it I'll break your neck' – she wisely refused to interfere at all, but instead generously picked up the tab for the processing. She felt that creating an opportunity should be enough encouragement in itself and, besides, she was very aware that personal style is something easily crushed by the influence of others.

As is customary in fate's control of these matters, the final burying of the hatchet with Tony came far too late. In October 1971, with the blessing of Lee and Roland, he left with two friends to drive around the world in a Land-Rover. He was away for more than three years, cabling perfunctorily from New Zealand that he had married Suzanna, a beautiful English girl who had joined him in Australia. On his return a new understanding immediately opened, greatly assisted by Suzanna, to whom Lee took an immediate liking. It was not all roses – no one could have a placid relationship with Lee – but there were no more fights or skilful assassinations of each other's emotions.

Lee watched with interest as Suzanna and Tony set up home in a nearby house on the farm. Suzanna was at first slightly awed by her mother-in-law. It is a little daunting as a young bride to invite a world famous gourmet to dinner, but the world famous gourmet was so full of warmth and approval that it did not take long for them to become friends. With her customary generosity, Lee pressed gadgets and the spoils of many competitions on Suzanna, but nothing seemed to give her more pleasure than when, the following year, they went shopping together for maternity clothes. 'I'm not buying anything for the baby,' Lee announced, 'Everyone else will do that as it's your first. Instead we're going to get you fitted out so you can feel good and look great.' At the end of the spree Suzanna's wardrobe was splendid and Lee had relented about the baby. The final purchase was a green cross-eyed hippopotamus.

In July 1976 Lee and Roland were invited to Arles by Lucien Clergue for the annual Photo Festival which was celebrating the work of Man Ray with an exhibition, workshops and seminars. Roland, whose book on Man Ray had been launched the previous year, gave a lecture, but in many ways it was Lee who was the star of the occasion, because Man Ray had asked her to stand in for him at the ceremony held in his honour. She was radiant with good humour, hugely enjoying the company of Marc Riboud, Lucien Clergue and David Hurn. Many young photographers were there to present their portfolios and Lee derived wry amusement from their prima donna-ish attitudes and their entourage of groupies.

That winter back in England, Tanja Ramm (now Tanja McKee) called on Lee while she was visiting London on a theatre trip. One of the greatest circles of Lee's life was joined at that moment. Over dinner she quietly

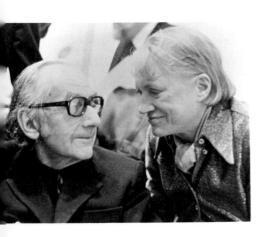

Man Ray and Lee at Man Ray's retrospective exibition at the ICA in 1975. (Eileen Tweedy)

mentioned to Tanja, 'It's rotten luck – I've just been told I've got cancer.' She went on, 'I don't want to talk about it, but I know it won't be long.' Then she resumed the conversation about London and the theatre as though nothing had happened.

In some mysterious way she had foreseen her demise two years previously when visiting Erik and Mafy. On her last evening in their house she had asked Mafy if she would come and share her room. They talked for most of the night about their good and bad times together that stretched back over more than forty years. By morning, when she left to board the London bound jet, Lee had made it quite clear that she did not expect to see either of them again.

The decline was swift. The last time she was able to come downstairs by herself was on 7 June 1977, the Queen's Silver Jubilee Day, when she had the added attraction of welcoming Tony back from a filming trip in Iran. As the inevitable grew closer, Roland hardly left her bedside. Patsy saw to her every need, preparing tempting morsels and trying to keep up with the many and varied demands that only Lee could think up. Suzanna was a frequent visitor, bringing Lee's infant granddaughter, whose appearance compared satisfactorily to baby photographs of Lee. Other friends came and went and, whatever the cost, Lee would always rally herself to greet them and make a few wisecracks. She faced her death fearlessly and with both interest and candour, as at the beginning of a great new adventure.

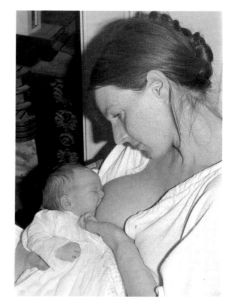

Suzanna Penrose and Amy. Burgh Hill, 1977. (Antony Penrose)

One hot, quiet afternoon she snapped out of a doze with a start. In a moment of panic she whispered to Tony, who was seated beside her, 'I feel I am on the edge of an abyss, and if I let go I will drop, and go on falling for ever.' 'No, it's not like that,' said Tony, drawing a sudden inspiration from the squeaking and chattering that came from the eaves. 'The baby house martins don't have a chance to practice either, but the moment they plunge from their nest they find they can wheel and swoop and soar for ever.' The idea seemed to satisfy Lee. A few days later, one bright clear dawn, she slipped away as Roland held her tightly in his arms.

When the obituaries started to appear they were mostly waffle. Who, after all, had ever been able to penetrate more than one, or two at the most, of the many sealed compartments that Lee had made of her life? Like watertight bulkheads in a ship, she defended the separate areas from ingression by others, certain that her vessel would founder if all the holds were penetrated by any one person. If there was such a thing as a fitting obituary, it was a poem written by Roy Edwards. Roy had first met Lee in 1947 in Downshire Hill, where, as a youth of eighteen, his insatiable thirst for Surrealist literature and poetry had led him. Roland had invited him for tea, but Lee, who was heavily pregnant at the time, could not be bothered with teapots that day, so she gave the lad a gin, thus earning his eternal admiration and friendship. He was fascinated by her green-painted toe-nails, the clarity of her perception and her sense of fun. In her he recognized a true Surrealist woman. Soon after her death he wrote a poem, of which the following is an extract:

LEE AND THE PHOTOGRAPHS

(She turns her head
to the seduction of lens and mirror)

Within the sights of an ancient landscape
parcels wrapped in the velvet dust
of forty years and five thousand miles
are taken from the stately clothes-press
and unwrapped: profiles of presidents
kings and queens are throttled by string unknotted or slashed
it is morning and dream rags fall away
but the air is still scented by smoke

(She turns her head
and it is seen that these negatives are the final distillation of light)

Savage and magnificent sculptures
meditate in the corners of their room
hearing the threat and prophecy
being spoken with a shimmer of silver
and wheat-heads cascading:
somewhere in the town or the forest
beyond these walls the wolves howl

      . . . . . .

(She turns her head
day and night make assignation at the nape of her neck)

The wolves the hounds the pack of boys and young girls
on all fours howl around mildewed cider presses
the fury discards cardboard boxes and tea-chests
plastic bags spilling rags and tatters
sufficient to stitch a patchwork quilt for the sea
but somewhere safe in the arms of this wild wind
is a house between trees and observed by Orion

(She turns her head
and the lightning conductor will fire voltages into the sky)

Clouds disperse and a vapour trail
dissolves across celestial blue
into the loops of love
cards marked by the terror of staves and swords
fall from the hand and are covered by snow
and after the thaw only an ace of hearts
will transcend the meltings
streaked by soot excrement
and a transparency of violet petals
The wind winnows through these pages
to find a sepia image confirming
the fragility the eternity of time made flesh

(She turns her head
and poetry countersigns the document of its surrender)

ROY EDWARDS[2]

Lee at Arles, 1976, near the end of a
long journey, with a spare hat for a
friend. (Marc Riboud)

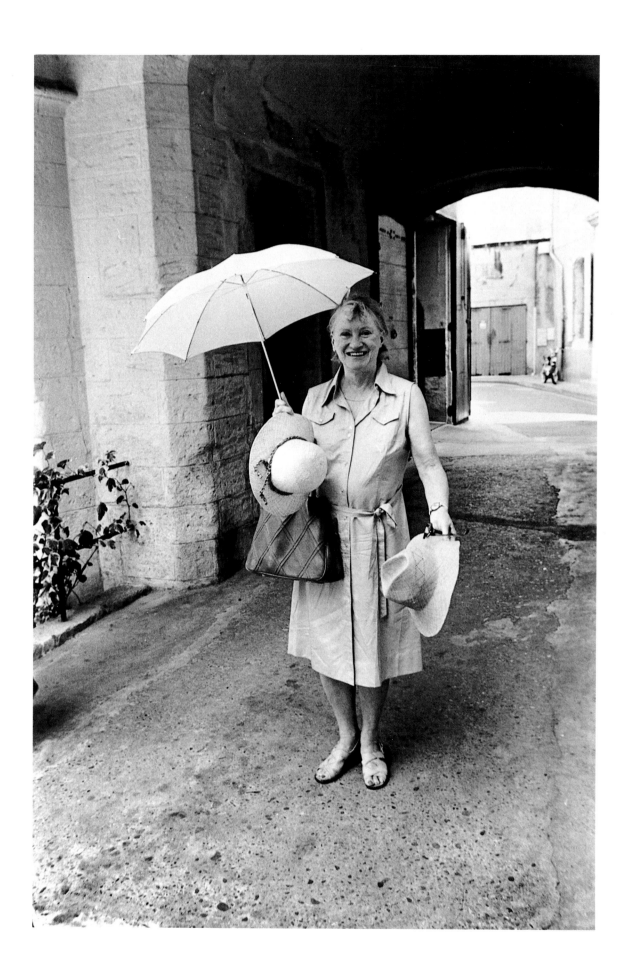

Postscript

Writing this biography has at times been like taking part in an elaborate treasure hunt contrived by Lee in one of her more sardonic moods. Blind alleys that stretched for days abounded, but so did unexpected rewards. The diverse and seemingly random clues were hidden in the masses of manuscripts, negatives and ephemera hoarded at Farley Farm. They led inexorably to New York, Chicago, Los Angeles and Paris, and, if time and money had permitted, the trail would have criss-crossed Europe, Egypt and the East.

The Lee I discovered was very different from the one I had been embattled with for so many years, and I am left with the profound regret that I did not know her better. This regret is bound to be shared by many, as Lee revealed only a small part of herself to any one person. It has often been those who were closest to her who have been given the biggest surprises by my researches, almost as though Lee had carefully planned a little posthumous mischief.

Notes

All quotations used in this book retain their original spelling and punctuation.

Chapter 1
1 Lee Miller, 'What They See in the Cinema' in *Vogue* (August 1956): 46.
2 Arthur Gold and Robert Fizdale, 'The Most Unusual Recipes You Have Ever Seen' in *Vogue* (April 1974): 160–87.
3 Horst P. Horst in conversation with the author, March 1984, New York City.
4 Background information on Condé Nast taken from Caroline Seebohm, *The Man Who Was Vogue*, New York 1982.

Chapter 2
1 Brigid Keenan, *The Woman We Wanted to Look Like*, London 1977, p. 136.
2 Quoted by Arturo Schwartz in *Man Ray*, London 1977, p. 321.
3 Man Ray, *Self Portrait*, London 1963, p. 168.
4 Mario Amaya, 'My Man Ray' (interview with Lee Miller), *Art in America* (May–June 1975): 55.
5 Cecil Beaton, *Vogue*, c. 1960.
6 Horst P. Horst in conversation with the author, March 1984, New York City.
7 Mario Amaya, 'My Man Ray', p. 57.
8 Ibid.
9 David Hurn in conversation with Lee Miller at Arles in 1976, reported to the author June 1984.
10 Julien Levy, *Memoir of an Art Gallery*, London 1977, p. 83.
11 'Rayograms' in *Time* (18 April 1932).
12 'Letters to the Editor' in *Time* (1 August 1932).
13 Erik Miller, tape-recorded notes, February 1979.
14 Lee Miller, unpublished ms.
15 Lee Miller, *Vogue* (August 1956): 98.
16 Julien Levy, *Memoir of an Art Gallery*, p. 121.
17 Man Ray in *This Quarter* (1932): 55. The letters from Man Ray to Lee Miller are held in the Lee Miller Archive, Burgh Hill House, Chiddingly, East Sussex.

Chapter 3
1 Unidentified newspaper article, November 1932.
2 Erik Miller, in conversation with the author, July 1974.
3 Julien Levy, *Memoir of an Art Gallery*, London 1977, p. 297.
4 David Travis, *Photographs from the Julien Levy Collection*, Chicago 1976, p. 53.
5 *New York Sun* (23 December 1932).

6 John Houseman, *Run Through*, London 1973, p. 96.
7 *Poughkeepsie Evening Star* (1 November 1932).
8 Erik Miller, tape-recorded notes, February 1979.

Chapter 4
1 The letters from Aziz Eloui and Lee to Lee's parents and Erik are held in the Lee Miller Archive, Burgh Hill House, Chiddingly, East Sussex. They were kept in Poughkeepsie by Theodore Miller, who handed them over to Lee in the mid-1960s.
2 Erik Miller, tape-recorded notes, February 1979.

Chapter 5
1 Roland Penrose, *Scrap Book*, London 1981, p. 104.
2 Ibid, p. 109.
3 Ibid, p. 118.

Chapter 6
1 Roland Penrose, *Scrap Book*, London 1981, p. 134.
2 Dave Scherman, unpublished ms., 1983.
3 Edward Murrow, *Grim Glory*, London 1940.
4 Dave Scherman, unpublished ms., 1983.
5 Caroline Seebohm, *The Man Who Was Vogue*, New York 1982, p. 244.

Chapter 7
1 Lee Miller, 'St. Malo' in *Vogue* (October 1944): 51.
2 Lee Miller, 'Paris' in *Vogue* (October 1944): 51.
3 Ibid, p. 78.
4 Christine Zervos, *Pablo Picasso*, vol. 14, Editions Cahiers d'Art, Paris 1963.
5 Lee Miller, unpublished ms., edited to form part of 'Paris Fashion' in *Vogue* (November 1944): 36.
6 Lee Miller, 'Colette' in *Vogue* (March 1945): 50.
7 Lee Miller, 'Pattern of Liberation' in *Vogue* (January 1945): 80.
8 Henry McNulty, 'High Spirits from White Alcohols' in *House & Garden* (April 1970): 182.
9 Lee Miller, 'Hitleriana' in *Vogue* (July 1945): 74.

Chapter 8
1 Lee Miller, unpublished ms. on Salzburg.

2 Lee Miller, condensed from an unpublished ms. on Salzburg.
3 Lee Miller, unpublished ms. on Salzburg.
4 Ibid.
5 Lee Miller, unpublished cable ms., 'Vienna'.

Chapter 9
1 John Phillips, *Odd World*, New York 1959, p. 197.
2 Lee Miller, 'Hungary' in *Vogue* (April 1946): 64, and unpublished parts of ms. of same.
3 Ibid.
4 Ibid.
5 Lee Miller, original ms. of 'Romania' in *Vogue* (May 1946): 64.
6 Ibid.
7 Ibid.

Chapter 11
1 From Patsy Murray's notebook:

MUDDLES GREEN GREEN CHICKEN
FOR EIGHT PEOPLE

4 chicken breasts (halved) – skinned and boned
2 lb celery with leaves
1 quart strong chicken stock
2 slices white toast without crusts
1 lb leeks
5 oz parsley with stalks
5 oz double cream
2 oz cooked cooled roux (in reserve)
1 oz butter
1 bouquet garni
Salt and pepper

Roughly chop celery and leaves with green tops. Put celery, leeks, parsley and toast in stock with bouquet garni and salt and pepper. Cook until very soft. Remove bouquet garni. Put all into food processor and process until smooth – aim for a thick purée soup. If too thin bring back to boil and add roux.

Put chicken pieces into hot butter to stiffen without colouring, then poach gently in purée until cooked. Add cream. Do not bring to boil again.

Serve in large soup dishes with scones and peas.

Other parts of chicken may be used, but remove skin.

2 Roy Edwards, *Chaka Speaks and Other Poems*, London 1981, p. 93. Copyright Roy Edwards 1981. Reprinted by kind permission of Geoffrey Lawson.

Index

Page numbers in *italics* refer to the illustrations and captions.